NICHE NEWS

Niche News

THE POLITICS OF NEWS CHOICE

Natalie Jomini Stroud

OXFORD UNIVERSITY PRESS

OXFORD
UNIVERSITY PRESS

Oxford University Press, Inc., publishes works that further
Oxford University's objective of excellence
in research, scholarship, and education.

Oxford   New York
Auckland   Cape Town   Dar es Salaam   Hong Kong   Karachi
Kuala Lumpur   Madrid   Melbourne   Mexico City   Nairobi
New Delhi   Shanghai   Taipei   Toronto

With offices in
Argentina   Austria   Brazil   Chile   Czech Republic   France   Greece
Guatemala   Hungary   Italy   Japan   Poland   Portugal   Singapore
South Korea   Switzerland   Thailand   Turkey   Ukraine   Vietnam

Published by Oxford University Press, Inc.
198 Madison Avenue, New York, New York 10016

www.oup.com

Oxford is a registered trademark of Oxford University Press

Library of Congress Cataloging-in-Publication Data
Stroud, Natalie Jomini.
Niche news : the politics of news choice / Natalie Jomini Stroud.
p.   cm.
Includes bibliographical references and index.
ISBN 978-0-19-975550-9 (hardcover : alk. paper)   ISBN 978-0-19-975551-6 (pbk. : alk. paper)
1. Mass media—United States—Audiences.   2. Mass media and public opinion—United States.
3. Press and politics—United States.   4. Television broadcasting of news—United States.
5. Radio journalism—United States.   I. Title.
P96.A832U67 2011
302.23—dc22   2010016330

1 3 5 7 9 8 6 4 2

Printed in the United States of America
on acid-free paper

Acknowledgments

THIS BOOK WAS supported by funding from multiple sources, including: the Annenberg School for Communication at the University of Pennsylvania; the Annenberg Public Policy Center; the Institute for the Study of Citizens and Politics (ISCAP) at the Annenberg Public Policy Center; the Annette Strauss Institute for Civic Participation at the University of Texas at Austin; the Knapp Fellowship, Reddick Award, Undergraduate Mentor Fellowship, and Junior Faculty Fellowship from the Department of Communication Studies and the College of Communication at the University of Texas at Austin; and a Special Research Grant from the University of Texas at Austin. I am thankful for the research support and the time made possible by these awards, fellowships, and organizations.

Several people provided helpful comments on portions of this manuscript, including Kathleen Hall Jamieson, Vincent Price, Joseph Cappella, Max McCombs, and Diana Mutz. I am particularly grateful to Vincent Price for his insights on earlier versions of this project. I am indebted to Kathleen Hall Jamieson for her sage advice, vision, and encouragement. At the helm of the Annenberg Public Policy Center and the National Annenberg Election Survey, she in many ways made this project possible. I also thank Kate Kenski, Sharon Jarvis, and Rod Hart for their friendship and words of wisdom at just the right moments. I also owe special thanks to the anonymous reviewers for this book whose questions and suggestions made this a far stronger project. I consider myself extremely fortunate to have worked with David McBride on my first book. He, Philip Wolny, and others at Oxford University Press have been invaluable in their assistance.

A host of colleagues and students helped with the content analyses and data collection reported in this book. Thanks to Ken Winneg and Eran Ben-Porath for their assistance in coding the media outlets and political candidates' agendas. Kristin Stimpson was especially helpful in the content analysis reported in chapter 6. Sarah Rayburn, Lauren Callahan, Nausheen Jivani, and Jace Wietzikoski dedicated many hours to this content analysis and I appreciate their hard work. I also thank Diana Mutz for supporting the magazine experiment and the ISCAP employees (Danielle, Lena, Qian, Andrew, and Michael) who helped to conduct the study. Additional thanks to Colene Lind, Ashley Muddiman, and Josh Scacco for their help with proofreading.

Portions of several chapters of this book were published previously in *Political Behavior* (reprinted with kind permission from Springer Science+Business Media: "Media use and political predispositions: Revisiting the concept of selective exposure," 30, 341-66: 2008) and the *Journal of Communication* (reprinted with kind permission from Wiley-Blackwell Publishing: "Polarization and partisan selective exposure," 60, 556-76: 2010). This project began as my dissertation and I am deeply honored that this earlier version was recognized by the Political Communication Division of the National Communication Association, by the Political Psychology Section of the American Political Science Association, and with the K. Kyoon Hur Award from the International Communication Association.

Several others in the Department of Communication Studies at the University of Texas also deserve thanks including Rene Dailey, Erin Donovan-Kicken, Deanna Matthews, Jennifer Betancourt, and Barry Brummett. This book would not have been possible without Rachel Brennan, Jess Grennan, Vani Henderson, and Lilach Nir. I am lucky to have such supportive friends. Thanks to my family: Val Murray, my wonderful parents, Pierre and Sandy Jomini, and my truly amazing brother, Paul Jomini, who all were an unending source of encouragement. My biggest thanks goes to my husband, Scott Stroud, who inspires me with his talent and with his insight. He read multiple drafts, talked with me for many hours about these ideas, and always believed in this project.

For Scott

Contents

NICHE NEWS

I

PARTISANS MAKE THE NEWS

INTERVIEWS WITH FORMER presidents tend to be routine and respectful. This was far from the case on September 24, 2006.

It was an important interview for *Fox News Sunday*'s host Chris Wallace. Ratings for the program had not been stellar. Nielsen ratings consistently showed the program in fourth place among the four main Sunday morning talk shows (NBC's *Meet the Press,* CBS's *Face the Nation,* and ABC's *This Week*). An interview with former president Bill Clinton, however, represented an opportunity to make some headway.

Wallace had interviewed Clinton on *Fox News Sunday* before. In a joint appearance with fellow former president George H. W. Bush on February 20, 2005, Clinton discussed relief efforts for the massive tsunami in Asia. The interview was typical; Clinton and Bush were cordial and conveyed a strong sense of bipartisanship. The program generated modest interest but failed to produce a noteworthy bump in the program's ratings.

But this Clinton interview would be different. Wallace would interview Clinton one on one and the interview stipulations gave Wallace quite a bit of latitude in the questions he could ask. Although half of the questions would be about Clinton's efforts to tackle global problems, the other half were left to the discretion of Fox News. And Wallace planned to use this freedom; he intended to ask Clinton several probing questions about how Clinton had handled the threat of terrorism during his presidency.

The interview was taped on Friday, September 22 in preparation for Sunday's show. By Friday afternoon, tantalizing details about an explosive Wallace/Clinton exchange appeared in the media. Fox News began heavily promoting the show. One provocative promotion showed an angered Clinton fending off criticism about his efforts to catch terrorist mastermind Al Qaeda leader Osama bin Laden. The promo abruptly ended with Clinton declaring, "So I tried and failed." The promotions swiftly appeared on YouTube. The blog Think Progress posted a transcript of the interview online. In the interview, online details revealed, the former president accused Fox News of having a conservative bias. Contributors to the blogosphere began commenting on the exchange. Their responses oozed with partisanship. On left-leaning blogs, commentators rallied behind Clinton and tore into Fox News. Many were elated that someone had chastised Fox News while being interviewed by the network. They speculated about how Fox might edit the interview to maximize its impact. On right-leaning blogs, commentators rallied behind Fox News and tore into Clinton. For the right, the interview showed Clinton losing his composure—yet again—and Wallace reacting gracefully to an unreasonably irate Clinton. Wallace's inbox overflowed with e-mails—some angry and some congratulatory.

The highly anticipated interview aired on Sunday, September 24, 2006. Wallace formally introduced the program by informing viewers that Clinton had agreed to an interview where half of the questions would focus on Clinton's philanthropy and the other half would focus on topics of Fox's choosing. Wallace also ended speculation about how the interview would be edited by telling viewers that the interview would be shown in its entirety. Wallace concluded his preface by acknowledging that the interview did not go according to plan.

The interview got under way quickly. Skimming over pleasantries, Wallace began the interview by asking Clinton about a statement he had made in the *New Yorker* regarding his philanthropic efforts. The response to the first question foreshadowed what was to come. Clinton responded that Wallace had not accurately captured the *tone* of his statement, after which Wallace reminded Clinton that the statement was a *direct quotation*. During Wallace's fourth question, the interview truly began to unravel. Wallace asked Clinton, "Why didn't you do more to put bin Laden and Al Qaeda out of business when you were president?" Clinton responded by angrily defending his record on terrorism. He accused both the Fox News Network and Chris Wallace of bias, labeling the interview a "conservative hit job." He charged, "I want to know how many people in the Bush administration you asked, 'Why didn't you do anything about the [2000 terrorist attack on the USS] Cole?' I want to know how many you asked, 'Why did you fire [counter-terrorism adviser] Dick Clarke?' I want to know how many people you asked...."

After several explosive moments, the exchange progressed awkwardly. Wallace asked the former president, "Would you like to talk about the Clinton Global Initiative?"

"No, I want to finish this now," Clinton responded. For the remainder of the interview, Wallace switched between soft questions about Clinton's philanthropy and hard questions about Clinton's acts as president. Clinton switched between vigorously (and sometimes venomously) defending his actions and proudly talking about his global initiatives. Wallace ended the interview with delightful candor: "Mr. President, thank you for one of the more unusual interviews."

The program was a journalistic and ratings coup. The last time *Fox News Sunday* had seen ratings that high was in 2003 when Iraqi leader Saddam Hussein had been pulled from his underground hideaway. Fox News milked the moment, airing the interview again at 10 P.M. and frequently showing clips from the exchange. The network dedicated a great deal of the next week's programming to analyzing the interview. Heavy-hitters clamored to comment; Secretary of State Condoleezza Rice, former first lady Hillary Clinton, former New York City mayor Rudy Giuliani, and Democratic National Committee Chairman Howard Dean all weighed in on the exchange. Political commentators surmised that Clinton's reaction had been a crafty political stunt designed to rally the Democratic base and to fend off criticism about the Democrats' ability to handle the war on terrorism. Others suspected that the emotion was a genuine reaction to an accusatory interview and a history of unfair media treatment by Fox News. Ratings continued to soar in the days following the interview. The Democratic National Committee sent an e-mail link to the video with a fundraising appeal. The Republican National Committee sent talking points to the media. Prominent media outlets including the *Washington Post,* the *New York Times,* and *USA Today* covered the story. International outlets also reported on the interview. Even today, the interview remains a matter of intense pride for *Fox News Sunday*—years later, the video file and transcript still can be found on the show's Web site and Wallace's online biography highlights his "explosive interview with former president Bill Clinton."

Only a few weeks later, Wolf Blitzer, host on Fox News's competitor CNN, found that he had a bit more in common with Chris Wallace than he might have anticipated. On October 27, 2006, Blitzer's guest was Lynne Cheney, wife of Vice President Dick Cheney. Cheney was no stranger to CNN; she had appeared on numerous occasions and had cohosted the CNN program *Crossfire* years earlier. She had been promoting her new children's book, *Our 50 States: A Family Adventure Across America,* which recently had hit bookstores. Though the interview was supposed to be about the book, room was left for political questions as well. Days after the interview, Blitzer would go on the record stating, "[Cheney] knew full well that we would be asking her serious political questions in addition to those questions that we asked her about her new children's book. That was reaffirmed with her staff only hours before the interview."

It was a good time to ask Cheney political questions—Vice President Dick Cheney recently had made headlines with a statement that some interpreted as an endorsement of the controversial interrogation technique called "water boarding." And Lynne Cheney had been brought into the political fray by Democrat James Webb, a senatorial candidate from Virginia. In defending himself against criticism for penning racy fiction books years earlier, Webb directed people to Cheney's fiction book *Sisters,* claiming that it was even steamier.

Blitzer began the *Situation Room* episode by hyping the upcoming interview with Cheney: "She's coming out swinging. You're going to want to see the fireworks in this interview." After repeatedly promoting the exchange, Blitzer turned to the interview late in the broadcast. Like Wallace, Blitzer specifically noted that CNN would play the entire interview. Blitzer began the interview by introducing Cheney and her new book. By Blitzer's third statement in the exchange, however, the topic had shifted considerably from children's literature. Blitzer asked Cheney about her husband's views on using water boarding as an interrogation technique. In response, Cheney charged that CNN's programming "seemed almost straight out of Democratic talking points." Blitzer countered by asserting, "This is reporting the news, which is what we do. We're not partisan," and by noting that Cheney once had been a CNN host. Tabling Cheney's request to return to a discussion of *Our 50 States,* Blitzer turned from his questions about water boarding to ask Cheney to comment on Webb's accusations. Cheney, seeming to direct her comment both to CNN and to Webb, responded, "Sex, lies, and distortion. That's what it is." Needless to say, Cheney seemed less than satisfied when Blitzer returned only briefly to the topic of her children's book at the close of the interview. The exchange ended on a spiteful note. Blitzer told Cheney, "You came armed. I guess you knew what you wanted to do," to which Cheney responded, "Wolf, I am always prepared for you to ask questions that maybe aren't quite fair, but they are pretty tough."

Though the interview generated less buzz than the Clinton/Wallace interview, the message was identical: News media outlets have political biases. And people got the message. In the blogosphere, public reaction closely resembled reactions to the Clinton/Wallace exchange, except, of course, that the tables were turned. Now, commentators on liberal blogs rallied behind the host and criticized the interviewee. And commentators on conservative blogs rallied behind the interviewee and criticized the host. Speculation swirled that this interview was a Republican response to the Wallace/Clinton exchange, designed to rally the Republican base in the days leading up to the midterm elections by attacking the liberal media.

Why start with these vignettes? After all, this book is about the behavior of *citizens,* about citizens' news choices and the consequences of their selections. Yet these vignettes are about clashes between political elites and prominent members of the media. I chose to start with these vignettes because citizens do not select news in a vacuum. News selections occur in a political context—whether prominent political figures critique media outlets in 2006 or prominent Federalists and Anti-Federalists sponsor competing newspapers in 1806. Today, the United States arguably is returning to an era of media partisanship. Former Fox News host and Bush White House Press Secretary Tony Snow echoed this observation:

> The Washington press corps is in the midst of a great leap backward. A century ago, newspapers proudly boasted their partisan loyalties. And although that kind of open political combat fell out of vogue long ago, it is enjoying a resurgence. An increasing number of reporters have picked sides in the pitched battles of the day....Too many journalists are letting their hearts rule their reporting. Facts take a back seat to prejudices. Banner headlines titillate us with allegations spun more out of speculation than truth.[1]

Indeed, today's political elites are signaling the role of partisanship in the media environment.

Interviews like those with Clinton and Cheney offer insights to numerous constituencies. For politicians, these interviews are powerful reminders to, in the words of Wolf Blitzer, "come armed" when appearing on a hostile program. For the media, these interviews raise important questions—what happened to objectivity, fairness, and balance? For academics, these interviews are intriguing artifacts, providing explosive evidence that the media environment in which we live is politically charged. And for the public, Clinton and Cheney reinforce the views of those already convinced of partisan biases in the media. For others, they teach important lessons: If you are a conservative or a Republican, you better flip away from CNN. If you are a liberal or a Democrat, Fox News is not your channel. Perhaps most important, Cheney and Clinton offer a more global lesson: Partisanship is an appropriate criterion for making news selections.

Politics may be at the heart of how citizens approach the news. Public trust in the news media has plummeted. Over the past two decades, trust in network television news has dropped by 18 percentage points and trust in major national newspapers has fallen by 21 percentage points.[2] At the same time, public perceptions of news media outlets have fractured along partisan lines as new sources have emerged. Today, Democrats and Republicans can live in completely different news environments. No longer do those craving televised news need to choose between a few national news broadcasts each evening. In the modern media environment, news media options are endless. Citizens can be picky about their news. They easily can filter out news on topics that are not of interest. And, most important for this project, citizens can readily find likeminded news. Conservative Republicans can depend on Bill O'Reilly for news and liberal Democrats can depend on Keith Olbermann. The use of politically likeminded news is known as *partisan selective exposure*. This type of exposure is the focus of this book. Do people prefer likeminded news? Why? With what effect?

Political leanings can influence not only where people turn for news but also their perceptions and memories of the news. When partisans interpret information in ways consistent with their political beliefs, they are engaging in selective perception. If, for example, learning that an article is from the *New York Times* or from the *Wall Street Journal* influences how partisans perceive the content, then there is evidence of selective perception. Memory also can be affected by existing partisan proclivities, a phenomenon known as selective retention. Partisans may remember likeminded information and fail to remember or *mis*remember contradictory information. Although I focus predominately on selective exposure, selective perception and retention are part of the story. Perceptions that an outlet favors the opposition, for example, may prompt partisans to avoid and discount the outlet. And remembering only the best aspects of coverage from a likeminded source may lead to entrenched patterns of likeminded news exposure.

DEMOCRATIC CONSEQUENCES OF PARTISAN SELECTIVE EXPOSURE

Should we worry about partisan selective exposure? Isn't it worth promoting exposure to political content no matter where people get it? The many possible answers to these questions have far-reaching implications for our democratic system. To follow, I review three possible answers that helped to motivate this project.

First, partisan selective exposure may energize citizen participation in politics. If this is the case, we might not need to worry about likeminded news use. Citizen political participation is a hallmark of a democracy. Without citizen involvement, the legitimacy of a democratic government is called into question. Do leaders have a mandate from the citizenry to govern? Are citizens acting as a necessary check on governmental power?

Despite its democratic importance, the frequency with which citizens participate in politics has fluctuated over time. Some eras are characterized by high levels of citizen participation while others are not. In looking over the historical trend of political participation in the United States, it is noteworthy that political participation soared during an era when the press was rampantly partisan.[3] Perhaps citizens find something compelling and motivating about partisan media. Partisan content can be highly engaging—it is hard to look away from the contentious Wallace/Clinton and Blitzer/Cheney interviews. And, thanks to these interviews, citizens *were* motivated to participate. Thousands logged their opinions in public, online forums. Fundraising appeals solicited a citizen response to the interviews.

Partisan media can provide explicit instructions about political participation. Consider the progressive Web site www.alternet.org, for example. The Web site provides users with the opportunity to donate to political causes, to sign petitions to Congress, and to get more involved in politics. More traditional media outlets also can get into the act by providing mobilizing information; in 2009, for example, Fox News posted online instructions on how to organize rallies to protest government spending and taxes, affectionately known as "tea parties."[4] By providing partisans with mobilizing information and energizing them to participate, partisan content can promote a politically active citizenry.

Even if partisan selective exposure inspires participation, a desirable outcome, there remains reason for concern. Partisan media could exacerbate existing divides in the public in terms of political participation. It is well known that not everyone participates in politics. Wealthy, educated, and older Americans are more apt to participate; among other acts of political participation, these citizens are more likely to vote, to attend candidate meetings, and to wear buttons supporting a preferred candidate.[5] If these same citizens are more likely to engage in partisan selective exposure, then partisan media may further energize groups that are already overrepresented in the political process. Although partisan selective exposure may contribute to higher levels of participation, it may not promote *equitable* participation. If some participate while others do not, the interests of those not participating may not be adequately represented.

Second, partisan selective exposure may affect what citizens know about politics. Ideally, democratic theorists contend, citizens should reach informed political decisions after carefully weighing arguments supporting various political perspectives. Though exactly how much information citizens need to adequately perform their democratic responsibilities is a matter of debate, the idea that citizens need at least *some* information to uphold their responsibilities is without question.[6]

Polls of the public, however, show that the public lacks background knowledge about numerous political matters.[7] And this ignorance can be consequential—without adequate political knowledge, citizens can make decisions that do not coincide with their interests. Lacking information about candidate issue stances, for example, citizens may vote for candidates who do not best match their issue preferences.[8]

The influence of partisan selective exposure on the public's store of political information is unknown. Citizens engaging in partisan selective exposure may be well versed in arguments supporting their own political perspective, yet severely lacking in a solid understanding of oppositional arguments. Political scientists Robert Lane and David Sears captured this sentiment when they wrote that "to be rational a man must expose himself to congenial and uncongenial matters alike; he must be able to look at both and perceive them as they are, not merely as what he would like them to be, and he must be able to retain this information in an undistorted form."[9] With one-sided information, citizens may not realize that they are not acting in their own—or society's—best interest. Partisan selective exposure, therefore, may lead to a less informed public.

Alternatively, partisan media may help citizens to learn about politics. Information presented by likeminded partisan sources may be more engrossing and more compatible with what people already know and believe, and thus, easier to remember. Simplifying the political world into two categories (liberal and conservative, Democrat and Republican) may help people to understand politics.[10] Instead of seeing politics as consisting of many different issues, candidates, processes, and events, politics may be easier to comprehend as a black and white, partisan phenomenon. If this is the case, we might celebrate partisan media for finding a way to make politics more accessible and understandable.

Third, partisan selective exposure may influence citizens' political attitudes and beliefs. Specifically, citizens using likeminded media may develop more polarized political attitudes and more fragmented political interests. At the turn of the twentieth century, philosopher John Dewey wrote extensively on the features of civic life that promote a healthy democracy. He argued that democracy functions best when citizens have common goals and interests.[11] The onslaught of diverse partisan media outlets may undercut the development of common goals, however, by leading to higher levels of polarization in the public. People may develop even stronger attachments to their own views and increasingly disdain oppositional views. Further, people's impressions of important issues may diverge due to partisan selective exposure. Without a shared issue agenda, allocation of limited resources, such as time and money, becomes more difficult. Partisan selective exposure, therefore, may stunt the ability of government officials to create policies that are responsive to the public's needs. Further, it may lead people to question the political legitimacy of public figures not sharing their political perspective.

In sum, there are good reasons to investigate the democratic consequences of partisan selective exposure. This behavior has the potential to affect how citizens reason about, react to, and act in the political world.

HISTORICAL PRECEDENTS

The effects of selective exposure have received only limited empirical attention, yet the concept of selective exposure has been around for decades. One of the earliest, and certainly the most cited, selective exposure scholars is psychologist Leon Festinger.[12] In the late 1950s and early 1960s, Festinger and his colleagues conducted numerous playful experiments to examine the conditions under which selective exposure occurs. Like Festinger, this project is concerned with what leads people to prefer likeminded information. Unlike Festinger, the focus is not on selective exposure in general, but on *partisan* selective exposure. Though the two share a common scholarly lineage, partisan selective exposure deserves to be analyzed as a distinct phenomenon. I return to this notion later. I also expand upon Festinger's interest in the *causes* of selective exposure by investigating the democratic *effects* of partisan selective exposure.

In the communication discipline, selectivity processes historically have been wedded to the study of effects—or rather, a lack of media effects. Selective exposure, for example, is seen as an explanation for the media's inability to powerfully affect citizens' beliefs. The logic is that if citizens are not exposed to information that conflicts with their beliefs, then they have no reason to change their beliefs. Joseph Klapper is remembered as a key figure in the limited media effects tradition; in 1960, he noted, "Selective exposure, selective perception, and selective retention have been shown...to be typically the protectors of predispositions and the handmaidens of reinforcement."[13] Though this project broadly agrees with Klapper's assessment—selective exposure and other selectivity processes can reinforce predispositions—it significantly parts ways with the limited effects tradition. Klapper's statement need not be read as a claim that the media have limited effects. On the contrary, Klapper's work can be seen as an invitation to study media effects in a more nuanced manner, by taking into account audience predispositions and by analyzing which media outlets audiences select. This project intends to do just this.

Despite early fanfare about selective exposure, research stalled in the 1970s. In the mid-1960s, scholars David Sears and Jonathan Freedman wrote chilling reviews of the research on selective exposure.[14] After reviewing published literature on the phenomenon, Sears and Freedman concluded that evidence of selective exposure was unconvincing. They offered a number of methodological critiques of prior research and challenged scholars to think more critically about the limited conditions under which selective exposure might occur. This project takes the critiques of Sears and Freedman seriously; these scholars have set a high bar for providing convincing evidence of selective exposure. Their work showcases that it is unlikely that everyone will seek out likeminded political news. Certain types of people under certain circumstances, however, are particularly likely to do so. In the end, this project reaches a different conclusion than Sears and Freedman. It documents the *occurrence* of partisan selective exposure and makes the case that the behavior can be politically consequential.

Work on selective exposure has been slow to re-emerge since Sears and Freedman wrote their reviews. In contemporary times, Cass Sunstein's *Republic.com* has played an important role in renewing interest in selective exposure.[15] Sunstein focused on the Internet and proposed that the new medium could make it easier to seek out like-minded others. By removing geographical constraints, the Internet provides a way for citizens with common predispositions to interact. "Echo chambers" could form, Sunstein worried, leading to more extreme attitudes and intolerance. Though Sunstein's normative questions are troubling, we don't yet have a comprehensive, empirical understanding of the effects of selective exposure. I aim to address this need.

Although insight can be gained from prior scholars, we have more to learn. Three questions guide this project's investigation into citizens' choices about which news to use: (1) To what extent do citizens' political beliefs guide their news selections? (2) What leads people to select news on the basis of their political beliefs? and (3) What are the consequences of partisan selective exposure? Chapter 2 reviews what we know about selective exposure and makes a case for focusing on partisan selective exposure. Chapter 3 asks whether people are using political media sources that express views matching their own. Chapter 4 examines how citizens learn about and learn from partisan media. It assesses perceptions of media outlets and considers what leads citizens to form impressions about partisanship in the media. Chapter 5 investigates whether partisan selective exposure affects, or is affected by, partisan involvement. I consider relationships between partisan selective exposure, political participation, the commitment to vote for a candidate, and political polarization. Chapter 6 tackles the notion of agenda setting—the idea that the media are responsible for determining which issues citizens see as important. This chapter explores whether partisan selective exposure influences citizens' issue priorities. The final chapter returns to questions about the implications of the partisan use of news, both for the conduct of media research and, more broadly, for the progress of democracy.

NOTES

1. Tony Snow, *Fox News Sunday,* June 14, 1998.

2. Pew Research Center for the People & the Press, *Internet News Audience Highly Critical of News Organizations: Views of Press Values and Performance 1985–2007* (Washington, DC, 2007).

3. Michael Schudson, *The Power of News* (Cambridge, MA: Harvard University Press, 1995).

4. Joshua Rhett Miller, "Organizers Give Recipes for Effective Tea Parties," www.foxnews.com/politics/2009/04/11/organizers-recipes-effective-tea-parties/, April 11, 2009.

5. Steven J. Rosenstone and John Mark Hansen, *Mobilization, Participation, and Democracy in America* (New York: Longman, 2003).

6. Michael Schudson, *The Good Citizen: A History of American Civic Life* (New York: Free Press, 1998).

7. Michael X. Delli Carpini and Scott Keeter, *What Americans Know about Politics and Why It Matters* (New Haven, CT: Yale University Press, 1996).

8. Larry M. Bartels, "Uninformed Votes: Information Effects in Presidential Elections," *American Journal of Political Science* 40 (1996): 194–230; Richard R. Lau and David P. Redlawsk, "Voting Correctly," *American Political Science Review* 91 (1997): 585–98; Richard R. Lau, David J. Andersen, and David P. Redlawsk, "An Exploration of Correct Voting in Recent U.S. Presidential Elections," *American Journal of Political Science* 52, 2 (2008): 395–411.

9. Robert E. Lane and David O. Sears, *Public Opinion* (Englewood Cliffs, NJ: Prentice-Hall, 1964): 73.

10. Schudson, *The Good Citizen,* 200.

11. John Dewey, *Democracy and Education* (Carbondale: Southern Illinois University Press, 1916/1985).

12. Leon Festinger, *A Theory of Cognitive Dissonance* (Stanford: Stanford University Press, 1957); Leon Festinger, *Conflict, Decision, and Dissonance* (Stanford: Stanford University Press, 1964).

13. Joseph T. Klapper, *The Effects of Mass Communication* (Glencoe, IL: The Free Press, 1960): 64.

14. Jonathan L. Freedman and David O. Sears, "Selective Exposure," in *Advances in Experimental Social Psychology,* edited by Leonard Berkowitz (New York: Academic Press, 1965), 2: 57–97; David O. Sears and Jonathan L. Freedman, "Selective Exposure to Information: A Critical Review," *Public Opinion Quarterly* 31 (1967): 194–213.

15. Cass Sunstein, *Republic.com* (Princeton: Princeton University Press, 2001); see also Cass Sunstein, *Republic.com 2.0* (Princeton: Princeton University Press, 2007).

2

SELECTIVE EXPOSURE IN THEORY AND IN PRACTICE

DO PEOPLE CRAVE likeminded information and eschew information that conflicts with their beliefs? This is the fundamental question of research on selective exposure. Early researchers were divided in their readings of the evidence and contemporary researchers seem no less at odds regarding whether they should embrace or dismiss selective exposure.[1] In 1960, sociology and communication scholar Joseph Klapper claimed that "The tendency of people to expose themselves to mass communications in accord with their existing opinions and interests and to avoid unsympathetic material, has been widely demonstrated."[2] Yet just a few years later, fellow academic William McGuire charged that "The survival of the human race for a period that even the most conservative estimates place at a minimum of 6000 years suggests that people seek information on some basis less primitive than seeking support of what they already know and avoiding any surprises."[3]

The debate on selective exposure persists today. Political scientist Donald Kinder argues that "Despite all of the early confidence, the evidence for selective exposure turns out to be thin. We now know that people do not, for the most part, seek out mass communications that reinforce their political predispositions."[4] Along similar lines, political scientist John Zaller notes that "Most people ... are simply not so rigid in their information-seeking behavior that they will expose themselves only to ideas that they find congenial. To the extent selective exposure occurs at all, it appears to do so under special conditions that do not typically arise in situations of mass persuasion."[5] On the contrary, psychologists Eva Jonas, Stefan Schulz-Hardt, and

Dieter Frey contend that "When searching for new information, people are often biased in favor of previously held beliefs, expectations, or desired conclusions."[6] After decades of research, why can't we reach a consensus about whether selective exposure occurs?

This chapter is dedicated to answering this question. In doing so, I have four main objectives. First, I review theoretical reasons to anticipate that people will seek out likeminded media. Second, I turn to an investigation of the diverse research findings on selective exposure. Third, I present a rationale for focusing on partisan selective exposure. Fourth and finally, I explain how this book contributes to what we already know and briefly describe how I will explore the existence, causes, and consequences of partisan selective exposure.

WHY SELECTIVE EXPOSURE OCCURS

Given a history of different conclusions about the existence of selective exposure, it is important to understand the theoretical basis for selective exposure. Why should we expect selective exposure to occur? Why would people select likeminded information?

There are numerous theories about what makes likeminded information particularly attractive. In the following pages, I describe four different theoretical reasons to anticipate that selective exposure will occur. Although these theories are interconnected, each offers unique insights into the psychological underpinnings of selective exposure.

Cognitive Dissonance

The most popular explanation for selective exposure is cognitive dissonance, a theory formally proposed by Leon Festinger in 1957.[7] According to this theory, people sometimes find themselves in situations where two of their ideas conflict. When a strong partisan finds himself agreeing with the opposition's stance on an issue, for example, his partisan attachment conflicts with his issue stance. This certainly can be disconcerting. It can lead the partisan to all sorts of challenging considerations. The partisan may think about how important this one issue is relative to all of the other issues on which he agrees with his party. Or he may question his partisan leaning. Or he may wonder whether he fully understands the issue. These types of questions signal the experience of the psychological discomfort that can arise when cognitions conflict. This is known as cognitive dissonance. Cognitive dissonance is important here because it can motivate people to engage in selective exposure. The partisan may seek information showing the weaknesses of the opposition's issue stance. By looking at this information, he may come to realize that his issue stance really isn't as out of alignment with his partisanship as he first thought. This would minimize his experience of dissonance. As this example shows, selective exposure serves as one way to resolve the psychologically uncomfortable state of cognitive dissonance.

People can experience different levels of dissonance. Festinger proposed that the amount of dissonance experienced is determined in part by how many consistent cognitions are held and by how many inconsistent cognitions are held. When holding only consistent cognitions, dissonance is nonexistent. No cognition conflicts with another. There is a sense of cognitive harmony. A mix of consistent and inconsistent cognitions, however, could result in dissonance. This is precisely what our partisan experiences—cognitions that cohere with his partisanship are inconsistent with the cognition that he agrees with the opposition on an issue. And if he disagreed with his party on several issues, then the dissonance experienced would be even greater.

The importance assigned to the cognitions also influences how much dissonance is experienced. If our partisan believed that the issue on which he disagreed with his party was an inconsequential one, then dissonance would be low. If he believed that the issue was quite important, however, then his experience of cognitive dissonance would be notably greater.

Whether people will engage in selective exposure, according to Festinger, is based on the amount of dissonance experienced. Festinger proposed that only the experience of moderate, or appreciable, levels of dissonance, as opposed to "extremely large amounts" or the "relative absence" of dissonance, would result in selective exposure; he wrote, "The existence of appreciable dissonance and the consequent pressure to reduce it will lead to the seeking out of information which will introduce consonances and to the avoidance of information which will increase the already existing dissonance."[8] Extremely large amounts of dissonance, Festinger believed, would motivate an individual to prefer dissonant information in order to return to a non-dissonant state. If the partisan kept finding new issues on which he disagreed with his party, at some point, he might begin seeking positive information about the other party. In this case, he would try to resolve his dissonance by switching his partisanship. In contrast, a relative absence of dissonance would not motivate seeking or avoiding information. Why closely monitor your information intake without any motivation to do so? Though Festinger proposed a nonlinear relationship between dissonance and selective exposure, few have investigated this idea empirically, and studies that have yield inconsistent findings.[9] What is clear from Festinger's theory is that the presence of dissonance can motivate selective exposure.[10]

Applying Festinger's theory of cognitive dissonance in political contexts is not a difficult task, and many have drawn from his theory to gain insight into people's political attitudes and behaviors.[11] The theory is important for my purposes because it suggests that selective exposure *should* occur. When people encounter political views unlike their own, the potential exists for the development of cognitive dissonance. This can occur when one recognizes a conflict between an issue preference and a party's issue stance—as in the case of the partisan. This also can occur when people use media expressing views unlike their own. When a Republican supporter reads a pro-Democratic pamphlet, for example, the behavior of reading the pamphlet is inconsistent with her candidate preference and can give rise to dissonance. And the development of cognitive dissonance can motivate selective exposure. The news media, therefore, can both cause dissonance by presenting contradictory views and resolve dissonance by presenting likeminded views.

Although Festinger's theory of cognitive dissonance is arguably the most prominent explanation for selective exposure, it is not clear that dissonance is the only reason that people would seek likeminded information.[12] People may prefer likeminded information even in the absence of dissonance. Given that people find dissonance psychologically uncomfortable, people may select consistent information and avoid inconsistent information not to dispel *existing* dissonance, but to prevent *future* dissonance. The idea that there are other motivations for seeking and avoiding information is a characteristic of the next theoretical rationales for selective exposure.[13]

Motivations beyond Dissonance

Several other theories for why selective exposure should occur begin in the same place as cognitive dissonance theory: People sometimes are *motivated* to seek likeminded information. These theories part ways with cognitive dissonance theory, however, in terms of whether *dissonance* is required for selective exposure to occur.

The theory of lay epistemics, as detailed by Arie Kruglanski and his colleagues, proposes that individuals are compelled to act based on different motivations that vary by individual and by situation.[14] Kruglanski outlined a 2 × 2 typology of different rationales, or epistemic motivations, that drive people: (1) a need for closure versus a need to avoid closure and (2) specific versus nonspecific closure. The occurrence of selective exposure depends on which of these motivations is occurring.

The first component of the typology is whether individuals need closure or need to avoid closure. Those needing closure crave an unambiguous answer, solution, or truth and will try to reach this conclusion as quickly as possible. With only a few moments to check the latest headlines and a need to know what is going on in the world, for example, the fastest and most easily accessible news Web site is enticing because it solves a need for closure.

Other individuals may be motivated by a need to avoid closure, or a need to avoid reaching a conclusion. If one were afraid of making an incorrect decision, for example, and had the luxury of unlimited time to gather information, one would experience a need to avoid closure. In a political context, when a person doesn't share the same political leaning as a group of dear friends, she may experience a need to avoid closure. The individual may not want to vote for a candidate whom her friends dislike. She also may not want to vote against her political leaning. In response to this need to avoid closure, she may avoid reaching a vote decision altogether.[15]

The second component of the typology is whether individuals are motivated by specific or nonspecific closure. A need for *specific* closure involves a desire to reach a preferred conclusion. For example, if one wanted to conclude that a certain candidate was the superior choice in a presidential election, one would have a need for specific closure. A need for *nonspecific* closure entails a desire to reach any conclusion. If one merely wanted to know which candidate was the superior choice and didn't have any preferences about which candidate would be preferable, one would have a need for nonspecific closure.

Kruglanski's typology has many implications for the study of selective exposure. The need to *avoid* closure leads people to seek conflicting information in the face of possible closure. And when the solution is sufficiently ambiguous, people would try to avoid subsequent information exposure. When motivated by this need, selective exposure should occur in instances when one is tempted to reach a conclusion that *dis*agrees with one's predispositions. Any time people experiencing a need to avoid closure get close to experiencing closure, they switch their exposure pattern.

A need for closure also could inspire selective exposure.[16] A need for *nonspecific* closure, or the need to find a solution without any regard for what the solution is, motivates a pattern of "seizing" and "freezing" in information seeking.[17] Here, people should seek any type of information that would facilitate reaching a conclusion. Once a conclusion is reached, however, people "freeze" upon it and avoid nonsupportive information because they do not want to encounter disagreement. If likeminded information would help someone reach a fast solution, then selective exposure would occur. And once a solution is reached, selective exposure would persist so that the solution needn't be revisited.

The need for *specific* closure, or the motivation to find a preferred answer, would be expected to bias one's information search in the direction of a preferred alternative. In other words, those with a need for specific closure would be expected to engage in selective exposure.

Related motivational theories also suggest that people sometimes are motivated to seek likeminded information. Ziva Kunda's theory of motivated reasoning, a close relative of the theory of lay epistemics, predicts that motivations will influence selective exposure.[18] Motivated reasoning is the idea that people are driven by different goals. Accuracy goals motivate people to find the *correct* solution. This results in more careful and intense information processing. Accuracy goals should not inspire selective exposure. Directional goals, however, motivate people to reach a *preferred* conclusion. Like a need for specific closure, this motivation can lead to the selection of likeminded information. Yet Kunda elaborates that this doesn't mean that a person can reach *any* desired conclusion. There are constraints. Kunda explains, "When one wants to draw a particular conclusion, one feels obligated to construct a justification for that conclusion that would be plausible to a dispassionate observer. In doing so, one accesses only a biased subset of the relevant beliefs and rules."[19] When motivated by directional goals, people will engage in selective exposure to the extent that they believe that they could justify this strategy as being relatively unbiased.

These theories have wide application in political contexts. Scholars have drawn on these ideas to explore the preference for likeminded groups, the processing of political information, and, most important for this project, the selection of likeminded information.[20] In a particularly informative experiment, communication scholar Young Mie Kim manipulated people's motivations and then examined their information selections.[21] In her study, participants were asked to review information about two political candidates. Half of the participants were asked to focus on reaching an accurate and objective decision about which of the two candidates was better. The other participants were asked to focus their attention on defending their initial candidate preference. Since the experiment was conducted online, Kim was able to track the information that participants accessed unobtrusively. The results showed that participants focused on making an accurate decision sought more information—and more balanced information—than those focused on defending their original preference. As this study shows, motivations do influence selective exposure. In addition, motivations can change in different contexts.

The theories of lay epistemics and motivated reasoning build on cognitive dissonance by suggesting that people can crave likeminded information even in the absence of dissonance. Some motivations, such as directional goals or the need for specific closure, should prompt selective exposure. We again have strong theoretical reasons to anticipate that selective exposure will occur in certain situations. Yet motivations aren't the only reasons to anticipate that people will engage in selective exposure.

Cognitive Misers

Another proposed reason that people will seek out likeminded information is that they are "cognitive misers." Wanting to conserve cognitive resources, people look for ways to simplify information processing tasks. A cognitive miser looks to "reach decisions as quickly as possible."[22] It turns out that information that runs counter to one's beliefs is more resource intensive to process than consistent information.[23] It takes more time and requires more energy to understand contradictory information. When seeking information, contradictory information may be avoided for the simple reason that it requires more cognitive resources to process. From this cognitive critique, there is a "greater expenditure for processing nonsupportive information, along with more potential rewards from supportive information," which gives "supportive information a much higher probability of selection."[24] Some evidence supports the idea that likeminded information is preferable when people are faced with limited information processing capacity. Noise, fatigue, and cognitive overload, for example, create a higher need for closure, which can result in more selective exposure.[25] By taxing one's cognitive resources, therefore, the desire for likeminded information can be enhanced.

The cognitive miser perspective proposes that it is not an attitudinal aversion that prompts selective exposure, but rather a desire to limit one's processing. This explanation may be somewhat disconcerting for those who see politics as a domain characterized by debates and careful reasoning. It may be difficult to imagine that people take cognitive shortcuts when it comes to news and politics. Yet we know that people often use cognitive shortcuts, or heuristics, when approaching politics.[26] Candidates' partisanship and political ideology, for example, often are used as heuristics. Based on this information, people can infer all sorts of things about political candidates: their issue stances, their networks of associates, even their personal preferences. If the use of heuristics that reduce mental effort is typical when thinking about politics, is it any surprise that people would look to minimize processing when gathering information about politics and other topics via the news media?

Perceptions of Information Quality

Instead of looking for an easy way out of intensive processing as the cognitive miser perspective suggests, other theories suggest that people have more thoughtful reasons to engage in selective exposure. When searching for information, what leads people to choose one piece of information over another? When Peter Fischer, Stefan Schulz-Hardt, and Dieter Frey asked participants in their study this question, the results were revealing.[27] Participants frequently replied that they chose the *highest quality* information.

At first, it seems that this notion has some benefits in terms of how we might *wish* people approached information selection. Wouldn't it be great if citizens systematically selected the best information available? Yet quality judgments are rather subjective.[28] In particular "The *perceived truth value* of supportive communications is greater than that of nonsupportive material."[29] And when selecting *high-quality* information, people often select *likeminded* information.

These findings are consistent with research on biased assimilation, the idea that attitude-consistent information is judged to be more convincing, more legitimate, and more credible than contradictory information.[30] In their influential study, psychologists Charles Lord, Lee Ross, and Mark Lepper asked proponents and opponents of capital punishment to evaluate research on the effectiveness of capital punishment as a crime deterrent.[31] Both those in favor of and those opposed to capital punishment believed that research supporting their perspective was more convincing and was conducted better than research opposing their view. Applied to this project, likeminded news should be seen as more credible and convincing than news from a nonlikeminded source.

Indeed, judgments about news quality are influenced by one's beliefs and predispositions. The hostile media phenomenon proposes that when partisans view a putatively neutral news report, they perceive that the coverage is biased against their political perspective.[32] They perceive the report to be unfair, to hold the opposition to lower standards, and to present a stronger and more favorable case for the opposition.[33] Nonneutral news, in contrast, is seen as more accurate, fairer, and more relevant to likeminded partisans compared to those with different views.[34] The implications for news choice are clear—people may select likeminded news because they see it as the higher-quality choice.

There is good reason to suspect that perceptions of quality promote selective exposure. When people select information, they can do so using any number of criteria. When they are prompted to focus on information quality, people tend to select likeminded information.[35] What is even more important, however, is that without any prompting at all, people faced with many informational choices naturally tend to focus on information quality, and thus make likeminded informational choices.[36]

Summary of Selective Exposure Mechanisms

Though these theories are distinct, they overlap in notable ways. For example, people wanting to limit cognitive resources may rationally use sources that they trust. Further, it may be dissonance arousing to read a source perceived to be untrustworthy. Which theory *best* explains selective exposure is a matter of debate.[37] It is possible that these theories work in concert to produce selective exposure in different instances. A recent series of studies have begun to tackle the issue of which explanation best accounts for patterns of partisan selective exposure. These studies suggest that perceptions of information quality do a better job of explaining selective exposure than other possible explanations, such as the dissonance and cognitive miser perspectives.[38] In examining partisan selective exposure and news media selections, the information quality explanation makes a good deal of sense. People's perceptions of news quality should guide their news selections. It would be surprising if people relied on news from sources they believed to be of poor quality if higher quality options were available. The information quality explanation also accounts for habitual news media selections. It predicts that audiences would return to the same high-quality news source repeatedly. Other explanations—such as dissonance and other motivations—arguably predict more variability in exposure over time as dissonance and motivations fluctuate. In terms of understanding news viewing habits, therefore, the information quality explanation has some appeal.

Irrespective of which theory best accounts for selective exposure, what is particularly noteworthy for my purpose is that each suggests that selective exposure *should* occur. These theories document motivational and cognitive reasons to anticipate that people will prefer likeminded information. Because likeminded information is easier to process and seen to be of higher quality, people should prefer it. And because of motivations to avoid dissonance and to find evidence for a preferred perspective, people should prefer likeminded information, at least under certain circumstances. But does the research provide support for these propositions?

SELECTIVE EXPOSURE RESEARCH

Despite theoretical reasons to anticipate the occurrence of selective exposure, scholars cannot seem to agree on whether selective exposure occurs in reality. Divergent conclusions about selective exposure stem from a rich history of conflicting research findings. When putting the theoretical propositions outlined previously to the test, scholars haven't found consistent support for selective exposure.

The research can be divided roughly into two categories based on the strategies used to investigate selective exposure. The first strategy tends to support the idea of selective exposure; however, it fails to account for other possible interpretations of the data. The second strategy, though remedying many of the concerns about the first, provides only mixed evidence for selective exposure. Both strategies are reviewed in turn.

The first strategy for investigating selective exposure involves determining the viewpoint advanced in a message and then evaluating whether the audience for the message consists mainly of individuals sharing that view. A number of studies using this strategy find support for selective exposure.[39] New car owners, for example, recognize and read advertisements about the cars they purchased more than advertisements about other cars that they considered but ultimately did not purchase.[40] People with signs of anorexia find media about fitness and dieting more interesting than others do.[41] Political partisans are more apt to tune in to political events hosted by their preferred party.[42] In general, evidence using this strategy tends to find that the audience for a communication message tends to agree with the message.

A second commonly employed strategy is to ask people to choose from a set of messages—some likeminded, some contradictory, and some neutral—and then to observe which messages people select. If people select likeminded messages more than contradictory messages, then there is support for selective exposure. Some studies using this approach provide good evidence for selective exposure.[43] In one experiment, for example, mothers were randomly assigned to listen to one of two talks about children's behavior.[44] One talk claimed that children's behavior was based on nature; the other claimed that children's behavior was based on nurture. Given the opportunity to obtain additional information afterward, the mothers preferred information that matched their original beliefs.

Although some studies using this second strategy offer resounding support for selective exposure, other studies find that people do not always select likeminded information. For example, students were asked which type of exams they preferred—essay exams or objective exams. After making a selection, students were given a list of six different article abstracts and asked to rank them in order of how much they would like to read each article. For some students, all six abstracts were positive—half describing the benefits of essay exams and half describing the benefits of objective exams. Here, selective exposure was apparent. Students who preferred essay exams wanted to read articles extolling the benefits of essay exams, and students who preferred objective exams wanted to read articles about the benefits of objective exams. For other students, however, all six article abstracts were negative, half describing the drawbacks of essay exams and half describing the drawbacks of objective exams. Here, there was little evidence of selective exposure—students showed no preference for articles supporting their exam preference.[45]

Other studies confirm that people are not always driven to select likeminded information. When making a judgment about an interviewee, for example, one study found that people nearly universally selected information that *disagreed* with their original assessment of the interviewee.[46] Another study found that regular smokers were more interested than nonsmokers in an article about the connection between smoking and lung cancer—quite the opposite of what selective exposure would predict.[47] Selective exposure, it seems, does not hold in every situation.

In the mid-1960s, after nearly a decade of sustained academic attention on the topic of selective exposure, scholars Jonathan Freedman and David Sears embarked on the important task of reviewing the research—taken as a whole, did the research confirm that selective exposure occurs?[48] In their influential assessments, Freedman and Sears concluded that the evidence was wholeheartedly unconvincing.

Freedman and Sears argued that the first strategy for investigating selective exposure—to examine the relationship between the beliefs of the audience and the message content—was unable to show a *motivation* to seek likeminded information. Instead, Freedman and Sears noted that this type of study only provided evidence of de facto selective exposure. In these studies, a similarity between people's beliefs and the messages to which they were exposed could have nothing to do with a preference for likeminded information. Instead, other factors, such as the availability of information, could be responsible for the similarity. For example, people living in a Republican-leaning city may be exposed to more Republican messages simply because Republican messages are more widely available, not because the city residents prefer Republican messages and avoid Democratic messages. Freedman and Sears concluded:

> There seems to be ample evidence, both systematic and anecdotal, for the existence of *de facto* selectivity. Most audiences for mass communications apparently tend to overrepresent persons already sympathetic to the views being propounded, and most persons seem to be exposed disproportionately to communications which support their opinions.[49]

The second strategy for investigating selective exposure, Freedman and Sears argued, *could* provide evidence of motivated selective exposure because each person is given access to the *same* messages. Yet research using this second strategy had produced inconsistent results, leading Freedman and Sears to conclude that the support for selective exposure was unimpressive.

These early reviews of the literature had a substantial impact on selective exposure research. Research on the topic declined.[50] And contemporary scholarship continues to dismiss selective exposure by citing these reviews.[51]

This is not to say, however, that the concept of selective exposure has been abandoned altogether. On the contrary, there has been a recent renewal of interest in studying selective exposure. Recent reviews have reached more supportive conclusions about the concept of selective exposure.[52] Providing an update to the reviews conducted by Freedman and Sears, two recent meta-analyses evaluated the evidence for selective exposure.[53] They both uncovered support for selective exposure that was small to moderate in magnitude.

Others have proposed that selective exposure results are mixed because selective exposure occurs only under certain conditions.[54] Exposure decisions can vary on the basis of the perceived refutability of arguments, for example.[55] If a person believes that it would be easy to refute a piece of contradictory information, then there is little reason to avoid the information. Several of the theories reviewed earlier also suggest that the selection of likeminded information would occur only under certain conditions. Directional goals and a need for specific closure, for example, should motivate selective exposure. Other goals, however, may not.

Still others suggest that the mixed findings could be due to a number of method-ological flaws plaguing earlier investigations of selective exposure.[56] For example, differences in the usefulness and attractiveness of information could account for different exposure patterns. If contradictory information seemed more useful or more attractive, people may have sought it out rather than avoiding it. Further, having subjects select information in an experimental setting where they are aware that their information selection is being monitored may cause them to be more balanced in their selections. The setting could motivate accuracy goals and thus reduce selective exposure.

These recent assessments suggest that the jury is still out on the extent to which selective exposure occurs. Though there are theoretical reasons to anticipate that people will select likeminded information, the research seems to provide only a modest case for the occurrence of selective exposure. It seems that sometimes people are motivated to select likeminded information, but not always. The next section aims to provide one way of reconciling the theoretical promise of selective exposure with the less promising track record of research findings.

PARTISAN SELECTIVE EXPOSURE

An important reason that selective exposure studies may have produced conflicting patterns of results is the diversity of topics that have been studied. Research on selective exposure has been conducted on topics as diverse as cars,[57] parenting techniques,[58] personal care products,[59] and political preferences.[60] In summarizing the research on selective exposure, reviews have tended to group all studies of selective exposure together irrespective of their topic.[61] Different topics, however, may influence the propensity to engage in selective exposure.[62] Political topics, as will be discussed shortly, may be particularly likely to inspire selective exposure.

The Importance of Partisanship

Selective exposure occurs when people's beliefs guide their exposure decisions. Not every belief can guide every selection—if one considered *all* of the beliefs that would favor exposure to a media outlet, for example, and all of the beliefs that would *not* favor exposure to the outlet, one would be at an impasse. Some beliefs, therefore, must be more likely to guide exposure decisions compared to other beliefs. Which beliefs are more likely to guide exposure decisions?

One possibility is that personally relevant beliefs, those beliefs related to a person's interests or self-concept, are more likely to influence exposure decisions.[63] If one cared little about politics, he would have little motivation to seek out politically likeminded media. From a cognitive perspective, personally relevant beliefs are more readily activated from memory and hence, are more likely to guide our thoughts—and, as advanced here, our media selections. As communication scholars Vincent Price and David Tewksbury explain, certain constructs are chronically accessible—irrespective of the situation, they are more likely to be used as a basis for processing information. They note that "Chronic accessibility may come from a variety of sources.…One example would be the degree to which a given construct is linked with a person's self-concept."[64] Political partisanship represents a construct that can be quite connected to one's self-concept.[65] In contrast to other topics, those with strong political leanings may be particularly likely to engage in selective exposure because their political beliefs are accessible and personally relevant.

A second, and related, possibility is that we have been trained to use some beliefs more than others when processing information. Processing routines that have been developed and honed in political contexts may be transferred easily to related contexts, such as choosing among news media. When processing political information to reach a vote decision, for example, people frequently rely on information about partisanship and ideology to draw inferences: "Party and ideological stereotypes or schemata are among the richest and most widely shared in American politics."[66] When asked to choose information in a related context—such as selecting a news article about politics—people may readily default to this accessible and familiar routine to guide their choice. In nonpolitical contexts, such as deciding between multiple-choice and essay exams, people might not have well-developed routines on which they can rely.

In the political realm, there is plenty of evidence to suggest that partisans respond to incoming information on the basis of their political beliefs.[67] After presidential debates, partisans are quick to claim victory for their preferred candidate.[68] In 2000, when the winner of the presidential election was undetermined, "Evaluations of seemingly arbitrary events (e.g., beliefs about appropriate policies for dealing with hanging chads, whether to count votes from certain counties) were consistently and predictably aligned with people's political identities."[69] In 2004, 68 percent of Republicans found the Swift Boat Veterans for Truth advertisement criticizing Democratic presidential nominee Senator John Kerry's Vietnam service very or somewhat believable compared to only 23 percent of Democrats and 44 percent of Independents.[70] In response to a *New York Times* article published on February 21, 2008, suggesting that Republican Senator John McCain had an improper relationship with a female lobbyist, 63 percent of Republicans and 22 percent of Democrats believed McCain's denial of the charge more than the *New York Times* article.[71] If people frequently process political information using partisanship as a guide, then they also may use partisanship as a guide for making news and information choices.

A third possibility is that topics inspiring an emotional response may trigger selective exposure. When stimuli elicit an affective response, people are more likely to engage in selective exposure in response to the stimuli.[72] Certainly for some, politics yields an affective response.[73] In particular, those with strongly held political beliefs may avoid media outlets producing negative affect and approach media outlets producing positive affect.

Selective exposure, therefore, may be contingent on whether the topic is personally relevant, whether there is an established routine for processing information on the topic, or whether the topic generates an affective response. For partisans, political topics may be particularly likely to inspire selective exposure.

Far from a relic of a bygone era, partisanship remains a defining feature of our political system. In the citizenry, levels of party support remain at high levels: "The fraction of the citizenry declaring themselves to be supporters of the Democrats or Republicans produced a 90% level of party support by 2000–2004 that was indistinguishable from the 92% level observed in the 1950s."[74] In 1960, the influential book *The American Voter* asserted the central position of political parties in the American electorate.[75] When the conclusions were revisited nearly a half century later in *The American Voter Revisited,* the results were astounding in at least one regard: the similarities.[76] Partisanship had retained its importance. Partisan voting patterns also are strong, resurging after a lull in the 1970s to levels similar to those in the 1950s.[77] Further, on certain matters of public policy, partisans starkly differ. In 2004, for example, a majority of Republicans saw the War in Iraq as a part of the war on terrorism. Democrats, however, believed that the two were distinct.[78] Even political ideology, once considered a distinct dimension of political identity, has become more aligned with partisanship as citizens sort into two groups: liberal Democrats and conservative Republicans.[79] And the prominence of partisanship is visible not only among the citizenry, but also in the voting patterns of Congress and in elite political discourse.[80]

Partisanship's Influence on Exposure

By activating these partisan sentiments, political topics may inspire selective exposure. The research investigating *partisan* selective exposure confirms this suspicion. Not only do we tend to discuss politics with likeminded others, but we also tend use likeminded political information. Both will be discussed in turn.

Although this book focuses on likeminded *media* exposure, there is much to be learned from looking at the people with whom we discuss politics. People tend to visit about politics with others sharing their political point of view. In their in-depth study of voting in the 1948 presidential election, Berelson, Lazarsfeld, and McPhee found that "By and large, the voter is tied into a network of personal associations that is both homogeneous and congenial."[81] Democrats talk with fellow Democrats and Republicans with fellow Republicans. Although it is challenging to estimate the extent to which this occurs, evidence indicates that political discussions with likeminded others are the norm. In 2000, for example, around 35 percent of Bush voters discussed politics with someone who voted for Gore. In contrast, 85 percent of Gore voters discussed politics with someone who also voted for Gore. A nearly identical pattern appears among those discussing politics with someone who voted for Bush.[82]

These patterns are less surprising when one considers that likeminded partisans tend to live in the same areas and that there is a pattern of increasing political homogeneity in our local communities.[83] Equipped with money, mobility, and the ability to choose where to live, people increasingly live among fellow partisans.

If people are surrounded by politically likeminded others, would we expect that they also use politically likeminded news? The answer to this question depends on *why* people surround themselves with likeminded partisans. If people simply prefer likeminded information, then partisan selective exposure should occur whether people are discussing politics or gathering information from the media. If, however, there is something unique about face-to-face political conversation that leads to a preference for likeminded discussion, then people might *not* be motivated to use likeminded media. Encountering contradictory political beliefs may produce anxiety when visiting with a neighbor, for example, but not when listening to the radio.

Another possibility is that likeminded political discussion occurs not because people crave likeminded conversation, but because they are simply more likely to encounter likeminded views in their day-to-day lives. This is the de facto selectivity argument. People may wind up living in politically homogeneous communities without having this objective in mind. When selecting a place to live, factors other than the partisan breakdown of the neighborhood typically govern the decision. Yet politically likeminded communities develop because partisans tend to look for similar features in a community. Basketball hoops in front yards and runners in the neighborhood versus tennis courts and soccer fields—in 1996, Bill Clinton's political team found that these activities were good indicators of how citizens vote.[84] In his book *The Big Sort,* Bill Bishop describes the process: "Those interested in seeing a recently released foreign film or the new documentary on Townes Van Zandt on the big screen need to live in a community that can fill the theater. Similarly, someone who wants to participate in a specialized sport, worship in a less than mainstream church, or catch the latest alt-country acts will be drawn to certain locations."[85] In the process of seeking these seemingly nonpolitical features in a neighborhood, ever more politically homogeneous communities form. Yet if people had their druthers, they might prefer more political diversity.

Exposure to diversity in the media may be one way to compensate for a deficit of diversity in social settings. Some evidence supports this idea. In 1996, people reported encountering more politically diverse views in the media than in interpersonal discussions.[86] Yet it isn't clear whether people *wanted* more political diversity and sought it from the media or if they *encountered* more diversity in the media, whether they wanted it or not. This is particularly relevant given the changes in the media environment since 1996. We simply have more choices. Fox News and MSNBC, for example, now enliven cable packages. Online options have exploded. Our choices are more diverse. No matter your politics, connecting to likeminded information is but a few clicks away. And these changes can make a difference: "As the number of potential news sources multiplies, consumers must choose among them, and that exercise of choice may lead to less diversity of political exposure."[87] Turning to the research on partisan selective exposure to mediated messages, it doesn't seem that citizens use the media to seek diverse perspectives.

Instead, overtly political messages tend to attract likeminded audiences.[88] This observation has a strong track record over time. In a classic study of the 1940 presidential campaign, Republicans were more likely to attend to Republican campaign material compared to Democrats.[89] In 1958, Republican Senator William Knowland's twenty-hour telethon attracted a Republican audience.[90] Attitudes about U.S. policy in Vietnam influenced whether people tuned in to presidential speeches in the 1960s.[91] And in the 1976 election, candidate speeches and pamphlets tended to reach likeminded audiences.[92] The results persist in contemporary contexts.[93] For example, when news media coverage largely supported President Bush in 2003, some who opposed Bush sought news from foreign sources online.[94]

Broadly, these survey results show correspondences between the political predispositions of the audience and the partisan leanings of the media that they use. As correlational studies, however, these results are open to the critique that they document de facto selectivity but fall short of demonstrating motivated selective exposure.[95]

As previously discussed, studies of selective exposure where people are given a fixed set of media choices and their selections are observed have produced decidedly mixed results. When we narrow our focus and look only at those studies about politics, however, the case for selective exposure markedly improves. Given a choice of political pamphlets, people are more likely to select a preferred candidate's pamphlet compared to the pamphlets of a candidate they oppose.[96] Further, people are more likely to return a preaddressed postcard when an exterior envelope indicates support for a preferred candidate as opposed to when it indicates support for a candidate from another party.[97] Computer simulations of election campaigns show that subjects are more likely to view information about candidates they like in comparison to candidates they do not like.[98] Even with respect to information about issues such as affirmative action and gun control, people prefer likeminded information more than contradictory information.[99]

This is not to say that there aren't some exceptions to this pattern—one study found that people preferred information about a favored candidate, irrespective of whether the information was positive or negative, for example.[100] Rather, the evidence suggests that a stronger case for selective exposure can be made when looking exclusively at studies of *partisan* selective exposure.

Others have noted that political beliefs are particularly likely to motivate exposure. In 1967, psychologist Aaron Lowin observed that "Political selective-exposure studies have met with more success than have others."[101] Even the most well-known critics of selective exposure acknowledge this possibility; Sears and Freedman claim that selective exposure is most likely to be found "on long-standing issues (such as those chronically contested by the two major political parties)."[102] A meta-analysis on selective exposure also uncovered stronger effects for political topics.[103] There seems to be something special about partisanship when it comes to selecting information.

REVISITING THE CONCEPT OF SELECTIVE EXPOSURE

Theoretically, *partisan* selective exposure seems likely. And the track record of research findings over the past fifty years is promising. Yet much remains to be discovered. Past research has tended to focus on people's exposure decisions in a single instance—exposure to a political movie,[104] exposure to a political pamphlet,[105] or exposure to a political speech.[106] Though these studies help us to understand factors that influence single-exposure decisions, they provide limited insight into factors that influence people's more *habitual* exposure decisions. A number of factors that can influence exposure decisions are more likely to operate in single-exposure instances. The presence of a photograph, for example, can increase exposure to a news story.[107] The wording of a lead paragraph in a news article can influence whether people read the entire article or stop short.[108] Although these features can affect exposure to a single article or report, more habitual exposure decisions, such as the cable news network one *typically* watches, would not be influenced by these factors. It is possible, therefore, that selective exposure patterns have been underestimated because decisions in single-exposure studies can be influenced by factors that may not affect more habitual exposure decisions.

Research that has investigated more habitual exposure patterns by asking people about their preferred cable news station or talk radio program tends to show that people's beliefs are related to their media selections.[109] Many of these studies, however, fall short of documenting causal relationships between people's beliefs and their media use.[110] Furthermore, most studies to date have examined selective exposure for a single media type (e.g., talk radio preferences) at a single point in time, instead of comprehensively considering people's media consumption patterns.

When the focus expands beyond a single-exposure decision, it is vital to consider what counts as selective exposure. Selective exposure *could* be seen as an either/or phenomenon. As such, selective exposure would either occur always or not at all. Either a person would use *only* likeminded information or he would not be engaging in selective exposure. Many studies of selective exposure could be seen as studying selective exposure in this way because they examine a single media choice. In these studies, participants have only two possible reactions: to engage in selective exposure or not. These studies approach selective exposure as a dichotomy based on the study design, however, not based on a deliberate statement about how selective exposure works in all instances.

The theories I reviewed earlier in this chapter suggest that selective exposure will not occur in all situations. Whether by accident or for a motivational reason, people sometimes will encounter nonlikeminded information. Definitions of selective exposure also leave room for some exposure to nonlikeminded information. Klapper, for example, defines selective exposure as "the tendency of people to expose themselves to mass communications in accord with their existing opinions and interests and to avoid unsympathetic material."[111] Festinger sees selective exposure as a "selective process that favors consonant over dissonant information."[112] These definitions suggest that selective exposure is a tendency or an inclination to use likeminded sources, not the exclusive use of likeminded information. When examining a situation in which people can make multiple likeminded or nonlikeminded choices, others also have considered a propensity to choose likeminded information as evidence of selective exposure.[113] Throughout this book, therefore, I look at selective exposure as a tendency to use likeminded information. In the following chapter, I assess the evidence for partisan selective exposure. Do our news choices tend to coincide with our partisan beliefs?

Main Datasets Used

To examine partisan selective exposure, this book uses data from numerous sources. I describe the main data sources briefly here. More information is available in the appendices. A multimethod approach is employed to take advantage of the strengths of various research methods in exploring selective exposure. Surveys are used to explore the prevalence of selective exposure and to examine the relationships between selective exposure and its possible causes and consequences. I also use experiments to try to isolate causal dynamics. Though I investigate causal relationships, assessing causality is tricky business, and there are few fool-proof ways to conclusively demonstrate causal relationships. Even experiments, the gold standard of internal validity, can generate findings that do not apply outside of the laboratory.[114]

In this project, I rely on survey data gathered from the National Annenberg Election Surveys (NAES).[115] The NAES employed random-sample, telephone surveys during the primary and general election presidential campaigns in 2000, 2004, and 2008. These extensive surveys collected data from tens of thousands of Americans about their political attitudes, beliefs, behaviors, knowledge, media use habits, and demographic characteristics. A subset of participants in the NAES were contacted at two points in time and asked identical questions. I analyze these panel surveys to understand how partisan selective exposure functions over time.

In addition to the NAES, I use data gathered by Knowledge Networks in 2008 to examine partisan selective exposure. Knowledge Networks has a national, randomly selected panel of people who take part in research conducted over the Internet. Respondents agreeing to take part are given a WebTV in order to complete studies—thus, even those without Internet access are included in the sample. I worked with Knowledge Networks to conduct several experiments about the nature of partisan selective exposure. I also asked respondents to assess various media outlets. The experimental components of the research conducted by Knowledge Networks provide evidence of *causal* relationships and the survey component provides additional insight into how citizens perceive the media environment.

Beyond these data sources, other experimental, survey, and content analysis results will be discussed. I describe other studies in the chapters where the results are presented. Additional details about all of the studies conducted and analyses used are provided in the appendices.

This multimethod approach has a number of advantages. First, this project uses large-scale, national, random-sample surveys to evaluate partisan selective exposure. Findings from a national sample are more generalizable than surveys done in a single locale. Further, the surveys contain a breadth of content-specific media questions; this allows for analysis of exposure to many different media types. Instead of results pertaining to a single type of media, I evaluate whether partisan selective exposure is a more general, cross-outlet pattern with consistent political antecedents and consequences. I also employed several methodologies in order to understand partisan selective exposure. In addition to cross-sectional survey analysis, panel surveys and experiments provide more insight into patterns of partisan media exposure. These substantial strengths help me to contribute to what we know about partisan selective exposure.

SUMMARY

This chapter has provided the groundwork for examining partisan selective exposure. With strong theoretical reasons to suspect that selective exposure will occur, the evidence to date is surprisingly weak. By narrowing the focus to *partisan* selective exposure, however, the evidence is stronger. Yet we still have much to learn. Data gathered for this project allow for a more comprehensive look at partisan selective exposure. Before evaluating the causes and consequences of partisan selective exposure, the next chapter explores the extent to which partisan selective exposure occurs in the first place.

NOTES

1. Lewis Donohew and Philip Palmgreen, "A Reappraisal of Dissonance and the Selective Exposure Hypothesis," *Journalism Quarterly* 48, 3 (1971): 412–20.

2. Joseph T. Klapper, *The Effects of Mass Communication* (Glencoe, IL: The Free Press, 1960): 19–20.

3. William J. McGuire, "Selective Exposure: A Summing Up," in *Theories of Cognitive Consistency: A Sourcebook,* edited by Robert P. Abelson, Elliot Aronson, William J. McGuire, Theodore M. Newcomb, Milton J. Rosenberg, and Percy H. Tannenbaum (Chicago: Rand McNally and Company, 1968): 800.

4. Donald R. Kinder, "Communication and Politics in the Age of Information," in *Oxford Handbook of Political Psychology,* edited by David O. Sears, Leonie Huddy, and Robert Jervis (New York: Oxford University Press, 2003): 369.

5. John R. Zaller, *The Nature and Origins of Mass Opinion* (New York: Cambridge University Press, 1992): 139.

6. Eva Jonas, Stefan Schulz-Hardt, and Dieter Frey, "Giving Advice or Making Decisions in Someone Else's Place: The Influence of Impression, Defense, and Accuracy Motivation on the Search for New Information," *Personality and Social Psychology Bulletin* 31, 7 (2005): 978.

7. Leon Festinger, *A Theory of Cognitive Dissonance* (Stanford: Stanford University Press, 1957).

8. Festinger, *A Theory of Cognitive Dissonance,* 127–8.

9. Dieter Frey, "Different Levels of Cognitive Dissonance, Information Seeking, and Information Avoidance," *Journal of Personality and Social Psychology* 43 (1982): 1175–83.

10. Festinger, *A Theory of Cognitive Dissonance.*

11. See, for example, Ryan K. Beasley and Mark R. Joslyn, "Cognitive Dissonance and Post-Decision Attitude Change in Six Presidential Elections," *Political Psychology* 22, 3 (2001): 521–40; Aaron Lowin, "Approach and Avoidance: Alternate Modes of Selective Exposure to Information," *Journal of Personality and Social Psychology* 6, 1 (1967): 1–9; James C. McCroskey and Samuel V.O. Prichard, "Selective-Exposure and Lyndon B. Johnson's 1966 'State of the Union' Address," *Journal of Broadcasting* 11, 4 (1967): 331–7; Wilbur Schramm and Richard F. Carter, "Effectiveness of a Political Telethon," *Public Opinion Quarterly* 23, 1 (1959): 121–7.

12. See Alice H. Eagly and Shelly Chaiken, *The Psychology of Attitudes* (Fort Worth, TX: Harcourt Brace Jovanovich College Publishers, 1993): 479. Though Festinger's cognitive

dissonance theory proposes dissonance as a motivator of selective exposure, he acknowledged that dissonance is likely not the only factor that contributes to exposure patterns; he writes, "Active curiosity and the sheer pleasure of acquiring information for its own sake cannot be ignored in any discussion of voluntary seeking out of new information." Festinger, *A Theory of Cognitive Dissonance,* 124.

13. There has been debate on whether other motivational theories can be accounted for by cognitive dissonance theory. For more details, I refer the reader to *Psychological Inquiry* 3, 4 (1992), where a number of scholars discuss the relationship between cognitive dissonance and other motivational theories.

14. Arie W. Kruglanski, *Lay Epistemics and Human Knowledge: Cognitive and Motivational Bases* (New York: Plenum Press, 1989); Arie W. Kruglanski, *The Psychology of Closed Mindedness* (New York: Psychology Press, 2004). See, for example, the individual-level measure of need for closure in Arie W. Kruglanski, Donna M. Webster, and Adena Klem, "Motivated Resistance and Openness to Persuasion in the Presence or Absence of Prior Information," *Journal of Personality and Social Psychology* 65, 5 (1993): 861–76. See also Donna M. Webster and Arie W. Kruglanski, "Individual Differences in Need for Cognitive Closure," *Journal of Personality and Social Psychology* 67, 6 (1994): 1049–62.

15. Diana C. Mutz, "The Consequences of Cross-Cutting Networks for Political Participation," *American Journal of Political Science* 46, 4 (2002): 838–55.

16. Peter Fischer, Dieter Frey, Claudia Peus, and Andrea Kastenmüller, "The Theory of Cognitive Dissonance: State of the Science and Directions for Future Research," in *Clashes of Knowledge: Orthodoxies and Heterodoxies in Science and Religion,* edited by Peter Meusburger, Michael Welker, and Edgar Wunder (New York: Springer, 2008): 191. Note, however, that these authors also question whether complexity, which leads to need for closure, is responsible for the increase in selective exposure when more choices are available; see Peter Fischer, Stefan Schulz-Hardt, and Dieter Frey, "Selective Exposure and Information Quantity: How Different Information Quantities Moderate Decision Makers' Preference for Consistent and Inconsistent Information," *Journal of Personality and Social Psychology* 94, 2 (2008): 231–44.

17. Arie W. Kruglanski and Donna M. Webster, "Motivated Closing of the Mind: 'Seizing' and 'Freezing,'" *Psychological Review* 103, 2 (1996): 263–83.

18. Ziva Kunda, "The Case for Motivated Reasoning," *Psychological Bulletin* 108, 3 (1990): 480–98.

19. Ibid, 493.

20. Republicans with a high need for closure, for example, were the least likely to watch *Fahrenheit 9/11,* a film known for its criticism of Republican President George W. Bush, for example; see R. Lance Holbert and Glenn J. Hansen, "*Fahrenheit 9/11,* Need for Closure and the Priming of Affective Ambivalence: An Assessment of Intra-Affective Structures by Party Identification," *Human Communication Research* 32 (2006): 109–129. For other applications of these theories, see Arie W. Kruglanski, James Y. Shah, Antonio Pierro, and Lucia Mannetti, "When Similarity Breeds Content: Need for Closure and the Allure of Homogeneous and Self-Resembling Groups," *Journal of Personality and Social Psychology* 83, 3 (2002): 648–62; Lilach Nir, *What We Think Others Think: A Motivated Reasoning Model of Public Opinion Perception and Expression,* Unpublished Dissertation (University of Pennsylvania, Philadelphia, 2004); Charles S. Taber and Milton Lodge, "Motivated Skepticism in the Evaluation of Political Beliefs," *American Journal of Political Science* 50, 3 (2006): 755–69.

21. Young Mie Kim, "How Intrinsic and Extrinsic Motivations Interact in Selectivity: Investigating the Moderating Effects of Situational Information Processing Goals in Issue Publics' Web Behavior," *Communication Research* 34, 2 (2007): 185–211.

22. Shelley E. Taylor, "The Interface of Cognitive and Social Psychology," in *Cognition, Social Behavior, and the Environment,* edited by John H. Harvey (Hillsdale, NJ: Lawrence Erlbaum Associates, 1981): 195–6.

23. Kari Edwards and Edward E. Smith, "A Disconfirmation Bias in the Evaluation of Arguments," *Journal of Personality and Social Psychology* 71, 1 (1996): 5–24.

24. Dean A. Ziemke, "Selective Exposure in a Presidential Campaign Contingent on Certainty and Salience," in *Communication Yearbook,* edited by Dan Nimmo (New Brunswick, NJ: Transaction Books, 1980), 4: 500.

25. See examples in Kruglanski, *The Psychology of Closed Mindedness.*

26. Richard R. Lau and David P. Redlawsk, "Advantages and Disadvantages of Cognitive Heuristics in Political Decision Making," *American Journal of Political Science* 45, 4 (2001): 951–71.

27. Fischer, Schulz-Hardt, and Frey, "Selective Exposure and Information Quantity."

28. Peter Fischer, Eva Jonas, Dieter Frey, and Stefan Schulz-Hardt, "Selective Exposure to Information: The Impact of Information Limits," *European Journal of Social Psychology* 35 (2005): 469–92.

29. David O. Sears, "The Paradox of De Facto Selective Exposure without Preferences for Supportive Information," in *Theories of Cognitive Consistency: A Sourcebook,* edited by Robert P. Abelson, Elliot Aronson, William J. McGuire, Theodore M. Newcomb, Milton J. Rosenberg, and Percy H. Tannenbaum (Chicago: Rand McNally and Company, 1968): 785.

30. See, for example, Arthur G. Miller, John W. McHoskey, Cynthia M. Bane, and Timothy G. Dowd, "The Attitude Polarization Phenomenon: Role of Response Measure, Attitude Extremity, and Behavioral Consequences of Reported Attitude Change," *Journal of Personality and Social Psychology* 64, 4 (1993): 561–74; Geoffrey D. Munro and Peter H. Ditto, "Biased Assimilation, Attitude Polarization, and Affect in Reactions to Stereotype-Relevant Scientific Information," *Personality and Social Psychology Bulletin* 23, 6 (1997): 636–54.

31. Charles G. Lord, Lee Ross, and Mark R. Lepper, "Biased Assimilation and Attitude Polarization: The Effects of Prior Theories on Subsequently Considered Evidence," *Journal of Personality and Social Psychology* 37, 11 (1979): 2098–109.

32. Robert P. Vallone, Lee Ross, and Mark R. Lepper, "The Hostile Media Phenomenon: Biased Perception and Perceptions of Media Bias in Coverage of the Beirut Massacre," *Journal of Personality and Social Psychology* 49, 3 (1985): 577–85.

33. Ibid.

34. Albert C. Gunther and Janice L. Liebhart, "Broad Reach of Biased Source? Decomposing the Hostile Media Effect," *Journal of Communication* 56 (2006): 449–66. Note that the authors do not find consistent evidence that quality perceptions mediate the relationship between article reach (large vs. small audience) or article source (journalist vs. student) and perceived bias.

35. Fischer, Schulz-Hardt, and Frey, "Selective Exposure and Information Quantity."

36. Ibid.

37. Ibid.; Fischer, Jonas, Frey, and Schulz-Hardt, "Selective Exposure to Information: The Impact of Information Limits."

38. Ibid.

39. Elliott McGinnies and Leonard L. Rosenbaum, "A Test of the Selective-Exposure Hypothesis in Persuasion," *Journal of Psychology* 61 (1965): 237–40; Schramm and Carter, "Effectiveness of a Political Telethon"; Guido H. Stempel III, "Selectivity in Readership of Political News," *Public Opinion Quarterly* 25, 3 (1961): 400–4.

40. Danuta Erlich, Isaiah Guttman, Peter Schönbach, and Judson Mills, "Postdecision Exposure to Relevant Information," *Journal of Abnormal and Social Psychology* 54 (1957): 98–102.

41. Kristen Harrison, "The Body Electric: Thin-Ideal Media and Eating Disorders in Adolescents," *Journal of Communication* 50, 3 (2000): 119–43.

42. Schramm and Carter, "Effectiveness of a Political Telethon."

43. Some research has shown that after making a choice, individuals are more likely to choose positive information about their own decision compared to positive information about the opposite decision. See, for example, Jusdson Mills, "Avoidance of Dissonant Information," *Journal of Personality and Social Psychology* 2, 4 (1965): 589–93; Judson Mills, Elliot Aronson, and Hal Robinson, "Selectivity in Exposure to Information," *Journal of Abnormal and Social Psychology* 59 (1959): 250–3; Sidney Rosen, "Postdecision Affinity for Incompatible Information," *Journal of Abnormal and Social Psychology* 63, 1 (1961): 188–90

44. J. Stacy Adams, "Reduction of Cognitive Dissonance by Seeking Consonant Information," *Journal of Abnormal and Social Psychology* 62, 1 (1961): 74–8.

45. Mills, Aronson, and Robinson, "Selectivity in Exposure to Information."

46. Jonathan L. Freedman, "Preference for Dissonant Information," *Journal of Personality and Social Psychology* 2, 2 (1965): 287–9.

47. N.T. Feather, "Cigarette Smoking and Lung Cancer: A Study of Cognitive Dissonance," *Australian Journal of Psychology* 14, 1 (1962): 55–64.

48. Jonathan L. Freedman and David O. Sears, "Selective Exposure," in *Advances in Experimental Social Psychology,* edited by Leonard Berkowitz (New York: Academic Press, 1965), 2: 57–97; David O. Sears and Jonathan L. Freedman, "Selective Exposure to Information: A Critical Review," *Public Opinion Quarterly* 31 (1967): 194–213.

49. Freedman and Sears, "Selective Exposure," 89–90.

50. Fischer, Schulz-Hardt, and Frey, "Selective Exposure and Information Quantity," 241.

51. See, for example, Zaller, *The Nature and Origins of Mass Opinion*; Kinder, "Communication and Politics in the Age of Information."

52. John L. Cotton, "Cognitive Dissonance in Selective Exposure," in *Selective Exposure to Communication,* edited by Dolf Zillmann and Jennings Bryant (Hillsdale, NJ: Erlbaum, 1985): 11–33; David D'Alessio and Mike Allen, "Selective Exposure and Dissonance after Decisions," *Psychological Reports* 91 (2002): 527–32; Dieter Frey, "Recent Research on Selective Exposure to Information," in *Advances in Experimental Social Psychology,* edited by Leonard Berkowitz (New York: Academic Press, 1986), 19: 41–80.

53. D'Alessio and Allen, "Selective Exposure and Dissonance after Decisions"; William Hart, Dolores Albarracín, Alice Eagly, Inge Brechan, Matthew J. Lindberg, and Lisa Merrill, "Feeling Validated Versus Being Correct: A Meta-Analysis of Selective Exposure to Information," *Psychological Bulletin* 135, 4 (2009): 555–88.

54. Cotton, "Cognitive Dissonance in Selective Exposure"; Frey, "Recent Research on Selective Exposure to Information."

55. Randall R. Kleinhesselink and Richard E. Edwards, "Seeking and Avoiding Belief-Discrepant Information as a Function of Its Perceived Refutability," *Journal of Personality and*

Social Psychology 31, 5 (1975): 787–90; Lowin, "Approach and Avoidance"; Aaron Lowin, "Further Evidence for an Approach-Avoidance Interpretation for Selective Exposure," *Journal of Experimental Social Psychology* 5 (1969): 265–71.

56. Cotton, "Cognitive Dissonance in Selective Exposure."

57. See, for example, Ehrlich, Guttman, Schönbach, and Mills, "Postdecision Exposure to Relevant Information."

58. See, for example, Adams, "Reduction of Cognitive Dissonance by Seeking Consonant Information."

59. See, for example, Judson Mills, "The Effect of Certainty on Exposure to Information Prior to Commitment," *Journal of Experimental Social Psychology* 1 (1965): 348–55.

60. See, for example, Schramm and Carter, "Effectiveness of a Political Telethon."

61. Cotton, "Cognitive Dissonance in Selective Exposure"; D'Alessio and Allen, "Selective Exposure and Dissonance after Decisions"; Freedman and Sears, "Selective Exposure"; Sears and Freedman, "Selective Exposure to Information."

62. Indeed, Freedman and Sears noted that the data indicated "substantial variations between issues, subjects, and situations in the degree of preference for supportive information," Freedman and Sears, "Selective Exposure," 91.

63. Wolfgang Donsbach, "Exposure to Political Content in Newspapers: The Impact of Cognitive Dissonance on Readers' Selectivity," *European Journal of Communication* 6 (1991): 155–86.

64. Vincent Price and David Tewksbury, "News Values and Public Opinion: A Theoretical Account of Media Priming," in *Progress in the Communication Sciences,* edited by George Barnett and Franklin J. Boster (Greenwich, CT: Ablex), 13: 190.

65. Donald Green, Bradley Palmquist, and Eric Schickler, *Partisan Hearts & Minds: Political Parties and the Social Identities of Voters* (New Haven, CT: Yale University Press, 2002); Richard R. Lau, "Construct Accessibility and Electoral Choice," *Political Behavior* 11, 1 (1989): 5–32.

66. Lau and Redlawsk, "Advantages and Disadvantages of Cognitive Heuristics," 953.

67. There has been scholarly debate on the extent to which partisanship influences and biases our perceptions and interpretations of information. The most recent work suggests that there is evidence that partisanship does have an influence. See Alan Gerber and Donald Green, "Misperceptions about Perceptual Bias," *Annual Review of Political Science* 2 (1999): 189–210; Larry M. Bartels, "Beyond the Running Tally: Partisan Bias in Political Perceptions," *Political Behavior* 24, 2 (2002): 117–50.

68. Geoffrey D. Munro, Peter H. Ditto, Lisa K. Lockhart, Angela Fagerlin, Mitchell Gready, and Elizabeth Peterson, "Biased Assimilation of Sociopolitical Arguments: Evaluating the 1996 U.S. Presidential Debate," *Basic and Applied Social Psychology* 24 (2002): 15–26; Lee Sigelman and Carol K. Sigelman, "Judgments of the Carter-Reagan Debate: The Eyes of the Beholders," *Public Opinion Quarterly,* 48, 3 (1984): 624–8; Yariv Tsfati, "Debating the Debate: The Impact of Exposure to Debate News Coverage and Its Interaction with Exposure to the Actual Debate," *The International Journal of Press/Politics* 8, 3 (2003): 70–86.

69. David K. Sherman and Geoffrey L. Cohen, "The Psychology of Self-Defense: Self-Affirmation Theory," in *Advances in Experimental Social Psychology,* edited by Mark P. Zanna (San Diego, CA: Academic Press, 2006), 28: 190.

70. Kathleen Hall Jamieson and Natalie Jomini Stroud, "Cable and Talk Radio Boost Public Awareness of Swift Boat Ad, National Annenberg Election Survey Shows," *National Annenberg Election Survey Press Release,* August 20, 2004.

71. Kate Kenski and Kathleen Hall Jamieson, "Public Believes McCain over *New York Times* Story 2 to 1, Annenberg Data Show," *National Annenberg Election Survey Press Release,* March 4, 2008.

72. Taber and Lodge, "Motivated Skepticism in the Evaluation of Political Beliefs."

73. See, for example, George E. Marcus, W. Russell Neuman, and Michael MacKuen, *Affective Intelligence and Political Judgment* (Chicago: University of Chicago Press, 2000).

74. John Richard Petrocik, "Measuring Party Support: Leaners Are Not Independents," *Electoral Studies* 28 (2009): 565.

75. Angus Campbell, Philip E. Converse, Warren E. Miller, and Donald E. Stokes, *The American Voter* (Chicago: University of Chicago Press, 1960).

76. Michael S. Lewis-Beck, William G. Jacoby, Helmut Norpoth, and Herbert F. Weisberg, *The American Voter Revisited* (Ann Arbor, MI: University of Michigan Press, 2008).

77. Larry M. Bartels, "Partisanship and Voting Behavior, 1952–1996," *American Journal of Political Science* 44, 1 (2000): 35–50; Petrocik, "Measuring Party Support."

78. Gary C. Jacobson, *A Divider, Not a Uniter: George W. Bush and the American People* (New York: Pearson Longman, 2007).

79. Matthew Levendusky, *The Partisan Sort: How Liberals Became Democrats and Conservatives Became Republicans* (Chicago: University of Chicago Press, 2009).

80. Gary C. Jacobson, "Partisan Polarization in Presidential Support: The Electoral Connection," *Congress & the Presidency* 30, 1 (2003): 1–37; Sharon Jarvis, *The Talk of the Party: Political Labels, Symbolic Capital, and American Life* (Lanham, MD: Rowman & Littlefield, 2005).

81. Bernard R. Berelson, Paul F. Lazarsfeld, and William McPhee, *Voting: A Study of Opinion Formation in a Presidential Campaign* (Chicago: University of Chicago Press, 1954): 94.

82. Robert Huckfeldt, Jeanette Morehouse Mendez, and Tracy Osborn, "Disagreement, Ambivalence, and Engagement: The Political Consequences of Heterogeneous Networks," *Political Psychology* 25, 1 (2004): 65–95. See also Diana C. Mutz, *Hearing the Other Side: Deliberative Versus Participatory Democracy* (New York: Cambridge University Press, 2006).

83. Bill Bishop with Robert G. Cushing, *The Big Sort: Why the Clustering of Like-Minded America is Tearing Us Apart* (Boston: Houghton Mifflin Company, 2008).

84. Douglas B. Sosnik, Matthew J. Dowd, and Ron Fournier, *Applebee's America: How Successful Political, Business, and Religious Leaders Connect with the New American Community* (New York: Simon & Schuster, 2006).

85. Bishop, *The Big Sort,* 202.

86. Diana C. Mutz and Paul S. Martin, "Facilitating Communication across Lines of Political Difference: The Role of Mass Media," *American Political Science Review* 95, 1 (2001): 97–114.

87. Ibid., 111.

88. See, for example, Stempel, "Selectivity in Readership of Political News."

89. Early research by Lazarsfeld, Berelson, and Gaudet provided the groundwork for later investigations of political selectivity. Paul F. Lazarsfeld, Bernard Berelson, and Hazel Gaudet, *The People's Choice* (New York: Columbia University Press, 1948). Note that the conclusions have been debated; see Charles. K. Atkin, "Reassessing Two Alternative Explanations of De Facto Selective Exposure," *Public Opinion Quarterly* 34, 3 (1970): 464–5; Freedman and Sears, "Effects of Expected Familiarity with Arguments."

90. Schramm and Carter, "Effectiveness of a Political Telethon."

91. McGinnies and Rosenbaum only found this relationship for females. Remarking on why they did not find the same relationship for males, they argued that "the limited spread of male initial attitudes provided no opportunity for selective exposure to operate." McGinnies and Rosenbaum, "A Test of the Selective-Exposure Hypothesis in Persuasion," 240. See also McCroskey and Prichard, "Selective-Exposure and Lyndon B. Johnson's 1966 'State of the Union' Address."

92. Ziemke, "Selective Exposure in a Presidential Campaign."

93. See, in addition to the other examples noted, Sandra J. Ball-Rokeach, Joel W. Grube, and Milton Rokeach, "'Roots: The Next Generation': Who Watched and With What Effect?" *Public Opinion Quarterly* 45, 1 (1981): 58–68; Adam Clymer, "Fahrenheit 9/11 Viewers and Limbaugh Listeners about Equal in Size Even Though They Perceive Two Different Nations, Annenberg Data Show," *National Annenberg Election Survey Press Release,* August 3, 2004; David L. Paletz, Judith Koon, Elizabeth Whitehead, and Richard B. Hagens, "Selective Exposure: The Potential Boomerang Effect," *Journal of Communication* 22, 1 (1972): 48–53; Natalie Jomini Stroud, "Media Effects, Selective Exposure, & *Fahrenheit 9/11,*" *Political Communication* 24, 4 (2007): 415–32; Steven H. Chaffee, Melissa Nichols Saphir, Joseph Graf, Christian Sandvig, and Kyu Sup Hahn, "Attention to Counter-Attitudinal Messages in a State Election Campaign," *Political Communication,* 18 (2001): 247–72; Shanto Iyengar and Kyu S. Hahn, "Red Media, Blue Media: Evidence of Ideological Selectivity in Media Use," *Journal of Communication* 59 (2009): 19–39; Shanto Iyengar, Kyu S. Hahn, Jon A. Krosnick, and John Walker, "Selective Exposure to Campaign Communication: The Role of Anticipated Agreement and Issue Public Membership," *Journal of Politics* 70 (2008): 186–200.

94. Samuel J. Best, Brian Chmielewski, and Brian S. Krueger, "Selective Exposure to Online Foreign News during the Conflict with Iraq," *The International Journal of Press/Politics* 10, 4 (2005): 52–70.

95. Freedman and Sears, "Selective Exposure"; Sears and Freedman, "Selective Exposure to Information."

96. Steven H. Chaffee and Jack M. McLeod, "Individual vs. Social Predictors of Information Seeking," *Journalism Quarterly* 50 (1973): 237–45; Jonathan L. Freedman and David O. Sears, "Voters' Preferences among Types of Information," *American Psychologist* 18 (1963): 375.

97. Dorothy L. Barlett, Pamela B. Drew, Eleanor G. Fahle, and William A. Watts, "Selective Exposure to a Presidential Campaign Appeal," *Public Opinion Quarterly* 38, 2 (1974): 264–70; Lowin, "Approach and Avoidance."

98. Michael F. Meffert, Sungeun Chung, Amber Joiner, Leah Waks, and Jennifer Garst, "The Effects of Negativity and Motivated Information Processing during a Political Campaign," *Journal of Communication* 56, 1 (2006): 27–51; David P. Redlawsk, "Hot Cognition or Cool Consideration?" *Journal of Politics* 64, 4 (2002): 1021–44.

99. Taber and Lodge, "Motivated Skepticism in the Evaluation of Political Beliefs."

100. Interestingly, Meffert and colleagues found that subjects also preferred negative information about their favored candidate. They propose that people may be more likely to expose themselves to negative information about their preferred candidate if they believe that it is easily refutable. See Meffert, Chung, Joiner, Waks, and Garst, "The Effects of Negativity." Several experimental studies provide support for this idea; see Lowin, "Approach and Avoidance"; Lowin, "Further Evidence for an Approach-Avoidance Interpretation."

101. Lowin, "Approach and Avoidance," 2.

102. David O. Sears and Jonathan L. Freedman, "Effects of Expected Familiarity with Arguments upon Opinion Change and Selective Exposure," *Journal of Personality and Social Psychology* 2, 5 (1965): 421.

103. Hart, Albarracín, Eagly, Brechan, Lindberg, and Merrill, "A Meta-Analysis of Selective Exposure to Information."

104. Ball-Rokeach, Grube, and Rokeach, "'Roots: The Next Generation': Who Watched and With What Effect?"; Clymer, "Fahrenheit 9/11 Viewers and Limbaugh Listeners"; Paletz, Koon, Whitehead, and Hagens, "Selective Exposure: The Potential Boomerang Effect"; Stroud, "Media Effects, Selective Exposure, & *Fahrenheit 9/11.*"

105. Chaffee and McLeod, "Individuals vs. Social Predictors of Information Seeking"; Freedman and Sears, "Voters' Preferences among Types of Information."

106. McCroskey and Prichard, "Selective-Exposure and Lyndon B. Johnson's 1966 'State of the Union' Address"; Schramm and Carter, "Effectiveness of a Political Telethon."

107. Dolf Zillmann, Silvia Knobloch, and Hong-sik Yu, "Effects of Photographs on the Selective Reading of News Reports," *Media Psychology* 3 (2001): 301–24.

108. Dolf Zillmann, Lei Chen, Silvia Knobloch, and Coy Callison, "Effects of Lead Framing on Selective Exposure to Internet News Reports," *Communication Research* 31 (2004): 58–81.

109. See, for example, Joseph N. Cappella, Joseph Turow, and Kathleen Hall Jamieson, *Call-in Political Talk Radio: Background, Content, Audiences, Portrayal in Mainstream Media* (Philadelphia: Annenberg Public Policy Center, 1996); Pew Research Center for the People & the Press, *Trends 2005* (Washington, DC, 2005).

110. A number of these studies rely on cross-sectional data without the presence of controls. These studies, therefore, are unable to show that people are motivated to select likeminded media. This follows the arguments of Freedman and Sears. Freedman and Sears, "Selective Exposure"; Sears and Freedman, "Selective Exposure to Information."

111. Klapper, *The Effects of Mass Communication,* 19.

112. Leon Festinger, *Conflict, Decision, and Dissonance* (Stanford: Stanford University Press, 1964), 64.

113. See, for example, Silvia Knobloch-Westerwick and Jingbo Meng, "Looking the Other Way: Selective Exposure to Attitude-Consistent and Counterattitudinal Political Information," *Communication Research* 36 (2009): 426–48, who look at length of exposure to attitude-consistent and counterattitudinal information, or Iyengar, Hahn, Krosnick, and Walker, "Selective Exposure to Campaign Communication", who look at number of subchapter visits.

114. Carl I. Hovland, "Reconciling Conflicting Results Derived from Experimental and Survey Studies of Attitude Change," *American Psychologist* 14 (1959): 8–17.

115. Daniel Romer, Kate Kenski, Kenneth Winneg, Christopher Adasiewicz, and Kathleen Hall Jamieson, *Capturing Campaign Dynamics 2000 & 2004: The National Annenberg Election Survey* (Philadelphia: University of Pennsylvania Press, 2006); Daniel Romer, Kate Kenski, Paul Waldman, Christopher Adasiewicz, and Kathleen Hall Jamieson, *Capturing Campaign Dynamics: The National Annenberg Election Survey: Design, Method, and Data* (New York: Oxford University Press, 2004).

3

USING NICHE NEWS

DESPITE DECADES OF attention, selective exposure remains theoretically promising, yet empirically illusive. Numerous studies call the concept into question.[1] The authors of several influential reviews note that selective exposure appears to occur only under limited circumstances.[2] Others urge the abandonment of the concept altogether.[3] The purpose of this chapter is to evaluate the evidence for selective exposure using contemporary data. I narrow the debate to a single domain: *partisan* selective exposure. I exclusively examine this domain for several reasons. Political topics can give rise to heated emotional reactions.[4] Citizens routinely view the world of politics through the lens of partisanship. And for some, partisanship is fundamentally connected to their identity.[5] These factors arguably make partisan selective exposure particularly likely to occur.

This chapter examines a wide variety of contexts in order to understand the extent to which our political leanings influence our media exposure decisions. The main question of this chapter is: Are people motivated to use politically likeminded media? I begin by evaluating situations in which partisan selectivity would be most expected and most easily demonstrated. I investigate who watches unmistakably partisan media by looking at the audiences for the national political conventions and the film *Fahrenheit 9/11*. Although these types of partisan media events can be politically influential, they don't occur every day. To evaluate whether partisan selective exposure is more pervasive, I assess habitual news media exposure—are our political beliefs related to where we typically turn for news? I then turn to experimental evidence. When given the opportunity to browse political magazines in a waiting room, for example, which magazines do people peruse? What about when they are given a free subscription to a political magazine? The final section of this chapter probes whether the contemporary media environment changes patterns of selective exposure. In particular, does the explosion of news media outlets exacerbate partisan selective exposure? With data from numerous sources, the findings of this chapter provide extensive evidence that partisan selective exposure is alive and well.

MEDIATED POLITICAL EVENTS

Do people watch some programs—and not others—on the basis of their political beliefs? To start, I examine media events with unambiguous partisan leanings. Do the political conventions, for example, inspire likeminded partisans to watch and the opposition to flip to another channel?

Political Conventions

During presidential campaigns, the Democratic and Republican conventions represent clear moments for observing partisan selective exposure. The partisanship of these events is blatant and prominent convention speeches are widely viewed. In 2008, for example, the nomination acceptance speeches at each major party's convention attracted between 38 million and 39 million viewers.[6] If selective exposure occurs, Democrats should be drawn to the Democratic National Convention (DNC) and Republicans should be drawn to the Republican National Convention (RNC). To evaluate this idea, I turned to the National Annenberg Election Surveys (NAES).

There are numerous ways to use survey data to analyze who watched the conventions. I could look at the percentage of Democrats and the percentage of Republicans watching the DNC, for example. But all sorts of people may both view the DNC and identify as Democrats. I want to know whether being a Democrat attracted viewers to the DNC and not something else, like race or gender. Instead of presenting the raw percentage of partisans viewing the DNC and the RNC, I use regression analysis to control for other factors. Rather than focus on the statistical details of each analysis in the main text, I instead present summary charts depicting the relationships uncovered. What should be noted is that the values shown in the figures throughout this book are based on analyses controlling for numerous other variables, including respondents' demographics, political habits and beliefs, and media use. Therefore, the results are appropriately interpreted as describing relationships where these other variables are held constant. One other detail of the analysis deserves note. I look at a combined measure of partisanship and political ideology, two components of one's political leaning that yield similar results if examined separately. For more details on the analysis and measurement, interested readers are encouraged to review the appendices. Figures 3.1 and 3.2 show the probabilities of watching the nomination speeches at each convention, holding other factors constant.

The data shown here, and elsewhere in the book, aren't for those with the strongest partisan and ideological attachments.[7] If I were to use this data, the patterns would be even more impressive. Instead, the results show the behavior of those with weaker political attachments (those one standard deviation away from the average political leaning in the study). Even among these individuals, the patterns are clear. Consistently—in 2000, 2004, and 2008—where people stood politically influenced their convention viewing. Liberals and Democrats watched Gore, Kerry, and Obama accept the Democratic presidential nomination. Conservatives and Republicans watched the Bush and McCain acceptance speeches. Though the data presented in Figures 3.1 and 3.2 go back only to 2000, partisan patterns of convention

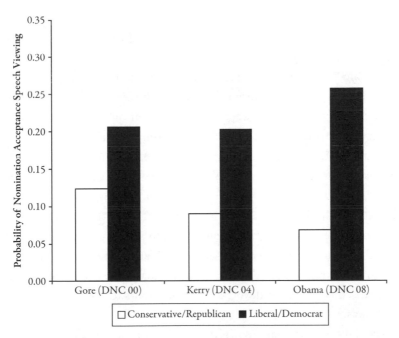

FIGURE 3.1 Probability of Watching Democratic Presidential Nomination Acceptance Speeches. Results based on logistic regression analyses predicting viewership of the entire nomination address. Analyses control for demographics, political orientations, and patterns of media use. Ideology/partisanship is significant in all analyses. Ideology/partisanship values are calculated using one standard deviation from the mean value. More details can be found in the technical appendix for this chapter.

Source: Data from the 2000, 2004, and 2008 NAES Rolling Cross-Sectional (RCS).

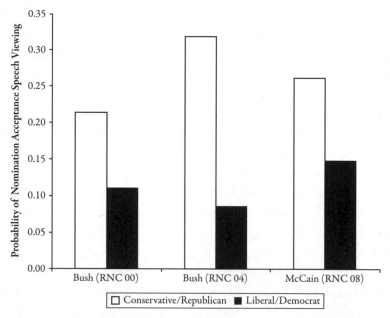

FIGURE 3.2 Probability of Watching Republican Presidential Nomination Acceptance Speeches. Analysis details are the same as those described below Figure 3.1.

viewing are not a recent phenomenon. Data from 1976 and 1988 also show a similar pattern.[8]

Ratings from The Nielsen Company—the television industry's gold standard for audience metrics—provide additional evidence that political conventions spark selectivity. Nearly half of those watching the conventions *watched only one* of the 2008 party conventions. Of those who watched only one, about half watched only the RNC and about half watched only the DNC. Although these data don't tell us whether *Democrats* tuned in to the DNC and *Republicans* the RNC, they do show us that citizens were selective in their convention viewing. Based on the NAES results, partisanship likely explains at least some of these differences. Further, the Nielsen figures may underplay the extent of selective exposure because I cannot tell based on these data whether people spent considerably more time watching one convention compared to the other. It is possible that some spent only ten minutes watching one convention but devoted numerous hours to the other based on their partisan beliefs.

As unambiguously partisan events, the conventions allow for a straightforward investigation of partisan selective exposure. The evidence is clear: Partisans are far more likely to watch a candidate accept *their* party's nomination than to watch the opposition. Do less routine media events also inspire selectivity? In the following section, I analyze the audience composition of a popular partisan film.

Political Film: Fahrenheit 9/11

In the summer of 2004, a notable political film stormed the box office: *Fahrenheit 9/11*. The film's anti-Bush sentiment was unmistakable. In the opening scene, filmmaker Michael Moore asks the audience whether the 2000 presidential election was perhaps "just a dream." How did Al Gore lose the election to George W. Bush? With bluegrass music twanging in the background, Moore pieces together an answer. Moore invites the audience to conclude that Bush—and his powerful family connections—rigged the voting process, influenced the Supreme Court, manipulated the news media via the Fox News election desk, and, ultimately, stole the election.

This popular film represents another excellent opportunity for examining partisan selective exposure. Given its blatant partisanship, would the film attract a mainly likeminded audience? Or would its critical acclaim, strong box office showing, and numerous film awards attract viewers from across the political spectrum? I examined data from the NAES to find out. The results confirmed my suspicion. The film's popularity did not signal bipartisan curiosity. Rather, the film mainly attracted a likeminded audience. After taking into account demographic and other political differences between those who went to see the film and those who did not, those with unfavorable attitudes toward Bush were far more likely to view the film. The probability of someone with a favorable attitude toward Bush going to see the film was 0.02. The probability of someone with an *un*favorable attitude toward Bush going to see the film was significantly greater—0.13.[9] Those with unfavorable impressions of Bush were more than six times more likely to watch the film. And those with favorable impressions of Bush opted to spend their money elsewhere.[10]

Partisan media events, such as political conventions and partisan films, attract likeminded audiences. Yet these events don't happen every day. And occasional instances of partisan selective exposure likely have only limited political influence. In the next section, I evaluate whether the occurrence of partisan selective exposure might be more prevalent than these isolated events would have us believe.

Habitual News Media Use

Partisan selective exposure occurs when viewing national party conventions and when deciding to watch a partisan film. Does the same thing happen in our day-to-day news selections? In the following section, I make three arguments. First, news exposure is common. This is not to say that everyone watches news. Just as the modern media environment allows people to find likeminded news, it also allows them to abandon the news if they so choose.[11] Rather, it is to document that the news remains an important part of the media landscape, particularly during presidential elections.[12] Second, audiences are selective. They don't want news from *any* outlet; they want news from *specific* outlets. I find very little evidence that people randomly make their news selections. Third, audience selectivity is predictable. Audiences are not turning en masse to the news media to seek the diverse views that they are lacking in their social circles. There is audience demand for politically like-minded news.

Newspapers

Over the past decade, newspaper circulation figures have declined precipitously.[13] Although circulation figures exceeded 60 million in the 1990s, they dropped to around 49 million by 2008.[14] Despite declining readership, newspapers remain influential. Leading national newspapers—such as the *New York Times*—can influence how other media outlets cover the news, for example.[15] And as more and more newspapers—and readers—venture online, the demise of the newspaper looks decidedly less certain. The Project for Excellence in Journalism reports that "Despite an image of decline, more people today in more places read the content produced in the newsrooms of American daily newspapers than at any time in years past."[16] I will return to partisan selectivity and the Internet shortly; for now, I focus on hard-copy newspaper reading.

Newspaper choices are different from other types of news media choices that we make. Compared to other media types, newspaper choices are constrained. Many communities have a single local newspaper of record. Residents of Helena, Montana who want to read a local newspaper, for example, have one choice: the *Independent Record*. In areas dominated by a single newspaper, residents still have an important choice; they can choose to read the newspaper or they can choose to forgo the paper. In other areas, though admittedly dwindling, there are competing newspapers: in Detroit, the *Detroit Free Press* and *The Detroit News*; in Fort Wayne, Indiana, *The Journal-Gazette* and the *News-Sentinel*; and in Las Vegas, the *Las Vegas Review-Journal* and *The Las Vegas Sun*. A number of these newspapers differ on political grounds—in each of the instances I just mentioned, one endorsed Democrat Barack Obama for president in 2008 and the other endorsed Republican John McCain. In these types of communities, citizens can choose which newspaper to read based on numerous criteria—one of which could be the partisan leaning of the paper. Beyond reading a local newspaper, citizens in some locations also have the option to read out-of-area newspapers. In Austin, Texas, for example, I can subscribe to the *Austin-American Statesman,* the *New York Times,* the *Wall Street Journal,* the *Dallas Morning News,* and *USA Today.*

Given that there is some—albeit limited—choice, which newspapers do people read? To evaluate this question, I turned to the NAES. As part of the survey, those who read a newspaper were asked to name the newspaper they read most often. Which newspapers do people read? Do they tend to read politically likeminded newspapers? In order to answer these questions, the thousands of newspapers that respondents to the NAES named needed to be grouped into partisan categories. This was a formidable challenge. How can one categorize nearly all of the newspapers in the United States? I opted to categorize the political leanings of the named newspapers based on the presidential candidate endorsed by the newspaper.

Measuring newspaper leanings based on endorsements raises a simple question: Are endorsements a valid measure of a newspaper's political leaning? There are numerous justifications for using endorsements as a proxy for newspaper leanings. Several studies have found evidence of a relationship between the tone newspapers use when covering candidates and newspapers' editorial endorsements.[17] In their meta-analysis, communication scholars Dave D'Alessio and Mike Allen, for example, found a relationship between the presidential endorsements made by newspapers and news coverage.

As a stand-alone measure, editorial endorsements represent an unambiguous statement of a newspaper's partisan sentiment. Anecdotally, newspaper endorsements have influenced exposure decisions. In 2004, for example, readers reacted when the *Statesman* from Austin, Texas, endorsed George W. Bush and the *Lone Star Iconoclast* from Crawford, Texas, endorsed John Kerry: "In Austin, more than 300 protesters gathered near the newspaper's building. In President Bush's adopted hometown of Crawford, almost half of the newspaper's 920 subscribers cut ties."[18] The evidence that editorial endorsements are uniquely influential, however, is admittedly limited.[19] Unlike previous researchers, however, I am not interested in isolating the effects of an endorsement by comparing attitudes before and after an endorsement is made, for example. Rather, I am using endorsements as a proxy for newspaper leanings.

Whether endorsements reflect the tone of the news, mirror the tone of the editorial page, or merely represent an unequivocal expression of editorial sentiment about the candidates, this proxy allows for the categorization of the thousands of different newspapers identified by respondents.

Data from the NAES provide evidence that people tend to read newspapers that endorse a likeminded presidential candidate. As shown in Figure 3.3, liberals and Democrats were more likely to read Kerry-endorsing newspapers compared to conservatives and Republicans. Further, conservatives and Republicans tended to read newspapers endorsing Bush more than liberals and Democrats.[20] Although results for those with moderate political leanings are shown in Figure 3.3, if I look at the strongest partisans, the pattern is even more obvious. A strong conservative Republican had a 0.24 probability of reading a Bush-endorsing newspaper

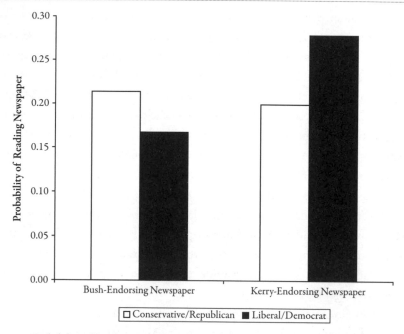

FIGURE 3.3 Probability of Reading Newspapers by Political Leanings. Results based on logistic regression analyses predicting newspapers named by respondents. Analyses control for demographics, political orientations, and patterns of media use. Ideology/partisanship is significant in all analyses. Ideology/partisanship values are calculated using one standard deviation from the mean value. More details can be found in the technical appendix for this chapter.

Source: Data from the 2004 NAES RCS.

compared to a 0.16 probability for a strong liberal Democrat, again controlling for other factors. The probability of reading a Kerry-endorsing newspaper was 0.33 for strong liberal Democrats and 0.18 for strong conservative Republicans.

The results displayed in Figure 3.3 do not prove that people *prefer* to read newspapers expressing views that match their political beliefs, however. This is a rather thorny issue. One reason that it is thorny is because there is a relationship between newspaper endorsements and the voting habits of the community in which the newspaper circulates.[21] In predominantly Republican communities, newspapers tend to endorse Republicans. In predominantly Democratic communities, newspapers tend to endorse Democrats. Considering market pressures, this is rather expected. Newspapers risk declining circulation if they defy the partisan sentiments of their readers. From the perspective of understanding partisan selective exposure, however, this makes my job more challenging. Do people *want* a likeminded newspaper or do they *settle* for a likeminded newspaper because no other local option is available?

Several details add weight to the idea that people purposefully select likeminded newspapers. First, I can statistically control for the partisan sentiment of each congressional district. If the districts' partisan sentiments are responsible for the observed relationship between newspaper reading and reader partisanship, then taking the district's voting habits into account should eliminate the observed pattern of partisan selective exposure. The results do not support this idea, however. It is true that living in a predominantly Republican district means that it is more likely you'll read a Republican-endorsing newspaper. And living in a predominantly Democratic district means that it is more likely you'll read a Democrat-endorsing newspaper. Yet irrespective of whether people live in predominantly Republican districts, predominantly Democratic districts, or districts with mixed partisan leanings, Republicans are still more likely to read a Republican-endorsing newspaper and Democrats are still more likely to read a Democrat-endorsing newspaper.

Second, communities served by more than one newspaper can be examined separately. If people are not driven by their partisan leanings to select likeminded news, then when they have the option to select more diverse news, they should embrace it. Yet this is far from the case. In communities served by more than one newspaper, people report that they encounter *more* likeminded information from the media.[22] This arguably is the case because people select newspapers that match their political inclinations. The newspaper market spanning New York City and surrounding areas offers a compelling case study. Here, newspapers were divided in 2004—the *New York Times* and *Newsday* endorsed Democrat John Kerry and the *New York Post* and *New York Daily News* endorsed Republican George Bush. Given the choice, New Yorkers opted for likeminded newspapers, as illustrated in Figure 3.4.

This calls into question the idea that people merely *settle* for a likeminded newspaper, but wish they could be reading more diverse news. They seem to seek out news that corresponds with their own predispositions.

Political Talk Radio

Overall, the genre of radio known as news/talk/information—of which a subset is political talk radio—reaches nearly 48 million listeners each week.[23] Popular talk radio hosts attract significant audiences. The most popular political talk radio program is hosted by Rush Limbaugh and attracts over 14 million people each week.[24] Compared to newspapers, talk radio has a greater potential to inspire partisan selectivity. Diverse political perspectives are readily available over the airwaves and many hosts clearly state their partisan leanings.

To examine talk radio listening patterns, I again turned to the NAES. Respondents listening to political talk radio identified the radio shows and hosts to which they listened. To determine whether people listened to likeminded radio programs, I categorized the thousands of hosts and programs named by respondents into partisan

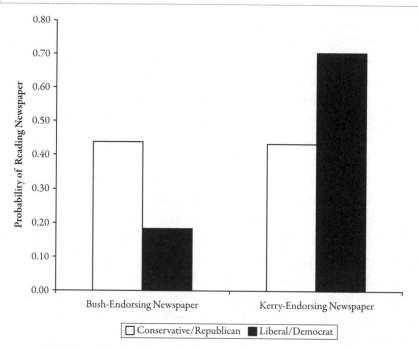

FIGURE 3.4 Probability of Reading New York Newspapers by Political Leanings. Analysis details are the same as those described below Figure 3.3. Given the left-leaning political inclinations of citizens in this newspaper market, ideology/partisanship values are calculated using two standard deviations from the mean value. Results are for residents of the New York/New Jersey newspaper market reading the *New York Times*, *New York Post*, *Newsday*, or *New York Daily News*.

categories on the basis of three criteria. First, many radio hosts and programs openly identify their political leanings. For example, Greg Garrison's promotional materials say, "Garrison brings his populist conservative values to the airwaves."[25] Second, the leading trade publication *Talkers* often notes the political leanings of various hosts and programs. For example, radio host Ed Schultz is labeled a "liberal talent" by *Talkers*.[26] Third, there has been extensive scholarly research on talk radio. Where applicable, I also examined how other scholars had categorized various hosts and programs.[27]

This coding scheme has several implications for my ability to assess partisan selective exposure. First, this categorization system is strict in the sense that ambiguous cases were not categorized as liberal or conservative. Only those hosts and shows where clear evidence about the political leanings could be obtained were categorized as liberal or conservative. It is possible that this strategy captures only the *most* partisan programs. This would limit the conclusions that could be drawn about listening to radio programs with less blatant partisanship. Second, this approach is conservative because classification errors would reduce support for partisan selective exposure. For example, there may be some instances where a program was not coded as having a partisan leaning because there wasn't adequate evidence but where, in actuality, the program does have a partisan bent. In the event that this occurred, my ability to detect partisan selective exposure would be obscured. If partisan selective exposure is occurring, meaning that there is a strong relationship between political beliefs and talk radio listening, incorrectly coding a nonpartisan program as partisan would yield *lower* estimates of partisan selective exposure. It is also possible, despite efforts to employ strict criteria in categorizing the radio programs, that a program was coded as partisan when in actuality, it is nonpartisan. Again, the effect of categorization errors is to make it more difficult for me to find evidence for partisan selective exposure. Errors in coding like these work against my hypothesis.

Using this coding scheme, the analysis reveals that talk radio listeners tend not to explore diverse political views when they tune in to the radio. The NAES encouraged people to name multiple hosts and programs to which they listened. Yet respondents infrequently reported listening to both liberal and conservative radio programs. Only 3 percent of those naming any partisan program identified that they listened to bipartisan radio hosts and programs. Talk radio listeners tended to tune in to radio programs and hosts that matched their political beliefs. The results are shown in Figure 3.5.

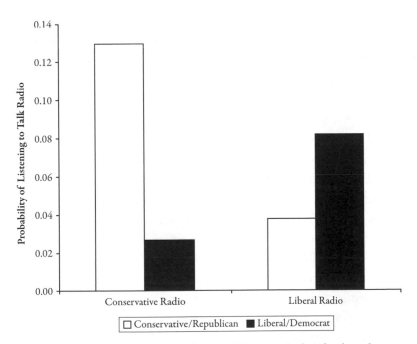

FIGURE 3.5 Probability of Talk Radio Listening by Political Leanings. Analysis details are the same as those described below Figure 3.3. Results based on logistic regression analyses predicting radio hosts and programs named by respondents.

As shown in Figure 3.5, partisanship does predict listening to talk radio. For the most extreme partisans, strong conservative Republicans have a 0.25 probability of listening to conservative talk radio and a 0.03 probability of listening to liberal talk radio. Strong liberal Democrats have a 0.01 probability of listening to conservative talk radio and a 0.13 probability of listening to liberal talk radio. Republicans and conservatives tune in to hear conservative hosts such as Rush Limbaugh, Sean Hannity, and Michael Savage. Liberal Democrats tune in to hear liberal hosts such as Ed Schultz, Al Franken, and Randi Rhodes. Crossing partisan lines in talk radio listening is hardly the norm.

Cable News

The twenty-four-hour breaking-news format adopted by the major cable news networks has met with substantial audience approval. For many Americans, cable news is their main source for political news and information.[28] In December 2006, CNN attracted over 70 million viewers; Fox News, 61 million; and MSNBC, 53 million.[29] Cable news ratings vary widely depending on news events.[30] For example, between 8 and 9 P.M. on September 29, 2008 (the day the economic bailout bill failed to pass the House of Representatives), over 9 million people watched cable news.[31] Presidential campaign season in particular has been a boon for cable news ratings. In an article entitled, "The News: Cable TV's Sleeper Hit," *Business Week* reported that Nielsen ratings for Fox News, CNN, and MSNBC increased by 16 percent during the 2008 primary season.[32]

Which cable news networks attract which viewers? NAES respondents identified the cable news network they watched most often. Of the two-thirds of respondents who watched cable news in the past week, 34 percent reported viewing Fox News most often, 45 percent CNN, and 12 percent MSNBC.[33]

Though the three major cable news networks, CNN, Fox News, and MSNBC, self-identify as objective news outlets, content analytic investigations suggest that some have identifiable political differences. CNN coverage of the 2003 Iraq War tended to be less supportive of Republican-initiated military efforts in comparison to Fox News coverage.[34] Compared to a host of other news sources, Fox News's 2003 coverage of affirmative action was more negative.[35] The think tanks and policy groups referenced by CNN's *News Night with Aaron Brown* were more liberal and less conservative in comparison to those referenced by Fox News's *Special Report*.[36] Relative to other media outlets, Fox News was more critical of Democratic presidential hopeful John Kerry compared to Republican incumbent President George Bush in the 2004 presidential election.[37] In their comprehensive project investigating several conservative media outlets, communication scholars Kathleen Hall Jamieson and Joseph Cappella presented substantial evidence that Fox News emphasizes a conservative take on the news.[38] Research on coverage of presidential approval polls also illustrates differences in cable news coverage. Fox News was more apt to report on a presidential approval poll when the results showed increasing approval for Bush. During the Clinton administration, however, Fox News more frequently covered polls showing declining presidential approval.[39] Though far fewer content analyses have been conducted on MSNBC coverage, the Project for Excellence in Journalism noted a liberal slant: "Although it was not explicitly marketed as such, MSNBC also appeared to be positioning itself as the liberal alternative news channel to Fox."[40] These analyses provide important justification for determining what should count as partisan selective exposure. Relative to Fox News, CNN and MSNBC are more consistent cable news choices for liberals and Democrats. Relative to CNN and MSNBC, Fox News is a more consistent cable news choice for conservatives and Republicans.

These categorizations are admittedly rough. There have been hosts on CNN and MSNBC who are not appropriately categorized as liberal (e.g., Glenn Beck and Joe Scarborough) and hosts on Fox News who are not appropriately categorized as conservative (e.g., Alan Colmes). If likeminded partisans view these programs, however, this would decrease the likelihood that I would detect patterns of partisan selective exposure because some Republicans would report viewing CNN or MSNBC and some Democrats would report viewing Fox News. Thus, finding consistent patterns of partisan selective exposure would be more of a feat. Further, it is noteworthy that conservative Glenn Beck switched from CNN Headline News to Fox News and liberal Alan Colmes left Fox News's *Hannity & Colmes* to pursue independent projects. It seems that the hosts are sorting based on partisanship, but are audiences?

Are people selective about their cable news exposure or are they news omnivores, flipping indiscriminately between various cable news channels? It may be that there are significant overlaps in cable television news viewing; those viewing one network also may spend equal time viewing other networks. Though it would be surprising if people didn't flip channels occasionally, it would be equally surprising if people didn't have a preferred outlet. The 2008 Knowledge Networks Survey asked respondents how many days in the past week they watched CNN, MSNBC, and Fox News. Of cable news viewers, only 12 percent watched all three channels with equal frequency. Forty-two percent watched CNN or MSNBC and not Fox News or watched Fox News and not CNN or MSNBC. Others watched one channel more often than the others.

NAES respondents had little trouble identifying which cable news outlet they watched *most frequently*. In response to this question, only 5 percent of respondents volunteered that they watched more than one network equally. Viewers' cable news selections are not haphazard. In fact, audiences seem to be rather discriminating. The results are shown in Figure 3.6.

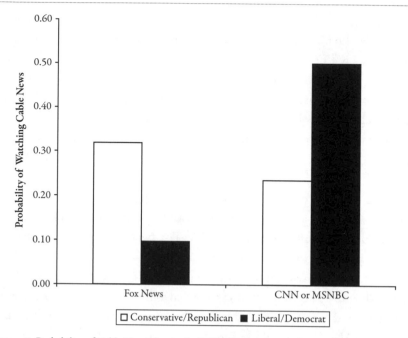

FIGURE 3.6 Probability of Cable News Viewing by Political Leanings. Analysis details are the same as those described below Figure 3.3. Results based on logistic regression analyses predicting most watched cable news network named by respondents.

Partisan viewing patterns appear for cable news viewing—those watching Fox News tend to be conservatives and Republicans and those watching CNN or MSNBC tend to be liberals and Democrats. Figure 3.6 shows cable news use for those with modest political leanings. For those with the most intense political leanings, the relationships are even stronger. Strong conservative Republicans have a 0.47 probability of naming Fox News their most watched cable news network and a 0.14 probability of naming either CNN or MSNBC. Strong liberal Democrats have a 0.05 probability of naming Fox News their most watched cable news outlet and a 0.58 probability of naming either CNN or MSNBC. Political beliefs seem to very much influence cable news network preferences.

Data from The Nielsen Company can further inform our understanding of the nature of cable news viewing. Previous reports using Nielsen data provide mixed evidence about the extent to which cable news networks attract different audiences. For one-time events like the national conventions, ratings reveal that the DNC and the RNC were most commonly viewed on different channels. In 2008, CNN ratings soared during the DNC and Fox News received some of its highest ratings during the RNC—both were ratings leaders during the respective conventions.[41] Since like-minded partisans tend to tune in to the national conventions, this suggests that partisans watched the conventions on cable news networks based on their political identity.

Data looking at whether those watching one cable news network flip to other news networks reveal more diverse viewing habits, however. In the first week of February 2003, 27 percent of the adult population spent at least one minute watching Fox News.[42] On average, this group devoted 7.5 percent of their television viewing time to Fox News. Yet they also spent 2.9 percent of their television time, on average, watching CNN, and 1.6 percent of their time watching MSNBC. Although these data show overlaps in viewing, it isn't clear how many viewers watch Fox News, CNN, and MSNBC. It also isn't clear how many spend most of their time with just one cable news network. Other evidence suggests that many people watch more than one cable news network. In December 2004, Fox News attracted 54 million viewers for at least six minutes. Yet only 14 million avoided all other cable news networks.[43] This measure, however, treats someone watching many hours of Fox News and only 10 minutes of CNN the same as someone watching 15 minutes of Fox News and 15 minutes of CNN. How many people watched *more* Fox News compared to other outlets? To provide a more complete picture of patterns of cable news viewership, I obtained data from The Nielsen Company. I use this data to examine two aspects of cable news use. First, how selective are cable news users? Second, how has selectivity changed over time?

Before turning to these analyses, it is important to note that Nielsen data cannot resolve debates about partisan selective exposure. This is true for at least two reasons. First, Nielsen doesn't record viewer partisanship, which means that we can't tell whether different viewing patterns are related to viewers' partisanship. Second, conclusions about selectivity based on Nielsen data critically depend on what is being measured. Estimates of selectivity vary depending on how the data are analyzed. If I look only at those viewing sixty minutes or more of cable news in a two week period, estimates of selectivity are higher than if I look at those viewing five minutes or more of cable news. If I consider selective viewing as watching sixty minutes or more of some cable news networks and *less than sixty* minutes of others, selectivity is higher than if I consider selective viewing as watching sixty minutes or more of some cable news networks and *less than fifteen* minutes of others. If I look at data for individuals, selectivity is higher than if I look at data for households. The list could go on. As each measurement is valid in the sense that it captures a different way of looking at selective viewing, I obtained a variety of different metrics from Nielsen for this project. Consistent with my analysis to this point, I examine patterns of cable news selectivity by contrasting Fox News viewers with viewers watching some combination of CNN and MSNBC.

To get started, I looked at those viewing cable news for a minimal amount of time—five minutes or more. In the last two weeks of October 2008, Nielsen data show that 50 percent of households turned to CNN and MSNBC or to Fox News for at least five minutes during a single day. Of these households, how many watched CNN or MSNBC and then flipped over to see Fox News? And how many Fox News households switched over to CNN or MSNBC? Forty-one percent watched CNN or MSNBC for five minutes or more *and* watched Fox News for five minutes or more. The other 59 percent of cable news–viewing households watched some networks more than others. Some spent five minutes or more with CNN or MSNBC and less than five minutes with Fox News. Others spent five minutes or more with Fox News and less than five minutes with CNN and MSNBC.

Watching cable news for only five minutes isn't very long, however. Who knows, five minutes of cable news viewing could be accidental! What about households tuning in to CNN, Fox News, or MSNBC for at least one hour? Here, patterns of selectivity are more striking. According to Nielsen, in the last two weeks of October 2008, just over 30 percent of households tuned in to CNN and MSNBC or to Fox News for an hour or more during a single day. Among these households, only 18 percent watched CNN or MSNBC for sixty minutes or more *and* watched Fox News for sixty minutes or more. The remaining 82 percent displayed a preference in terms of devoting more than sixty minutes either to CNN and MSNBC or to Fox News and devoting less than sixty minutes to the other network(s).

What about different combinations of cable news viewing? What about those watching sixty minutes or more of Fox News and fifteen minutes or less of CNN and MSNBC, for example? To look at these types of combinations, Nielsen computes the data somewhat differently. Here, the data capture those spending sixty or more minutes viewing cable news over the entire two-week period, instead of during a single day.[44] This means that a person watching five minutes of cable news each day over a two-week period would count as watching 60 minutes of cable news. Of the 27 percent watching CNN and MSNBC for sixty minutes or more, 52 percent watched Fox News for less than fifteen minutes. In other words, around half of the households viewing CNN and MSNBC devoted significantly more time to CNN and MSNBC than to Fox News. Fox News households were more likely to spend time with CNN or MSNBC. Of the 18 percent watching Fox News for sixty minutes or more, only 33 percent watched CNN or MSNBC for less than fifteen minutes.

Increasing the threshold of viewing time to 120 minutes, patterns of selectivity are clearer. Of the 21 percent of households watching CNN or MSNBC for 120 minutes or more, half checked out Fox News for less than fifteen minutes. The 14 percent of households watching Fox News for 120 minutes or more were equally selective. Here, 46 percent flipped to CNN or MSNBC for fifteen minutes or less. In both instances, around half of frequent cable news–viewing households rarely checked out the other network(s). The patterns are even more pronounced if I look at the individual data, as opposed to household data. For example, nearly 60 percent of those watching 120 minutes or more of CNN and MSNBC or of Fox News rarely check out the other network(s).

As this discussion shows, it is not possible to arrive at a single estimate of selective viewing using Nielsen data. The results show evidence of selectivity but also confirm that many cable news viewers do not focus exclusively on one news network. A larger percentage of viewers exhibit selectivity by devoting more time to some cable news networks than others, but again, estimates of how many viewers do so vary depending on how the number is calculated.

Although the amount of selectivity is not easily pinned down, Nielsen data offer more clear-cut information about how selectivity has changed over time. Irrespective of the metric used, two patterns are apparent. First, cable news viewing has increased. More people watched cable news in 2008 than in 2004. Between October 2004 and October 2008, the percentage of households watching CNN or MSNBC jumped from 21 percent to 27 percent. Fox News viewing rose more modestly from 16 percent to 18 percent.

Second, selective cable news viewing has increased. When looking across years— comparing levels of selectivity in 2004 with levels of selectivity in 2008—selectivity has risen. In the last two weeks of October 2004, 44 percent watched CNN and MSNBC for 60 minutes or more and watched Fox News for less than fifteen minutes. This increased to 52 percent in the last two weeks of October 2008. A similar, though less dramatic, pattern appears for households watching 60 minutes or more of Fox News. In late October 2004, 31 percent watched CNN and MSNBC for less than 15 minutes. By late October 2008, 33 percent did so. There is evidence, therefore, that cable news loyalty is on the rise. This occurs when looking at any combination of viewing, be it among those watching five minutes, sixty minutes, or 120 minutes of cable news. It also occurs whether looking at individual or household data. The increases in selectivity were not large—typically only a few percentage points—but the pattern is consistent across these different ways of analyzing the data.

Nielsen data show that cable news selectivity has increased at least somewhat, but without knowing the partisanship of the viewers, it is not possible to know from Nielsen data alone whether *partisan* selective exposure has increased. Other evidence, however, suggests that this is the case. Public opinion research shows that from 1998 to 2004, partisanship increasingly predicted cable news use.[45] The CNN audience became increasingly Democratic and the Fox News audience became increasingly Republican. Although not completely resolving the issue, the combination of public opinion and Nielsen data suggests that partisan patterns of cable news use are becoming more entrenched.

In sum, cable news outlets attract significant audiences, and in some instances, they attract distinct audiences. Conservatives and Republicans watch Fox News more often than liberals and Democrats. Liberals and Democrats watch CNN and MSNBC more often than conservatives and Republicans. Further, cable news audiences have become increasingly fragmented over time, dedicating more of their viewing time either to Fox News or to CNN and MSNBC.

Political Internet

The Internet has become an increasingly important source of political news. During the 2008 presidential campaign, 55 percent of Americans obtained news and information about the campaign from the Internet.[46] News Web sites receive substantial traffic. In October 2008, for example, CNN's Digital Network recorded over 38 million unique hits, over 20 million visited nytimes.com, and the Fox News Web site garnered over 14 million hits.[47]

The Internet, in particular, provides ample opportunities to encounter information that either complements or contradicts one's political predispositions. In embracing this freedom of choice, it is an open question whether people will seek out likeminded or opinion-challenging online content. On one hand, it is possible that people will use the Internet to fragment into ever more specific likeminded groups.[48] Indeed, visitors to candidate Web sites tend to share the political outlook advanced by the Web site.[49] On the other hand, people may use the Internet to explore diverse opinions. In-depth interviews have revealed that people discussing politics online tend not to mention that they purposefully seek out likeminded others. Instead, they report that they enjoy hearing diverse views.[50] Further, research by R. Kelly Garrett suggests that Internet users do not *avoid* counterattitudinal partisan messages online.[51] Yet the extent to which people *encounter* counterattitudinal messages is an open question. Whether the Internet inspires different patterns of selective exposure in comparison to other media types warrants exploration.

Around three-fourths of NAES respondents had access to the Internet and just over a third of those with access reported that they had obtained information about the presidential campaign online during the previous week. They went to numerous online locations to access information. Twelve percent of respondents accessing campaign information online visited a candidate's Web site. Sixty percent reported visiting an online news organization.[52] Thirty-two percent reported going to another political Web site. Respondents identifying another website were asked where they went. Their open-ended responses were reviewed and coded as to whether the sites were conservative or liberal.[53] Results for who uses partisan sites are shown in Figure 3.7.

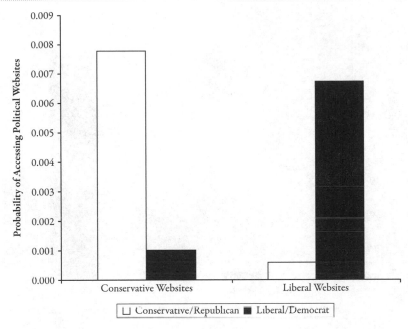

FIGURE 3.7 Probability of Web Site Accessing by Political Leanings. Analysis details are the same as those described below Figure 3.3. Results based on logistic regression analyses predicting Internet Web sites named by respondents.

Few respondents named another Web site and even fewer named a partisan site. Among those who did, partisan Web site viewing was concentrated among like-minded partisans. Those accessing liberal Web sites nearly universally identified as liberal Democrats and those accessing conservative Web sites nearly universally identified as conservative Republicans. And the results persist in the face of multiple controls, as shown in Figure 3.7.

Although the results shown in Figure 3.7 support the idea of partisan selective exposure, only a small group of respondents were asked to report their online behavior as part of the NAES. The Pew Research Center, however, obtained more extensive data about where people go to obtain their news online. In the Pew survey, 64 percent reported that they go online to access the Internet or to send and receive e-mail. Of those respondents, 92 percent reported going online to get news. These online news gatherers were asked to name a few of the Web sites that they accessed most often. As before, the Web sites were categorized as liberal, conservative, or neither. Results are shown in Figure 3.8.

Again, partisans were more likely to use likeminded Web sites. Liberals and Democrats accessed more liberal Web sites than conservatives and Republicans. Although less common, conservatives and Republicans accessed conservative Web sites more than liberals and Democrats. If I look at those with the most intense

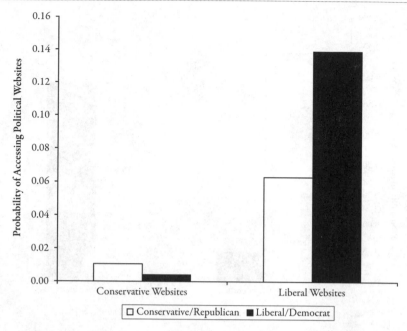

FIGURE 3.8 Probability of Web Site Accessing by Political Leanings, 2008. Results based on logistic regression analyses predicting Web sites named by respondents. Analyses control for demographics, political orientations, and patterns of media use. Ideology/partisanship is significant in all analyses. Ideology/ partisanship values are calculated using one standard deviation from the mean value. More details can be found in the technical appendix for this chapter.

Source: Data from the May 2008 Media Consumption Survey sponsored by the Pew Research Center for the People and the Press.

political leanings, conservative Republicans have a 0.05 probability of accessing a conservative Web site and a 0.02 probability of accessing a liberal Web site. Liberal Democrats have a 0.19 probability of accessing a liberal Web site and less than a 0.01 probably of accessing a conservative Web site.

Partisan Selective Exposure across Media Types

Before continuing, it is important to take stock of the measurement strategy employed to this point. Throughout this project, I contrast two political perspectives: those who identify as liberals and Democrats and those who identify as conservatives and Republicans. This is obviously an oversimplification of the political views represented in the public. There are numerous other political perspectives. Categorizing media outlets into two political categories also is an over-simplification. This categorization scheme does not capture subtleties and nuances between media outlets. Some outlets certainly are more liberal or more conservative than others. However, establishing ways to more finely measure political leanings in the media would undoubtedly be a difficult endeavor. What's more, it is not clear that this would improve upon the current categorization scheme since members of the public may not consistently make these distinctions when making their media choices.

The media measures employed here have other limitations. Though these measures allow for the most complete understanding of partisan selective exposure that we have, they only go so far. For example, NAES respondents were encouraged to name only one newspaper and only their most frequently watched cable news station. Whether respondents used other newspapers and cable news networks and how frequently they did so cannot be discerned. All we know is which newspapers and cable news networks respondents used most. Respondents were asked to name all of the radio hosts and programs to which they listened, but there is no way to know whether some programs were used more frequently than others. I also don't have complete information about all of the Web sites respondents accessed.[54]

Improving upon these measures, however, demands caution. Media measures must balance the desire for discriminating measurement with the ability of respondents to provide accurate information. An ideal survey might include measures of all outlets used, the amount of time spent with each outlet, the amount of attention paid to each outlet, the amount of trust in each outlet, and the amount of information absorbed from each outlet. This level of detail, however, is inconceivable and so we're left with less-than-perfect measures.

What is truly impressive here is that even though the survey respondents were asked about their media use in different ways and even though I categorized the media outlets in different ways, *the effects are consistent.* It doesn't matter whether I analyze use of newspapers, radio, cable television, or the Internet; political leanings are related to media selections. There seems to be something attractive about media outlets that are more in accord with one's political predispositions.

When looking across all of the media categories, two distinct groupings emerge. First, reading newspapers endorsing Bush, listening to conservative talk radio, watching Fox News, and accessing conservative Web sites tend to go together. Conservatives and Republicans are more likely to use all of these sources. And if you use one of these sources, chances are greater that you use another of these sources.[55] Second, reading newspapers endorsing Kerry, listening to liberal talk radio, watching CNN or MSNBC, and accessing liberal Web sites tend to go together. Using one of these sources increases the odds that you use another. And liberals and Democrats are more likely to use these sources.

Based on these findings, I created two indices of media exposure: an index of *conservative media use* and an index of *liberal media use.* These labels are admittedly rough categorizations, but I believe they represent a compelling way to assess patterns of partisan selective exposure. "Liberal media use" is more consistent for liberals and Democrats than "conservative media use," and vice versa for conservatives and Republicans. These labels are helpful in delineating the two types of media use under investigation here.

There are many advantages to using the indices as opposed to conducting an outlet-by-outlet analysis. First, the indices and individual media outlets theoretically capture the same phenomenon—partisan media use. Summing the equivalent concepts of media use, therefore, makes good theoretical sense. Second, the findings are easier to present using the indices. As opposed to summarizing eight relationships from the outlet-by-outlet analyses, two findings capture the same expected relationships. Third, the findings are generally similar. In subsequent chapters, I first will establish that the proposed relationships hold for the individual media outlets before proceeding with analysis using the indices.

Prevalence of Partisan Selective Exposure

It is challenging, yet important, to think about the prevalence of partisan selective exposure. Am I documenting patterns that occur among only a select few Americans, driven by extreme partisan impulses? Or are these patterns more far reaching, extending to a broad range of Americans? The answer to these questions is tricky in a handful of ways. First, it requires that partisans be identified. Who should count? Only those with the most extreme partisan ideas? Or can those with more modest leanings also use likeminded media? Second, it requires decisions about which outlets count as partisan. Third, it requires determining which patterns count as partisan selective exposure. Does the use of only one likeminded outlet qualify?

As these questions show, any estimate of the prevalence of partisan selective exposure requires a host of assumptions and should be treated with appropriate caution. Armed with these caveats, I offer a rough estimate. First, I divided the public into three groups: those identifying as conservative and Republican, those identifying as liberal and Democrat, and those with other partisan and ideological affiliations. Second, I looked at all of the outlets named by a respondent—the newspapers, radio programs, cable news networks, and Web sites. I looked at whether the outlets were classified as liberal or conservative, using the criteria discussed previously.

Dividing the world up in this way reveals the following five categories. First, 21 percent don't use any sources that were classified as liberal or conservative. This includes those using news sources like *USA Today,* which did not make a presidential endorsement, and Yahoo! News, which wasn't coded as having a clear partisan bent. This also includes those who don't use any news media at all. Second, 18 percent use some sources categorized as liberal *and* some sources categorized as conservative. Third,

10 percent of those who use sources of only one partisan stripe do not have consistent partisan and ideological leanings. For these individuals, it isn't clear what pattern of media exposure is likeminded. Fourth, 16 percent identify as liberal Democrats or as conservative Republicans and use only nonlikeminded sources. The fifth and final category—the most important for the purpose of this book—is those who identify as liberal Democrats or as conservative Republicans and who use likeminded sources without using any nonlikeminded sources. These are the respondents that most clearly engage in partisan selective exposure. Thirty-four percent of all respondents are in this group—the largest of any of the categories.

On one hand, this way of measuring partisan selective exposure is overly lenient. Some of the survey media measures ask only about frequently used outlets—less frequent use of nonlikeminded sources may not be reliably captured. On the other hand, this way of measuring partisan selective exposure is overly strict. I considered any mention of a nonlikeminded source as indicating that the respondent did not engage in selective exposure. Even if a person mentioned a hometown newspaper that endorsed a nonlikeminded presidential candidate and another paper that endorsed a likeminded presidential candidate, the person was *not* treated as engaging in partisan selective exposure. Even if a person named a radio program with hosts on two sides of the political spectrum (e.g., *Left, Right, and Center*), the person was not treated as engaging in partisan selective exposure. I did this because it is possible that the respondent relied more heavily on the nonlikeminded source than the others. Based on the evidence to this point, however, it is conceivable that those using both likeminded and nonlikeminded sources devote more time to the likeminded sources. As such, the estimate of partisan selective exposure may be conservative. Given these limitations, the magnitude of selective exposure uncovered here indicates that those engaging in partisan selective exposure are not a majority, but they also are not a small minority.

CAUSALITY AND PARTISAN SELECTIVE EXPOSURE

There is evidence that partisan selective exposure exists. Whether in terms of political conventions, partisan movies, newspapers, cable news networks, talk radio programs, or Web sites, political beliefs are related to media selections. Regardless of the medium, partisanship guides news media use.

To this point, the data on which I have relied show a *correlation* between media use and political beliefs but fall short of establishing a *causal* relationship. When given the option, do people purposefully choose likeminded media? To document a *causal* relationship, I would need to show that people's political beliefs occur before their media selections and that the observed relationships between political beliefs and media selections cannot be explained by other factors.

It is possible that the temporal order is reversed. Viewing partisan media may lead audiences to adopt the media's political leanings. Economists Stefano DellaVigna and Ethan Kaplan, for example, found that Republican vote shares increased when Fox News became available.[56] They attribute at least part of this effect to the Fox News channel persuading people to vote more conservatively. Yet decades of research on media effects have not provided strong evidence that the media are capable of dramatically *changing* citizens' partisan and ideological attachments. Democrats generally do not become Republicans (or vice versa) as a consequence of media programming. Rather, the primary effect of the media in political contests seems to be the reinforcement of political beliefs.[57] Party identification and political ideology are fairly stable among individuals and in the electorate.[58] Even vote intentions vary little over the course of an election. In their classic study of voting behavior, Lazarsfeld, Berelson, and Gaudet found that citizens in Erie County, Ohio, rarely changed their presidential vote intentions between May and October of 1940.[59] The trend persists today. In 2008, over 95 percent of those who intended to vote for Republican nominee John McCain or Democratic nominee Barack Obama before election day later reported that they actually did so.[60] If the media influence political identities, one would anticipate more variation as people switch between media programs and then update their beliefs.

Empirical evidence adds to this argument. A series of panel surveys, where respondents were contacted at two points in time and asked identical questions, were conducted as part of the NAES. For example, those completing the survey before the presidential and vice presidential debates were recontacted after the debates to evaluate how their thoughts and behaviors may have changed. As with the other analyses presented to this point, I include the technical details in the appendices. For the panel analyses conducted in this chapter and in subsequent chapters, however, several features are worth noting. First, I continue to control for differences in respondents' demographics, political habits and beliefs, and media use just as I did in the cross-sectional analyses. I also control for debate viewership for the panel surveys conducted before and after the debates and for convention viewing when analyzing panel data gathered around the conventions. This helps to address concerns that the relationships between partisan media use and political beliefs are spurious and could be accounted for by other variables.

Second, each panel analysis is designed to predict an outcome variable measured during the survey postwave while controlling for the value of the outcome variable during the survey prewave. For example, after taking into account whether a respondent watched Fox News in the prewave, what's the probability that the respondent watched Fox News in the postwave? Were Republicans particularly likely to watch and not Democrats? If so, this is evidence of partisan selective exposure.

Third, panel surveys can provide some insight into the causal direction of the relationships—whether political leanings motivate media use or whether media use influences political leanings. Panel surveys help in making this assessment because I can analyze whether political leanings in the prewave of a panel predict likeminded media use in the postwave of the survey.[61] Using the NAES, I am able to analyze data from several panel surveys. This has an important advantage: It allows for a stronger test of the causal direction. This is true because any one panel survey will have numerous distinctive features: the time period during which it is fielded, the time that elapses between the pre- and postwaves of the survey, even the sample size. Each of these factors can influence the ability to detect the causal direction of a relationship.

For example, drawing conclusions about causal direction from panel surveys assumes that the amount of time that elapses between the pre- and postwaves of the survey is optimal in terms of how long it takes for an effect to occur. Time lags that are too long or too short can obscure the ability to detect the causal direction.[62] As a solution, one can vary the amount of time that elapses between a prewave and a postwave survey.[63] If longer time lags consistently produce results but shorter time lags do not, then one has evidence that the effect takes more time to occur. As the amount of time between the prewave and postwave of the NAES panel surveys varies, the NAES allows for this possibility.

Of course, the amount of time that elapses between the pre- and postwave of a panel survey is not the only factor that distinguishes panel surveys. It is not possible to vary only the amount of time that elapses because circumstances change as time advances. Here, panel surveys were conducted at different points during the election—some were conducted during the conventions, another during the debates, and another over the course of the general election. This limits my ability to tell *which* difference between panels is responsible for different findings, but it strengthens my ability to detect the causal direction because I have multiple opportunities to do so.

In terms of the relationship between political leanings and media use, the evidence from the NAES panel surveys is consistent: Political leanings predict media preferences, even after controlling for media preferences in the panel prewaves.[64] Liberals and Democrats were more likely to read newspapers endorsing Kerry, to listen to liberal talk radio, to watch CNN or MSNBC, and to access liberal Web sites after the election, even after taking into account use of these media before the election. Much the same, conservatives and Republicans were more likely to listen to conservative talk radio, to watch Fox News, and to access conservative Web sites after the election even after controlling for their use of these outlets before the election. Conservatives and Republicans also were more likely to read Bush-endorsing newspapers, but not significantly so. Overall, the evidence supports the idea that political leanings predict news media use.

Given the evidence to this point, there is good reason to conclude that partisan selective exposure occurs. As Sears and Freedman remarked in the 1960s, however, studies where all respondents are given the same access to information are necessary to document that people are motivated to pick likeminded media.[65] I now turn to this type of evidence.

The next section adds to our understanding of partisan selective exposure in another way. In a media environment increasingly characterized by choice, there is limited potential for *incidental* selectivity, whereby people just happen to use likeminded media sources without intending to do so. Citizens are both empowered and burdened by extensive media choice. When faced with more options, do people use their freedom to select politically likeminded or diverse media?

EXPERIMENTAL EVIDENCE

The answer to this question is vitally important given that the number of available news sources seems to grow daily. Consumers have access to more media options and more diverse content than ever before. Cable television and the Internet in particular have redefined the media landscape. The number of television channels has dramatically increased; in 1985, households received an average of 18.8 television channels.[66] By 2008, however, households received an average of 130.1 television channels.[67] And with a click of the mouse, the Internet connects users to innumerable options. Instead of a few outlets battling to capture a mass audience, a host of niche outlets cater to the interests of more specialized audiences.[68] And while locating a media source espousing a likeminded viewpoint may have been difficult decades ago, it is now a relatively simple pursuit.

Structural changes in the media environment arguably change audience behavior. The opportunity to pick from so many media options empowers audiences to make selections coinciding with their preferences—*if* they so desire. But what do audiences actually do when faced with so much choice? Do they carefully and systematically scrutinize their options, eventually settling on those that best match their preferences? Or do they browse, using their freedom of choice to explore new outlets, perspectives, and ideas?

The evidence to date provides important clues as to what we can expect the public to do when confronted with numerous choices. In terms of their television viewing behavior, viewers hardly take advantage of all of the available channels. In 2008, The

Nielsen Company reported that the average household watched only 14 percent of available channels for at least ten minutes during a week.[69] And what people choose to watch is growing less—not more—diverse. When given more options, people gravitate toward their preferred genres of programming.[70] Political scientist Markus Prior, for example, finds that those preferring entertainment select more entertainment when they are given the option.[71]

Research on the influence of the number of media choices makes two general points. First, people's exposure patterns change based on the number of choices available. Second, as choice increases, people are more likely to choose materials supporting their beliefs and opinions.[72] Psychologists Peter Fischer, Stefan Schulz-Hardt, and Dieter Frey conducted an interesting study where they investigated whether people selected different information depending on how many information choices they had. Fischer and his colleagues gave people a case study to read—either a legal scenario or a personnel decision—and asked them to make a decision based on what they had read. Afterward, Fischer and colleagues gave the study participants the opportunity to view additional information—some of it supporting and some of it contradicting their decision. Some participants were given only a few pieces of information and others were given many pieces of information. The results showed more selective exposure when more choices were available.[73]

By providing consumers with excessive choice, the media environment arguably facilitates selective exposure. Yet we don't have much information about the effects of more choices on *political news media* choices. I conducted two studies to examine partisan selective exposure experimentally. With access to multiple partisan options, do people pick those that match their political beliefs? And how do more options influence people's choices?

The Magazine Experiment

Enter any waiting room and chances are you won't be too surprised by what you find. Some chairs. Pictures or instructions on a wall. A table. And, most important for this study, magazines.

To examine partisan selective exposure in the news media environment, I examined people's magazine selections as they waited in a waiting room. People had no idea they were participating in a study. They thought they were merely waiting to participate in another study. In a sense, they were. Community members from Philadelphia *were* recruited to participate in another study about a popular television series. Yet their waiting room behavior was exactly what I was interested in observing.

Upon arriving at the study site (a room within a university library), a research assistant informed each participant that the study was running late and asked the participant to wait in a small waiting area just outside of the study room. In the waiting area, there was a chair and a set of magazines placed on a table. Before each participant arrived, either three or five magazines were randomly arranged on the waiting room table. The magazines spanned the political spectrum. In addition to a putatively neutral magazine, an equal number of liberal- and conservative-leaning magazines were placed on the table.

The waiting area had a rather distinctive feature that made it particularly conducive to this study: There was a large window in the back of the waiting area that connected the library to an adjacent lobby. Seated unobtrusively at a table outside of this window was a confederate who appeared to be a student engaged in his studies. The confederate observed and recorded the subject's magazine choices. Participants remained in the waiting area for up to five minutes before the research assistant reappeared and invited the participant into the study room. Once in the study room, participants completed the other study, which included viewing a popular television program for approximately forty-five minutes and then answering a battery of questions about the program and their beliefs.

Following their completion of the other study, subjects were told that as a thank you for their participation, they could select a free magazine subscription. The same magazines that had been available in the waiting area were presented to the subjects. Once they had completed their magazine selection, subjects were surprised when we divulged that the magazines were a study in their own right. And they were glad to learn that they actually would receive their free magazine subscription.

In conducting this study, I wondered how people would negotiate these media choices. Which magazines would people browse in the waiting room? Which magazines would they select for their subscription? Would people's political beliefs influence the magazines they chose? Certainly the magazines' political leanings were just one of many possible criteria people could use when selecting a magazine. Photographs, headline size, article placement, lead paragraphs—all sorts of different factors influence people's reading decisions.[74] These factors easily could outweigh any preference for politically likeminded magazines.

Particularly when people had only three magazines from which to choose, many miscellaneous, nonpolitical reasons could govern their choice. As the number of choices increase, however, the likelihood that a miscellaneous, nonpolitical reason would determine magazine selection declines. In more concrete terms, suppose that a liberal Democrat was making a choice between several nonliberal magazines and just one liberal magazine. In this choice set, there are many reasons that the subject would not choose the liberal magazine. The liberal magazine's cover picture may be unattractive. The lead story may be on a topic that is not of interest. Given two liberal magazines, however, it is less likely that *both* of the liberal magazines would fail to meet the miscellaneous nonpolitical criteria.

The waiting room and subscription contexts have noteworthy similarities to the types of media choices people routinely make in the contemporary media environment. Surfing the Web and flipping through channels on television are both activities that allow people to browse different media outlets with little commitment. The magazine browsing condition parallels these situations. Other media selections, however, require more of a commitment on behalf of a consumer. Signing up for a magazine or a newspaper subscription is a prime example. In addition, consider the debate surrounding whether cable customers should be able to select channels à la carte, as opposed to purchasing predetermined bundles. Permitting cable viewers to select specific television channels for long-term commitments could parallel people's magazine subscription decision making. The manipulation of magazine choice also squares with changes in the media environment. On the radio, for example, partisan voices have gained popularity on the airwaves, thus increasing the number of partisan choices available.

Clearly, I am not the first to conduct an experiment to examine the occurrence of selective exposure. In designing this study, I had the benefit of examining numerous previous experiments. The strengths and limitations of prior research inspired the design of the current study in a number of ways.

First, participants were unaware that their magazine selections were being studied. In some previous studies, participants likely were aware that their information choices were part of the study.[75] When participants are aware that their selections are being observed, they may modify their behavior to be more ideologically balanced in their exposure decisions.[76] Second, subjects were allowed to use any strategy they wanted when deciding which magazine to view. They could have looked at the covers of all of the magazines, then decided which one best matched their beliefs. They could have picked up the first one they saw without any reflection. This is a particularly important component of this study because people likely employ different strategies depending on whether they encounter many options or just a few.[77] Experimental procedures requiring subjects to employ certain selection strategies can influence how subjects behave. Past studies, for example, have asked subjects to review and rate numerous article summaries as to how much they wanted to read each article before they read any articles.[78] Requiring subjects to make multiple selections before viewing any content reduces the observed level of selectivity.[79] Third, actual behavior was observed in this study. Asking respondents to rate their interest in reading articles based on headlines or brief summaries may result in thoughtless engagement in an experiment if respondents perceive that their preferences are without meaning—they may be aware that they never actually have to *read* any of the articles. When people believe that they will be asked to read the articles that they select, they are more likely to select likeminded articles.[80] Including these design features in my study reduces the chances of *underestimating* the extent to which selective exposure occurs.

Other design features of this experiment are included to minimize the probability of observing inflated levels of selective exposure. First, I used widely available magazines for this study. Although studies that have examined people's exposure decisions based on a list of one-sentence article summaries provide important insights into certain aspects of media selection,[81] this experiment more realistically captures a choice that people actually encounter. Though this design feature means that it is more likely that idiosyncratic features of the magazines (e.g., the cover photo) will influence exposure decisions, it enables results that are more generalizable. Second, an attempt was made to include a magazine rated as ideologically neutral in all of the experimental conditions since providing only polar opposite choice options theoretically could lead to an overestimation of selective exposure.[82] This turned out to be far more difficult in practice than in theory. On average, people did perceive the *Economist* as neutral. This was true both in pretesting and among those who took part in the study. Yet comparing partisan reactions to the *Economist* confirmed the existence of the hostile media phenomenon, whereby partisans on both sides of the political spectrum detected a hostile bias. Liberal Democrats found the *Economist* to be conservative leaning. Conservative Republicans found the *Economist* to be liberal leaning. In essence, the search for a neutral magazine resulted in an important observation in its own right: *Neutral* sources are illusive. Including a more diverse range of options, however, may help to prevent overestimating the occurrence of selective exposure. All of these design features helped to make this experiment better able to document the extent of selective exposure.

I first examined partisan selective exposure in the waiting room by looking at the percentage of time people spent with conservative magazines and the percentage of time people spent with liberal magazines. I used percentages because some participants did not spend the full five minutes viewing the magazines. Did people gravitate toward likeminded magazines?

Using this measure, there was evidence of partisan selective exposure when subjects browsed magazines in the waiting room. As shown in Figure 3.9, conservatives and Republicans spent more time with conservative magazines compared to liberals and Democrats. Other methods of analyzing magazine browsing in the waiting room, such as modeling all magazines viewed or examining which magazine was chosen by respondents last, yield similar results. Evidence of partisan selective exposure is consistent with the evidence presented thus far in this chapter. People's political beliefs seem to influence even their browsing decisions.

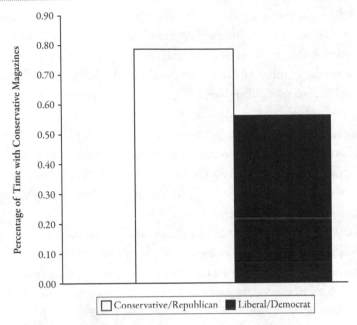

FIGURE 3.9 Waiting Room Magazine Viewing by Political Leanings. Results based on a regression analysis predicting the percentage of time spent with conservative magazines. Analysis controls for the number and type of magazines provided and political knowledge. Ideology/partisanship is significant in the analysis. Ideology/partisanship values are calculated using one standard deviation from the mean value. More details can be found in the technical appendix for this chapter.

Source: Data from the Magazine Experiment.

The pattern from Figure 3.9 persists when examining the free magazine subscriptions selected by study participants. Here, partisans on both sides of the political spectrum tended to choose likeminded subscriptions. Conservatives and Republicans were more likely to select conservative magazine subscriptions compared to others. The more conservative and Republican the participant, the odds of their choosing a conservative magazine increase by 15 percent. This relationship was marginally significant. Liberals and Democrats were more likely to select liberal magazine subscriptions compared to others. The more liberal and Democrat the participant, the odds of their choosing a liberal magazine increase by 43 percent.[83]

Throughout the magazine study, people's political leanings played a role in their magazine selections—even when browsing magazines in a waiting room. In all cases, the relationship between the participants' political proclivities and their magazine choices were in the expected direction, and in both the waiting room and subscription conditions, there was evidence that people's political preferences directed their magazine choices. This provides additional support for partisan selective exposure.

But did the *number* of magazines influence which magazines were chosen? With more choice, did people select more likeminded magazines? In this study, there was limited evidence that more options increased partisan selective exposure. In the waiting room, the number of magazines on the table did not make partisans any more or less likely to select likeminded magazines. Whether there were three or five magazines on the table, conservatives and Republicans were more likely and liberals and Democrats were less likely to read conservative magazines. In the subscription condition, however, there was some evidence that the number of choices matters. When respondents had five options as opposed to three, conservatives and Republicans were somewhat less likely and liberals and Democrats were somewhat more likely to select liberal magazines.[84]

Would the same effects of political leanings and choice hold in other contexts? After all, the results here could be due to the use of political magazines as opposed to other, more popular, news media choices. These magazines were not particularly well known to the respondents, and few had previous opinions about the partisan leanings of these choices. Before conducting the magazine study, I had taken a stack of magazines to the 30th Street train station in Philadelphia. As people waited for their trains to arrive, I asked them to browse through magazines and answer a short questionnaire about the magazines' political leanings. Though the perceived magazine leanings showed that some magazines were perceived to be liberal and others conservative, it is worth noting that the differences were not large. This may have reduced the observed occurrence of partisan selective exposure.

When faced with better-known sources, partisans may be more drawn to likeminded content. Subsequent experimental research adds weight to this idea. In one study, participants were given four different online news stories and asked to indicate which, if any, they would most like to read.[85] Unbeknownst to the study participants, researchers Shanto Iyengar and Kyu Hahn varied the *source* of the article. Articles were randomly attributed to CNN, Fox News, NPR and the BBC. The results tell a story consistent with this chapter: The source mattered. Fox News labels attracted Republicans and repelled Democrats. Although the effects were weaker, CNN and NPR labels attracted Democrats and repelled Republicans. The same general pattern appeared irrespective of whether the articles were all soft news or all hard news. Building on these results, the Google News study described next also uses more widely known sources to examine news selections.

In the magazine study, there was only limited evidence that choice increases selectivity. Why? It is possible that the complexity of the novel stimuli—with different covers, headlines, features, and pictures—may have led people to use so many different criteria for their magazine selections that partisanship wasn't much more likely to be used when respondents had more options. Taking this into account, I designed another study to replicate and extend the findings of the magazine study by using more popular media choices and by more carefully controlling the choice criteria that respondents *could* use.

The Google News Experiment

News aggregator Web sites—such as Yahoo! News, AOL News, and Google News—are popular online sources for news and information. In October 2008, all three were among the top news sites according to Nielsen Research.[86] These sites compile news from multiple sources onto a single Web site, giving the user many news options from which to choose. Aggregators offer only limited details about each news story on a single page, giving the user only a few details to use when deciding whether or not to click on a story and read more. Typically, a headline and the name of the information source are provided. Sources vary widely; on news aggregators like Google News, wire stories from Reuters and the Associated Press are mixed with stories from newspapers and cable news outlets, such as CNN and Fox News. These Web sites can facilitate selective exposure by allowing people to select news stories from preferred media outlets. News aggregators thus are a natural place to observe selective exposure. The Google News experiment aimed to answer two questions: (1) Does the source of a story matter? and (2) When given the opportunity to select stories with interesting topics and likeminded sources, do people select more likeminded news?

Although partisan selective exposure is my main focus, partisanship is not the only factor governing news selection. Indeed, numerous other factors can influence news selections. Issues, for example, can inspire selective exposure. A series of creative experiments provide ample evidence. Political science and communication scholars Shanto Iyengar, Kyu Hahn, Jon Krosnick, and John Walker found that certain demographic characteristics known to prompt issue interest also prompt issue selectivity.[87] Health care workers, for example, gravitate toward health care information and Catholics toward abortion information more than other citizens. Subsequent research has provided even more evidence that issues can influence exposure. Citizens believing that an issue is important are drawn toward information about that issue.[88] And people with a stance on an issue access and devote more time to information favoring their perspective.[89] The Google News study draws from these findings by incorporating the opportunity to engage in both issue and partisan selectivity.

The Google News study also provides an important opportunity to return to the results of the magazine study in another context. I made several important adjustments to the experimental design. Rather than including a neutral news source, this study includes only Fox News and CNN. This change was made for several reasons.

First, for well-known media outlets, choices that all partisans would label as neutral simply do not exist. Even in the magazine study, where subjects had little experience with the magazines, strong partisans tended to believe that the neutral magazine was biased against their beliefs. Here, the news outlets are recognizable—both in terms of the brand names and in terms of their perceived trustworthiness. These two sources garner similar amounts of distrust from partisans. Pew Research finds that 22 percent of Republicans believe all or most of what CNN says compared to 32 percent of Democrats. Exactly the opposite, 22 percent of Democrats believe all or most of what Fox News has to say compared to 32 percent of Republicans.[90] CNN and Fox News send ideological signals to Democrats and Republicans, influencing both their news selections and their perceptions of bias.[91] Whether more choices exacerbate these inclinations, however, has not been examined.

A second reason that I used only CNN and Fox News was so that each respondent had an equal chance of randomly selecting CNN or Fox News regardless of which version of the Web site they saw. In the previous study, the probability of randomly selecting a likeminded or a nonlikeminded magazine was higher in the high-choice condition (a two in five chance) than in the low-choice condition (a one in three chance). Although this arguably follows a trend of increasing partisanship in the media, in the Google News study, the probability of randomly choosing a like-minded or nonlikeminded source is identical across conditions.

This study also more carefully controls the criteria that people can use when making a choice. In the magazine study, the partisan leaning of the magazine was one criterion that people could use to pick a magazine, but a host of other possible reasons for selecting one magazine over another were possible. The Google News study gave respondents two explicitly featured criteria: the topic of an article and the source of an article.

Several versions of the Google News Web site were created. Four stories were selected to display on the Google News site. Each story mentioned both 2008 presidential candidates and was about an important issue from the campaign, either the floundering economy and domestic issues or the conflicts in Afghanistan and Iraq and national security. For each story, the source was randomly varied. For example, for some study participants, the story "Clash on Iraq highlights rivals' differences" was attributed to Fox News. For others, this story was attributed to CNN.

Further, participants randomly were given either a Google News Web site displaying two articles or a Google News Web site displaying four articles. In each condition, half of the articles were attributed to CNN and half to Fox News. An image of the Web site is shown in Figure 3.10. Participants were asked to select the news story that they would most like to read.

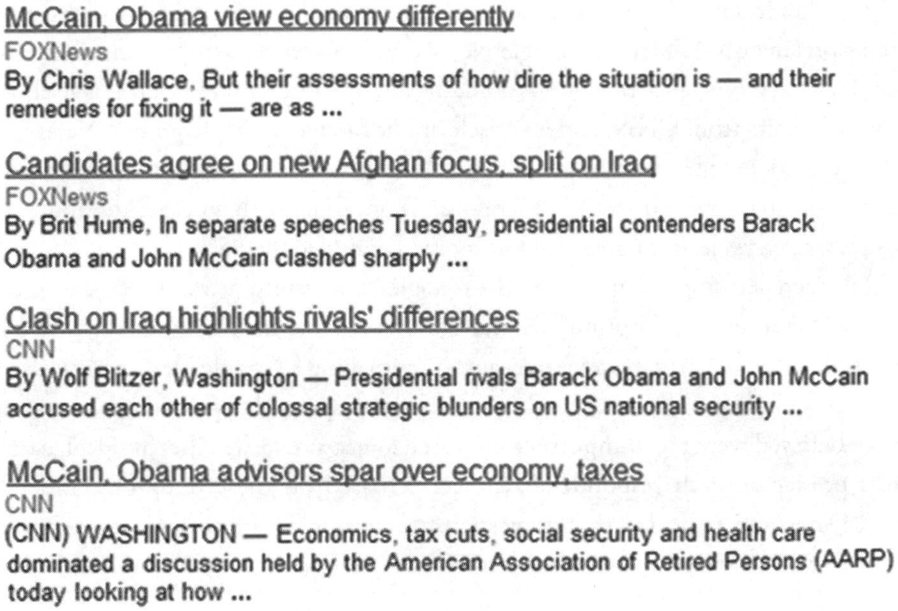

McCain, Obama view economy differently
FOXNews
By Chris Wallace. But their assessments of how dire the situation is — and their
remedies for fixing it — are as ...

Candidates agree on new Afghan focus, split on Iraq
FOXNews
By Brit Hume. In separate speeches Tuesday, presidential contenders Barack
Obama and John McCain clashed sharply ...

Clash on Iraq highlights rivals' differences
CNN
By Wolf Blitzer, Washington — Presidential rivals Barack Obama and John McCain
accused each other of colossal strategic blunders on US national security ...

McCain, Obama advisors spar over economy, taxes
CNN
(CNN) WASHINGTON — Economics, tax cuts, social security and health care
dominated a discussion held by the American Association of Retired Persons (AARP)
today looking at how ...

FIGURE 3.10 Google News Web Site.

Based on the layout of the Google News Web site, users had at least two possible
criteria that they could employ in making their decisions. They could make a selection based on which *issue* they found to be most interesting or based on the *source*
that they preferred.

When only two articles were displayed, some respondents were able to make an
ideal selection because both *source* and *issue* criteria would lead them to pick the
same article. Those who preferred CNN and wanted to read about domestic issues,
for example, would luck out half of the time and see an article displayed on the
Google News site about domestic issues from CNN. The other half of the time,
however, the choice would be more difficult. If the Google News Web site showed
two articles—one about domestic issues from Fox News and one about foreign
affairs from CNN—then people would need to decide whether to pick a preferred
source or a preferred issue.

Even when four articles were displayed, there were some instances when people
would need to pick based either on their preferred *source* or their preferred *issue*.
When both domestic affairs articles were attributed to CNN and both foreign
policy articles were attributed to Fox News, then those who wanted to read about
domestic affairs and would ordinarily turn to Fox News had to choose: Would they
rather read about domestic issues or read an article from Fox News?

In other instances, the four article conditions would allow people to maximize their preferences. When the Google News site displayed an article about domestic affairs from CNN, an article about domestic affairs from Fox News, an article about foreign affairs from CNN, and an article about foreign affairs from Fox News (see Figure 3.10), people could have the best of both criteria—their favorite source and their preferred topic. This study, therefore, is concerned with whether the ability to use *more criteria* leads people to select more likeminded media.

For each person participating in the Google News study, it was possible to identify whether an "ideal option" was randomly available in their choice set. It was possible to make this assessment because after making a Google News article selection, respondents identified their political leanings and reported which issues they believed were most important. I created a measure of whether an ideal article was present in each respondent's choice set based on these questions. Liberals and Democrats believing that domestic issues were most important, for example, had an ideal article in their choice set when a domestic article from CNN was displayed.

So which articles did participants choose? For all respondents, the topic of the article most influenced their selection. They tended to choose articles containing issues they found to be most important. It didn't matter how many articles were present or whether an ideal article was in their choice set—the topic of the article influenced which article people chose. Those thinking domestic issues were important tended to choose articles that addressed this issue.

When an ideal article was present—one that allowed respondents to pick a source consistent with their partisanship and a topic consistent with their interests—there was some evidence that liberals and Democrats tended to choose articles from CNN and that conservatives and Republicans tended to choose articles from Fox News.[92] This suggests that partisanship exerts more influence in news selection when an article with a compelling topic and a likeminded source is available.

Yet only some citizens have established opinions about CNN and Fox News. And the Google News site used in this study did not provide any additional information about these outlets. Respondents could not draw any inferences about these news outlets from the site itself—they had to possess knowledge about these outlets *before* participating in the study in order for the news source to influence their selections. To take this into account, I repeated the analysis, but only for those respondents who had *different* opinions about CNN and Fox News. For these individuals, the article they selected depended on whether the source of the article and the topic of the article coincided with their preferences. As before, respondents identifying domestic issues as most important were drawn toward articles about domestic affairs. Respondents also were drawn to articles based on their political beliefs. Liberals and

Democrats were more likely to select an article from CNN. Conservatives and Republicans were more likely to select an article from Fox News.

The Google News experiment adds to our understanding of selective exposure and choice. Without an ideal article to choose, people can choose either a like-minded article *or* an article about a compelling topic—they can't use both criteria. Of course, they also may use other criteria, but the source and issue were most prominently featured in this study. Faced with this choice, some select an article about a topic they find important and forgo their source preference. Yet when an ideal choice is present—when people can use both issue and source criteria for selecting an article—they are drawn to that article. It seems that the ability to use *more criteria* influences what people select. When people can find sources that match multiple criteria, the source is more appealing. What is most important about these results is that they confirm that partisanship is an important factor governing news selection. These results also have implications for media choice in the contemporary media environment. When additional choices allow people to use more criteria for decision making, people take advantage of these additional options. With more diverse choices, people are increasingly able to choose news sources matching their interests and beliefs.

Summary

The accumulated evidence in this chapter documents that the theory of selective exposure should not be relegated to history books. Whether looking at newspapers, talk radio, cable television, news magazines, political films, national party conventions, or Web sites, I find evidence of partisan selective exposure. And the evidence suggests that this behavior is on the rise. The analysis of the panel surveys suggests that partisan selective exposure persists over time. Nielsen and over-time survey data provide consistent evidence that cable news audiences have become increasingly fragmented. And given more and more niche news options, there is good reason to anticipate that people will increasingly seek likeminded news sources.

From the results reported in this chapter, it is clear that partisanship can influence news selections at many different points. At the broadest level, political predispositions may influence whether people choose to use the news at all. If all news media were biased against a political perspective, those holding the perspective may avoid news altogether. This arguably occurred when Republicans avoided DNC coverage and Democrats avoided RNC coverage.

At a second level, news users must consider which medium to use—television? Radio? The Internet? Numerous factors, including availability and convenience, may affect the choice. Partisanship also may play a role. Conservatives and Republicans, for example, may be drawn to talk radio, where the most popular hosts are conservative.[93] Liberals and Democrats may prefer to use Internet news sites, where the most popular sites include CNN.com and nytimes.com.[94] Indeed, NAES data confirm both of these suspicions. Liberals and Democrats are more apt to use Internet news and conservatives and Republicans are more apt to obtain news from talk radio. [95] Upon choosing to use a certain medium, the next choice is which outlet to use: which cable news network, radio program, Web site, newspaper, or magazine? The results in this chapter offer strong evidence that partisanship influences these selections.

At the narrowest level, political predispositions may influence whether audiences attend to specific articles, segments, online posts, or subsections thereof. Indeed, the results of the Google News experiment suggest that partisanship can influence article selections. It is possible that different types of selective exposure—issue versus partisan, for example—occur more frequently at some levels compared to others. We simply don't know. What we do know is that our political sentiments influence our media exposure patterns, irrespective of level.

Despite the evidence that partisan selective exposure occurs, it is clear that not everyone uses likeminded news. Perhaps only certain sorts of individuals drive this phenomenon that all of these different measures and studies detect. We need more insight into *what types of people* use partisan media, other than those with stronger partisan attachments. What leads people to use likeminded media? We also have little insight into the consequences of partisan selective exposure. Is this behavior commendable or deplorable? The next chapters explore the answers to these questions.

NOTES

1. N.T. Feather, "Cigarette Smoking and Lung Cancer: A Study of Cognitive Dissonance," *Australian Journal of Psychology* 14, 1 (1962): 55–64; Jonathan L. Freedman, "Preference for Dissonant Information," *Journal of Personality and Social Psychology* 2, 2 (1965): 287–9; Michael F. Meffert, Sungeun Chung, Amber J. Joiner, Leah Waks, and Jennifer Garst, "The Effects of Negativity and Motivated Information Processing During a Political Campaign," *Journal of Communication* 56, 1 (2006): 27–51.

2. Jonathan L. Freedman and David O. Sears, "Selective Exposure," in *Advances in Experimental Social Psychology,* edited by Leonard Berkowitz (New York: Academic Press, 1965), 2: 57–97. David O. Sears and Jonathan L. Freedman, "Selective Exposure to Information: A Critical Review," *Public Opinion Quarterly* 31, 2 (1967): 194–213.

3. See, for example, William J. McGuire, "Selective Exposure: A Summing Up," in *Theories of Cognitive Consistency: A Sourcebook,* edited by Robert P. Abelson, Elliot Aronson, William J. McGuire, Theodore M. Newcomb, Milton J. Rosenberg, and Percy H. Tannenbaum (Chicago: Rand McNally and Company, 1968): 797–800.

4. George E. Marcus, *The Sentimental Citizen: Emotions in Democratic Politics* (University Park, PA: Pennsylvania State University Press, 2002); George E. Marcus, W. Russell Neuman, and Michael MacKuen, *Affective Intelligence and Political Judgment* (Chicago: University of Chicago Press, 2000).

5. Donald Green, Bradley Palmquist, and Eric Schickler, *Partisan Hearts & Minds: Political Parties and the Social Identities of Voters* (New Haven, CT: Yale University Press, 2002).

6. Nielsen Media Research, "Audience Estimates for the 2008 Republican National Convention," September 5, 2008.

7. Those labeled "Conservative/Republican" include roughly 28 percent strong Republicans with a moderate political ideology and 69 percent not strong or leaning Republicans with a conservative ideology. Those labeled "Liberal/Democrat" include roughly 50 percent strong Democrats with a moderate ideology and 47 percent not strong or leaning Democrats with a liberal ideology.

8. Dean A. Ziemke, "Selective Exposure in a Presidential Campaign Contingent on Certainty and Salience," in *Communication Yearbook,* edited by Dan Nimmo (New Brunswick, NJ: Transaction Books, 1980), 4: 497–511; ABC News, ABC News Democratic Convention Poll, July 1988 [Computer file]. Radnor, PA: Chilton Research Services [producer], Ann Arbor, MI: Inter-university Consortium for Political and Social Research [distributor], 1990. doi:10.3886/ICPSR09070. ABC News. ABC News Republican Convention Poll, August 1988 [Computer file]. Radnor, PA: Chilton Research Services [producer], Ann Arbor, MI: Inter-university Consortium for Political and Social Research [distributor], 1990. doi:10.3886/ICPSR09071.

9. Data from the 2004 National Annenberg Election Survey. Analysis controls for demographics, media use, and political orientations. The figures are based on one standard deviation above and below the mean level of Bush favorability. Full logistic regression equations are reported in Natalie Jomini Stroud, "Media Effects, Selective Exposure, & *Fahrenheit 9/11*," *Political Communication* 24, 4 (2007): 415–32.

10. One potential concern is that this finding may represent de facto selectivity rather than selective exposure. This would be the case if the film was released in Democratic areas and not in Republican areas. I conducted additional analysis on the make-up of the film's audience controlling for the district's voting habits. The results continued to hold: Those with less favorable attitudes toward Bush were more likely to view the film. Anecdotal evidence also suggests that the film was widely distributed; a *Los Angeles Times* article published on June 28, 2004 noted, "Informal surveys of theaters and rival studios also indicated that the film was attracting crowds wherever it played in the GOP-leaning 'red states' as well as the Democrat blue. Much of the audience was predictably left of center, but in addition to places like the liberal enclave of Santa Monica it was doing well even in several cities in the president's home state of Texas."

11. Markus Prior, *Post-Broadcast Democracy: How Media Choice Increases Inequality in Political Involvement and Polarizes Elections* (New York: Cambridge University Press, 2007).

12. Kathleen Hall Jamieson and Kate Kenski, "Why the National Annenberg Election Survey?" in *Capturing Campaign Dynamics: The National Annenberg Election Survey,* edited by Daniel Romer, Kate Kenski, Paul Waldman, Christopher Adasiewicz, and Kathleen Hall Jamieson (New York: Oxford University Press, 2004): 1–11.

13. Number of Daily Newspapers, "Newspaper Association of America," *Editor & Publisher International Yearbook,* http://www.naa.org/TrendsandNumbers/Total-Paid-Circulation.aspx.

14. Ibid.

15. Guy Golan, "Inter-Media Agenda Setting and Global News Coverage: Assessing the Influence of the *New York Times* on Three Network Television Evening News Programs," *Journalism Studies* 7, 2 (2006): 323–33; Stephen D. Reese and Lucig H. Danielian, "Intermedia Influence and the Drug Issue: Converging on Cocaine," in *Communication Campaigns about Drugs: Government, Media, and the Public,* edited by Pamela J. Shoemaker (Hillsdale, NJ: Lawrence Erlbaum Associates, Publishers, 1989): 29–45; Lucig H. Danielian and Stephen D. Reese, "A Closer Look at Intermedia Influences on Agenda Setting: The Cocaine Issue of 1986," in *Communication Campaigns about Drugs: Government, Media, and the Public,* edited by Pamela J. Shoemaker (Hillsdale, NJ: Lawrence Erlbaum Associates, Publishers, 1989): 47–66.

16. The Pew Research Center's Project for Excellence in Journalism, "The Changing Newsroom," July 21, 2008, http://www.journalism.org/node/11961.

17. Dave D'Alessio and Mike Allen, "On the Role of Newspaper Ownership on Bias in Presidential Campaign Coverage by Newspapers," in *Mass Media Effects Research: Advances through Meta-Analysis,* edited by Raymond W. Preiss, Barbara Mae Gayle, Nancy Burrell, Mike Allen, and Jennings Bryant (Mahwah, NJ: Lawrence Erlbaum Associates, 2007): 429–53; James N. Druckman and Michael Parkin, "The Impact of Media Bias: How Editorial Slant Affects Voters," *Journal of Politics* 67, 4 (2005): 1030–49; Kim Fridkin Kahn and Patrick J. Kenney, "The Slant of the News: How Editorial Endorsements Influence Campaign Coverage and Citizens' Views of Candidates," *American Political Science Review* 96, 2 (2002): 381–94; Jeffrey E. Cohen, *Going Local: Presidential Leadership in the Post-Broadcast Age* (New York: Cambridge University Press, 2009). For an intriguing exception, see Russell J. Dalton, Paul A. Beck, and Robert Huckfeldt, "Partisan Cues and the Media: Information Flows in the 1992 Presidential Election," *American Political Science Review* 92, 1 (1998): 111–26.

18. Michelle Koidin Jaffe, "Endorsements Fire Up Readers: In Polarized Presidential Race, Papers' Picks Sparking Unprecedented Outrage," *San Antonio Express-News,* October 29, 2004, 1A.

19. Robert S. Erikson, "The Influence of Newspaper Endorsements in Presidential Elections: The Case of 1964," *American Journal of Political Science* 20, 2 (1976): 207–33; Michael G. Hagen and Kathleen Hall Jamieson, "Do Newspaper Endorsements Matter? Do Politicians Speak for Themselves in Newspapers and on Television?" in *Everything You Think You Know About Politics…And Why You're Wrong,* edited by Kathleen Hall Jamieson (New York: Basic Books, 2000): 155–9.

20. At first glance, Republicans appear to be less selective; they have nearly the same probability of reading Bush-endorsing newspapers as reading Kerry-endorsing newspapers. This conclusion is not warranted, however, since this does not take into account the availability of various newspapers. Newspapers endorsing Kerry had larger circulations compared to those endorsing Bush, for example. See, for example, Greg Mitchell, "Yes, Newspaper Endorsements Matter," *Editor & Publisher,* October 17, 2008, www.editorandpublisher.com/eandp/news/article_display.jsp?vnu_content_id=1003875478.

21. Matthew Gentzkow and Jesse M. Shapiro, "Media Bias and Reputation," *Journal of Political Economy* 114, 2 (2006): 280–316.

22. Diana C. Mutz and Paul S. Martin, "Facilitating Communication Across Lines of Political Difference: The Role of Mass Media," *American Political Science Review* 95, 1 (2001): 97–114. Note that Druckman and Parkin, however, do not find partisan differences between the readers of competing newspapers the *Star Tribune* and the *St. Paul Pioneer Press,* indicating that this relationship may not hold in all instances. See Druckman and Parkin, "The Impact of Media Bias."

23. Arbitron, *Radio Today* 2008 *Edition, 2008,* http://www.arbitron.com/downloads/radiotoday08.pdf.

24. Talkers, *The Top Talk Radio Audiences,* 2008, http://talkers.com/online/?p=71.

25. Greg Garrison, http://www.wibc.com/garrison.

26. Thom Hartmann, "Suggested Approach: Programming a Liberal Talk Radio Line-Up," *Talkers,* 152 (2004): 37.

27. C. Richard Hofstetter, David Barker, James T. Smith, Gina M. Zari, and Thomas A. Ingrassia, "Information, Misinformation, and Political Talk Radio," *Political Research Quarterly* 52, 2 (1999): 353–69; Joseph N. Cappella, Joseph Turow, and Kathleen Hall Jamieson, *Call-In Political Talk Radio: Background, Content, Audiences, Portrayal in Mainstream Media* (Philadelphia: Annenberg Public Policy Center, 1996); William G. Mayer, "Why Talk Radio is Conservative," *Public Interest* 156 (2004): 86–103; Michael Harrison, "New Format for Heavy Hundred: The 100 Most Important Hosts Now Ranked Leading Elite Group of 250," *Talkers Magazine* 165 (2006); Kathleen Hall Jamieson and Joseph N. Cappella, *Echo Chamber: Rush Limbaugh and the Conservative Media Establishment* (New York: Oxford University Press, 2008). Using these criteria, statements that the hosts or programs were liberal, progressive, Democratic, anti-Bush, pro-Kerry, or supportive of issue positions known to be related to the Democratic Party were coded as liberal. Statements that hosts or programs were conservative, Republican, pro-Bush, anti-Kerry, or supportive of issue positions known to be related to the Republican Party were coded as conservative.

28. Pew Research Center for the People & the Press, *Internet Now Major Source of Campaign News,* October 31, 2008, http://pewresearch.org/pubs/1017/internet-now-major-source-of-campaign-news.

29. Project for Excellence in Journalism, *State of the News Media 2008,* http://www.stateofthenewsmedia.com/2008/index.php.

30. Project for Excellence in Journalism, *State of the News Media 2004,* http://www.stateofthenewsmedia.com/2004/index.php.

31. Nielsen Media Research, "Americans Flock to TV, Internet for 'Bailout' News," October 1, 2008, http://blog.nielsen.com/nielsenwire/online_mobile/americans-flock-to-tvs-internet-for-bailout-news/.

32. Ronald Grover and Burt Helm, "The News: Cable TV's Sleeper Hit," *Business Week,* July 3, 2008.

33. Note that the measure did not distinguish between CNN and CNN Headline News.

34. Sean Aday, Steven Livingston, and Maeve Hebert, "Embedding the Truth: A Cross-Cultural Analysis of Objectivity and Television Coverage of the Iraq War," *The International Journal of Press/Politics* 10, 1 (2005): 3–21.

35. Center for Media and Public Affairs, *The Diversity Debate: Media Coverage of Affirmative Action in College Education,* (Washington, DC, 2003).

36. This admittedly is a simplification of Groseclose and Milyo's extensive analysis. These authors model ADA scores for media outlets based on the ADA scores for legislators and their references to various policy groups and think tanks. Tim Groseclose and Jeffrey Milyo, "A Measure of Media Bias," *The Quarterly Journal of Economics* CXX, 4 (*2005*): 1191–237.

37. Center for Media and Public Affairs, *Campaign 2004: The Summer: How the Media Covered the Presidential Campaign During Summer 2004* (Washington, DC, 2004); Center for Media and Public Affairs, *Campaign 2004: The Media Agenda* (Washington, DC, 2004); Project

for Excellence in Journalism, *The Debate Effect: How the Press Covered the Pivotal Period of the 2004 Presidential Campaign* (Washington, DC, 2004).

38. Jamieson and Cappella, *Echo Chamber.*

39. Tim Groeling, "Who's the Fairest of Them All? An Empirical Test for Partisan Bias on ABC, CBS, NBC, and Fox News," *Presidential Studies Quarterly* 38, 4 (2008): 631–57.

40. Project for Excellence in Journalism, *The State of the News Media* 2008: *An Annual Report on American Journalism,* March 17, 2008, http://www.stateofthenewsmedia.org/2008/index.php.

41. Dusty Saunders, "Political TV Ratings Peak during Conventions," *Rocky Mountain News,* September 10, 2008, http://www.rockymountainnews.com/news/2008/sep/10/political-tv-ratings-peak-during-conventions/; Jim Rutenberg and Brian Stelter, "Conventions, Anything but Dull, Are a TV Hit," *New York Times,* September 6, 2008, http://www.nytimes.com/2008/09/06/us/politics/06ratings.html?fta=y; Lisa de Moraes, "My Friends, That's a Record Audience for a Convention Speech," *Washington Post,* September 6, 2008, http://www.washingtonpost.com/wp-dyn/content/article/2008/09/05/AR2008090503406.html.

42. James G. Webster, "Beneath the Veneer of Fragmentation: Television Audience Polarization in a Multichannel World," *Journal of Communication* 55, 2 (2005): 366–82.

43. Prior, *Post-Broadcast Democracy,* 157–8.

44. When the same amount of time is used to examine both CNN/MSNBC and Fox News (e.g., looking at viewing for five or sixty minutes or more for both channels), the data represent those instances when at least sixty minutes were watched during a *single* day. Nielsen data are somewhat different for the calculations that involve mixed amounts of time (e.g., sixty minutes versus fifteen minutes). Here, the sixty minutes could occur at any point over the course of the two weeks (e.g., ten minutes on Thursday, ten minutes on Friday, etc.). This produces some differences in the data. When the sixty minutes is required to be watched within a single day, 21 percent watch CNN/MSNBC and 15 percent watch Fox News. When the sixty minutes can occur at any point during the two weeks, 27 percent watch CNN/MSNBC and 18 percent watch Fox News. Also note that the minimum viewing time is thirty-one seconds, which is counted as a minute. If a person were to view a cable news network for thirty-one seconds each day during a two-week period, he would be counted as watching the network for ten minutes or more.

45. Jonathan Morris, "The Fox News Factor," *The International Journal of Press/Politics* 10, 3 (2005): 56–79.

46. Aaron Smith, *The Internet's Role in Campaign* 2008, Pew Internet and American Life Project (Washington, DC, 2008).

47. Jennifer Saba, "Top 30 News Sites for October," *Editor & Publisher,* November 13, 2008, http://www.editorandpublisher.com/eandp/news/article_display.jsp?vnu_content_id=1003890933.

48. Cass Sunstein, *Republic.com* (Princeton: Princeton University Press, 2001); Cass Sunstein, *Republic.com 2.0* (Princeton: Princeton University Press, 2007).

49. Visitors to Gore's presidential campaign Web site in 2000 tended to be Democrats, while visitors to Bush's presidential campaign Web site tended to be Republicans; see Bruce Bimber and Richard Davis, *Campaigning Online: The Internet in U.S. Elections* (New York: Oxford University Press, 2003). Of those who got political news online in 2004, for example, 31 percent of Kerry voters visited the Kerry campaign Web site, while only 12 percent of Bush voters did. Sixteen percent of Bush voters visited the Bush campaign Web site, followed by 14 percent of Democrats. Lee Rainie, Michael Cornfield, and John Horrigan, *The Internet and Campaign* 2004, Pew Internet & American Life Project (Washington, DC, 2005).

50. Jennifer Stromer-Galley, "Diversity and Political Conversations on the Internet: Users' Perspectives," *Journal of Computer-Mediated Communication* 8, 3 (2003).

51. John Horrigan, R. Kelly Garrett, and Paul Resnick, *The Internet and Democratic Debate*, Pew Internet & American Life Project (Washington, DC, 2004); R. Kelly Garrett, "Politically Motivated Reinforcement Seeking: Reframing the Selective Exposure Debate," *Journal of Communication* 59, 4 (2009): 676–99; R. Kelly Garrett, "Echo Chambers Online?: Politically Motivated Selective Exposure among Internet News Users," *Journal of Computer Mediated Communication* 14, 2 (2009): 265–85.

52. The NAES did not ask respondents to specify which candidate Web sites or which online news organizations they visited.

53. In order to validate this coding scheme, a subset of fifty open-ended responses were selected and coded by a second coder. The intercoder reliability, computed using Krippendorff's *alpha*, was 0.96. Details about Krippendorff's *alpha* can be found in Klaus Krippendorff, *Content Analysis: An Introduction to its Methodology* (Thousand Oaks, CA: Sage, 2004), 2.

54. Note that there is some debate about the accuracy of survey-based media exposure measures; see, for example, Vincent Price and John Zaller, "Evaluation of Media Exposure Items in the 1989 NES Pilot Study." Technical Report to the National Election Studies Board of Overseers. (Ann Arbor: Institute for Social Research, 1990); Markus Prior, "The Immensely Inflated News Audience: Assessing Bias in Self-Reported News Exposure" *Public Opinion Quarterly* 73 1 (2009): 130–43. Two components of the analysis conducted here, however, may boost confidence in the measures. First, the media variables measure content-based exposure (as opposed to frequency of exposure), which may be easier for respondents to accurately recall. Second, in most cases, respondents were asked open-ended questions about their media exposure, so they would have to recall the name of the media program or outlet in order to answer the question.

55. This was determined by running forty-eight logistic regression analyses—six for each partisan media category. For example, I analyzed whether those listening to liberal talk radio, watching CNN, and accessing liberal Web sites were more likely to read a Kerry-endorsing newspaper and whether those listening to conservative talk radio, watching Fox News, and accessing conservative Web sites were less likely to read a Kerry-endorsing newspaper. Without any controls, 79 percent of the forty-eight analyses confirm the cross-media hypotheses, 8 percent contradict, and 13 percent are not significant. With controls for demographics, political orientations, and media use (including ideology/partisanship, political knowledge and interest, and use of various media types), 40 percent confirm the hypotheses, 8 percent contradict, and 52 percent are not significant.

56. Stefano DellaVigna and Ethan Kaplan, "The Fox News Effect: Media Bias and Voting," *Quarterly Journal of Economics*, 122, 3 (2007): 1187–234.

57. See, for example, Shanto Iyengar and Jennifer A. McGrady, *Media Politics: A Citizen's Guide* (New York: W.W. Norton & Company, 2007).

58. Donald Green, Bradley Palmquist, and Eric Schickler, *Partisan Hearts and Minds: Political Parties and the Social Identities of Voters* (New Haven, CT: Yale University Press, 2002); Jon A. Krosnick, "The Stability of Partisan Preferences: Comparisons of Symbolic and Nonsymbolic Attitudes," *American Journal of Political Science* 35, 2 (1991): 547–76. This is not to deny some variation in partisanship (see Jamieson and Cappella, *Echo Chamber*).

59. Paul F. Lazarsfeld, Bernard Berelson, and Hazel Gaudet, *The People's Choice: How the Voter Makes Up His Mind in a Presidential Campaign* (New York: Columbia University Press, 1944/1968): 3.

60. The American National Election Studies (ANES; www.electionstudies.org). The ANES 2008 Time Series Study [dataset]. Stanford University and the University of Michigan [producers]. These materials are based on work supported by the National Science Foundation under grants SES-0535334, SES-0720428, SES-0840550, and SES-0651271, Stanford University, and the University of Michigan. Any opinions, findings and conclusions or recommendations expressed in these materials are those of the author and do not necessarily reflect the views of the funding organizations.

61. See Ronald C. Kessler and David F. Greenberg, *Linear Panel Analysis: Models of Quantitative Change* (New York: Academic Press, 1981).

62. Kessler and Greenberg, *Linear Panel Analysis*; Michael D. Slater, "Operationalizing and Analyzing Exposure: The Foundation of Media Effects Research," *Journalism and Mass Communication Quarterly* 81, 1 (2004): 168–83.

63. William P. Eveland Jr., Andrew F. Hayes, Dhavan V. Shah, and Nojin Kwak, "Understanding the Relationship between Communication and Political Knowledge: A Model Comparison Approach Using Panel Data," *Political Communication* 22 (2005): 423–46.

64. Looking at the indices of media use across the 2004 NAES panel surveys, liberal Democrats consumed significantly more liberal media in the postwave after taking into account their prewave liberal media use in the DNC, debate, and general election panels. Conservative Republicans consumed significantly more conservative media in the postwave after taking into account their prewave conservative media use in the DNC, debate, and general election panels. More details can be found in the technical appendix for this chapter.

65. Freedman and Sears, "Selective Exposure"; Sears and Freedman, "Selective Exposure to Information."

66. Nielsen Media Research, "Average U.S. Home Now Receives a Record 104.2 TV Channels, According to Nielsen," March 19, 2007.

67. Nielsen Media Research, "Television Audience 2008."

68. Steven H. Chaffee and Miriam J. Metzger, "The End of Mass Communication?" *Mass Communication & Society* 4, 4 (2001): 365–79; David Tewksbury, "The Seeds of Audience Fragmentation: Specialization in the Use of Online News Sites," *Journal of Broadcasting & Electronic Media* 49, 3 (2005): 332–48; Joseph Turow, *Breaking Up America: Advertisers & The New Media World* (Chicago: The University of Chicago Press, 1997); James G. Webster, "Audience Behavior in the New Media Environment," *Journal of Communication* 36, 3 (1986): 77–90.

69. Nielsen Media Research, "Television Audience 2008."

70. Sug-Min Youn, "Program Type Preference and Program Choice in a Multichannel Situation," *Journal of Broadcasting & Electronic Media* 38 (1994): 465–75.

71. Prior, *Post-Broadcast Democracy*; see also Jatin Atre and Elihu Katz, "What's Killing Television News? Experimentally Assessing the Effects of Multiple Channels on Media Choice," (Paper presented at the International Communication Association Conference, New York, 2005).

72. Peter Fischer, Stefan Schulz-Hardt, and Dieter Frey, "Selective Exposure and Information Quality: How Different Information Quantities Moderate Decision Makers' Preference for Consistent and Inconsistent Information," *Journal of Personality and Social Psychology* 94, 2 (2008): 231–44; Dieter Frey and Robert A. Wicklund, "A Clarification of Selective Exposure: The Impact of Choice," *Journal of Experimental Social Psychology* 14 (1978): 132–39.

73. The relationship uncovered by Fischer and colleagues wasn't linear—having four choices produced significantly more selective exposure than having two choices, but having ten choices

did not produce significantly more selective exposure than having four choices. The result suggests that the influence of more choice on selectivity may be nonlinear—at some point, more choices may not enhance selective exposure. See Fischer, Schulz-Hardt, and Frey, "Selective Exposure and Information Quality." Yet other studies of more choice and selectivity suggest that higher amounts of choice *do* influence exposure patterns. See, for example, Atre and Katz, "What's Killing Television News"; Prior, *Post-Broadcast Democracy*.

74. Silvia Knobloch, Matthias Hastall, Dolf Zillmann, and Coy Callison, "Imagery Effects on the Selective Reading of Internet Newsmagazines," *Communication Research* 30, 1 (2003): 3–29; David Tewksbury and Scott L. Althaus, "Differences in Knowledge Acquisition Among Readers of the Paper and Online Versions of a National Newspaper," *Journalism & Mass Communication Quarterly* 77, 3 (2000): 457–79; Dolf Zillmann, Lei Chen, Silvia Knobloch, and Coy Callison, "Effects of Lead Framing on Selective Exposure to Internet News Reports," *Communication Research* 31 (2004): 58–81; Dolf Zillmann, Silvia Knobloch, and Hong-sik Yu, "Effects of Photographs on the Selective Reading of News Reports," *Media Psychology* 3, 4 (2001): 301–24.

75. See, for example, Jonathan L. Freedman, "Preference for Dissonant Information," *Journal of Personality and Social Psychology* 2, 2 (1965): 287–9.

76. John L. Cotton, "Cognitive Dissonance in Selective Exposure," in *Selective Exposure to Communication*, edited by Dolf Zillmann and Jennings Bryant (Hillsdale, NJ: Erlbaum, 1985): 11–33.

77. Eva Jonas, Stefan Schulz-Hardt, Dieter Frey, and Norman Thelen, "Confirmation Bias in Sequential Information Search after Preliminary Decisions: An Expansion of Dissonance Theoretical Research on Selective Exposure to Information," *Journal of Personality and Social Psychology* 80, 4 (2001): 557–71.

78. Judson Mills, Elliot Aronson, and Hal Robinson, "Selectivity in Exposure to Information," *Journal of Abnormal and Social Psychology* 59 (1959): 250–53.

79. Jonas, Schulz-Hardt, Frey, and Thelen, "Confirmation Bias in Sequential Information Search after Preliminary Decisions."

80. Brock, for example, replicated Feather's selective exposure study but included a manipulation where subjects were led to believe that they would actually have to consume the articles they said that they preferred. Brock found higher levels of selective exposure when subjects believed they would be reading their article choices. Note that this change was confined to smokers who rated articles claiming there was no link between smoking and cancer more highly when they were led to believe they would have to read the article. Timothy C. Brock, "Commitment to Exposure as a Determinant of Information Receptivity," *Journal of Personality and Social Psychology* 2, 1 (1965): 10–19; Feather, "Cigarette Smoking and Lung Cancer."

81. See, for example, Mills, Aronson, and Robinson, "Selectivity in Exposure to Information."

82. Lavine, Borgida, and Sullivan, for example, evaluated selective exposure by having respondents rate a pro- and an anti-affirmative action article. Note that the purpose of their study was to investigate the relationship between selective exposure and other variables, however, not to determine the absolute level of selective exposure. Howard Lavine, Eugene Borgida, and John L. Sullivan, "On the Relationship between Attitude Involvement and Attitude Accessibility: Toward a Cognitive-Motivational Model of Political Information Processing," *Political Psychology,* 21, 1 (2000): 81–106. In support of this, studies including a neutral or more balanced option find that the neutral option is chosen by respondents; see Steven H. Chaffee and Jack M. McLeod, "Individuals vs. Social Predictors of Information Seeking," *Journalism Quarterly* 50 (1973): 237–45.

83. These results come from discrete choice analyses not including an interaction between choice, magazine selection, and ideology/partisanship. The results incorporating this interaction are discussed shortly and displayed in the appendix.

84. The relationship was marginally significant. More details are available in the appendix.

85. Shanto Iyengar and Kyu S. Hahn, "Red Media, Blue Media: Evidence of Ideological Selectivity in Media Use," *Journal of Communication* 59 (2009): 19–39.

86. Jennifer Saba, "Top 30 News Sites for October," *Editor & Publisher,* November 13, 2008, http://www.editorandpublisher.com/eandp/news/article_display.jsp?vnu_content_id=1003890933.

87. Shanto Iyengar, Kyu S. Hahn, Jon A. Krosnick, and John Walker, "Selective Exposure to Campaign Communication: The Role of Anticipated Agreement and Issue Public Membership," *Journal of Politics* 70 (2008): 186–200.

88. Young Mie Kim, "Issue Publics in the New Information Environment: Selectivity, Domain Specificity, and Extremity," *Communication Research* 36 (2009): 254–84.

89. Silvia Knobloch-Westerwick and Jingbo Meng, "Looking the Other Way: Selective Exposure to Attitude-Consistent and Counterattitudinal Political Information," *Communication Research* 36 (2009): 426–48.

90. The Pew Research Center for the People & the Press, *Pew Research Center Biennial News Consumption Survey* (Washington, DC, 2006).

91. Matthew A. Baum and Phil Gussin, "In the Eye of the Beholder: How Information Shortcuts Shape Individual Perceptions of Bias in the Media," *Quarterly Journal of Political Science* 3 (2008): 1–31; Iyengar and Hahn, "Red Media, Blue Media"; Joel Turner, "The Messenger Overwhelming the Message: Ideological Cues and Perceptions of Bias in Television News," *Political Behavior* 29 (2007): 441–64.

92. The relationship was marginally significant. More details are available in the appendix.

93. *Talkers* magazine from October 2004 lists the top radio hosts by audience size. The most popular hosts are Rush Limbaugh and Sean Hannity.

94. Nielsen Media Research reports that in March of 2009, the five top global news sites included MSNBC global network, CNN digital network, Yahoo! News, AOL News, and NYTimes.com. Nielsen Media Research, "MSNBC, CNN Top Global News Sites in March, NY Times Top Paper," April 21, 2009, http://blog.nielsen.com/nielsenwire/online_mobile/msnbc-and-cnn-top-global-news-sites-in-march/.

95. Results computed using the 2004 NAES RCS. I conducted two regression analyses to arrive at this result. The first predicted use of Internet news and the second use of talk radio. All other controls used in creating Figure 3.3 were incorporated into the analysis.

4

LEARNING PARTISAN SELECTIVITY

NEWS SELECTIONS ARE influenced by partisanship. As the previous chapter shows, partisans tend to choose likeminded newspapers, magazines, radio programs, cable news networks, and Web sites. Partisanship may be particularly likely to influence news use for many reasons. For some citizens, partisanship is closely related to their personal identity, which may increase the chances that it guides exposure decisions. There also are environmental reasons that citizens link partisanship with the news media. Discussions of partisan media bias are everywhere. Citizens are frequently prompted to think about the news media in partisan terms.

Sometimes citizens are told, blatantly, about partisan leanings in the media. An advertisement for the *Kimmer Show*, for example, boasts, "Get your daily dose of un-apologetic, America-loving, wussy-liberal-blasting, hard-news and ever-so-slightly-biased commentary here!" And Bill Press's radio program is touted as a "new 'liberal way' to start your day."

With advertisements like these, it is clear that you don't even have to tune in to some programs to understand their partisan leanings. In the absence of these types of unambiguous partisan declarations, citizens still form impressions about media outlets—even those that they do not use regularly. In the Knowledge Networks study, for example, over half of the respondents who had not watched cable news on Fox News or CNN recently were perfectly willing to comment on these networks. Even though they explicitly were given the opportunity to opt out of answering the questions, numerous participants provided an opinion about the trustworthiness, fairness, political bias, and accuracy of news networks that they had not viewed recently. Some respondents may have formed impressions of these networks based on prior, but not recent, exposure. Others could have formed impressions on the basis of other information, however.

One possible source of information about partisan media bias comes from political elites, such as candidates for public office, their surrogates, and government representatives. Even without attending to the media, the public can learn about which media outlets lean which way thanks to clues from political elites. In addition to the Lynne Cheney and Bill Clinton examples described in chapter 1, consider the following:

- In the third presidential debate on October 15, 2008, Democratic presidential hopeful Senator Barack Obama described the *Chicago Tribune* as "a Republican-leaning newspaper."
- Steve Schmidt, a strategist for Republican Senator John McCain's 2008 presidential campaign, labeled MSNBC "a partisan advocacy organization that exists for the purpose of attacking John McCain."[1]

Statements like these influence public perceptions. In their research, Mark Watts, David Domke, Dhavan Shah, and David Fan investigated public reactions to elite statements about media bias.[2] They found that political elites frequently said that the media favored liberal views and Democratic candidates in the 1988, 1992, and 1996 presidential campaigns. In 1992, for example, the popular Republican refrain rang "Annoy the Media—Re-Elect George Bush." Watts and his colleagues found that when the media covered political elites' accusations of media bias, public perceptions of media bias followed suit. When political elites claimed that the media were liberally biased, a substantial portion of the public came to believe that the media were, in fact, liberally biased. Though most of the media bias accusations in the late 1980s and early 1990s were about the media *in general,* the same process should occur for accusations of bias in *specific* media outlets, such as the statements about bias made by Obama and Schmidt. Indeed, when political elites accuse a media outlet of biased reporting, some subsequently adopt the belief that the outlet is biased.[3]

Yet one doesn't need to be a *news* consumer to learn about media partisanship. Accusations of news media bias have become a staple in popular culture.

- In the song "Sly Fox," Nas raps, "Watch what you watchin'...Fox keeps feeding us toxins."
- Updating the lyrics to his well-known "Family Tradition" song for the 2008 McCain-Palin campaign, Hank Williams Jr. sings, "The left wing liberal media have always been a real close knit family. But, most of the American People don't believe 'em anyway ya see...."

- In Jodi Picoult's fiction book *Nineteen Minutes, A Novel,* she starts one chapter as follows: "You can tell a lot about people by their habits.... There are those who watched CNN and those who watched Fox News."[4]
- In the popular women's magazine *Marie Claire,* Democratic presidential nominee Barack Obama is asked whether he believes that his wife is misunderstood. He responds, "Not by people who've been paying attention. I think that if you've been watching Fox News then probably she's misunderstood, because I do think there's been a fairly systematic attempt by the conservative press to paint her in a completely false way."[5]
- *Vogue* magazine labels MSNBC host Rachel Maddow a "liberal commentator" and notes that "cable news shows on Fox and MSNBC are clearly defined outlets of the left and the right."[6]

Whether paying attention to the news, listening to music, browsing a women's magazine, or reading a novel, messages of media bias and selectivity are pervasive. Attentive citizens should have no problem learning to think about the news media in partisan terms. But do they? This chapter looks at how citizens learn about and learn from partisan media. I examine what partisans think about media bias and find that partisans frequently reach different conclusions about the presence of bias. Factors that one would hope might help citizens to keep their partisanship in check when evaluating the media don't seem to help much at all. Perceptions about the media are critical for my purposes because they help to explain why citizens are drawn toward likeminded media. Political knowledge emerges as a key factor in understanding not only perceptions of media bias but also partisan selective exposure. As the results in this chapter reveal, political knowledge both causes and to some extent is influenced by partisan selective exposure.

PERCEPTIONS OF PARTISAN MEDIA BIAS

Ideally, citizens would be able to detect bias even in the absence of a blatant alert about its presence. School curricula, critical thinking texts, and news media literacy campaigns all emphasize the detection of bias as an important skill.[7] The rationale is that by recognizing signs of bias, citizens can discount biased information and reach more accurate understandings about the world.

The ability to recognize bias is important here because it relates directly to the possible consequences of partisan selective exposure. If citizens can recognize signs of media bias and discount biased information, then despite dire predictions, partisan selective exposure would not be terribly worrisome. When using any type of news media source, citizens would recognize biases and interpret the information accordingly. If citizens have trouble detecting biases, however, they may inappropriately rely on biased information and discount unbiased accounts. All citizens may not be equally capable of examining bias in the media, however; some citizens may be better equipped. Attentive citizens—those with higher levels of political knowledge and interest—should have the requisite background and motivation to ascertain the presence of partisan bias. There are at least two reasons that this should be the case. First, politically knowledgeable and interested citizens are particularly receptive to political information. They know about candidate issue stances, the inner workings of the U.S. government, and the political happenings of the day.[8] Equipped with a store of political information and an interest in learning, these citizens are better able to process, organize, and subsequently recall contemporary political facts.[9] Learning about partisanship in the media may occur in much the same way that citizens learn who their senators are and where the political parties stand on the issues. With higher levels of political knowledge, partisans may be better *able* to assess bias in the media. With stronger political leanings and heightened political interest, partisans may be more *motivated* to examine bias in the media.

Second, knowledgeable and interested citizens have a more developed sense of how politics is structured. They tend to organize their attitudes ideologically and they are better able to categorize political statements based on partisanship.[10] They know when a policy statement represents a Democratic position and when it represents a Republican position. Just as they can sort issue positions into partisan categories, knowledgeable and interested citizens should be able to sort media outlets into categories based on partisan leanings.

To evaluate whether politically knowledgeable and interested citizens are more likely to pick up on partisan details about the media, I first turned to the 2004 National Annenberg Election Surveys (NAES) general election panel. Respondents were asked to identify which presidential candidate their newspaper endorsed.

Consistent with other studies, the percentage of people correctly identifying their newspapers' endorsement was underwhelming.[11] Examining only those instances in which the respondent's newspaper endorsed either Bush or Kerry, 47 percent of respondents knew which presidential candidate was endorsed by the paper that they read during the previous week. What is more interesting for this chapter, however, is *who* was more likely to know the endorsement.

If the aforementioned ideas are correct, politically knowledgeable and interested citizens should be more likely to correctly identify the candidate endorsed by their newspaper. On the NAES, respondents were asked to rate their level of interest in the presidential campaign. I evaluated political knowledge based on how many questions people were able to answer correctly on a quiz about general political facts. Which party has the most members in the U.S. House of Representatives? Who decides whether a law is constitutional—the president, the Congress, or the Supreme Court? How much of a majority is required for the U.S. Senate and House to override a presidential veto? These types of questions have been used extensively in political science and communication to measure political knowledge.[12] I combined these measures with the interviewer's assessment of how knowledgeable the respondent was—those who answered more quiz questions correctly also tended to be rated as more politically informed by their interviewer.[13] Measured in this way, political knowledge is a relatively stable, enduring measure of an individual's knowledge about politics and the government in general. I anticipated that these measures would be related to knowing who one's newspaper endorsed. The results are shown in Figure 4.1.

As expected, the politically knowledgeable were more likely to know who their newspaper endorsed. Although following the expected trend, the politically interested were no more likely than those with less interest to know who their newspaper

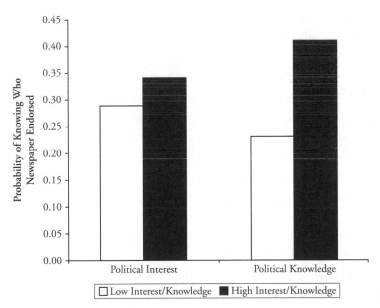

FIGURE 4.1 Knowledge of Newspaper Endorsement by Political Knowledge and Interest. Results based on a logistic regression analysis predicting knowledge of which presidential candidate was endorsed by the newspaper read most in the past week. Results are for respondents who read a newspaper at least once in the past week and who read a newspaper endorsing Bush or Kerry. Analysis controls for demographics, political orientations, and patterns of media use. Political knowledge is significant in predicting knowledge of one's newspaper endorsement. Political knowledge and interest values are calculated using one standard deviation from the mean values. More details can be found in the technical appendix for this chapter.

Source: Data from the 2004 NAES General Election Panel.

endorsed. Consistently, in fact, political knowledge emerges as a stronger and more consistent factor in how partisans approach the media. For this reason, I focus more on the contributions of political knowledge in this chapter.

Although attentive citizens recognize newspaper endorsements, skepticism about citizens' ability to detect bias is warranted. When it comes to making assessments about less clear-cut indicators of partisanship, citizens don't have a strong track record. Citizens' partisan attachments often influence their perceptions. For example, partisans tend to judge putatively neutral media as hostile to their viewpoint.[14] Democrats believe that the coverage favors Republicans. Republicans believe that the coverage favors Democrats. Even when asked to evaluate a *biased* news source, partisans do not reach identical conclusions about the presence of bias.[15] To draw from chapter 2, "The *perceived truth value* of supportive communications is greater than that of nonsupportive material."[16] A strong belief in a partisan perspective can make a likeminded source seem to be presenting correct, factual, and unbiased information. Looking at the same source, however, nonlikeminded partisans may be blown away by what they perceive as extensive bias. Even if partisans agree on the direction of bias in an unquestionably biased source, likeminded partisans *still* will tend to see less intense bias than those with opposing views.

Perhaps there are individuals, however, who can shed their partisan outlooks and recognize signs of media bias. Given that the politically knowledgeable are better informed about newspaper endorsements, an easily verified fact, they also may be more attentive to partisan biases in media sources.

I examined the extent to which liberals and Democrats reach similar conclusions about the presence of bias compared to conservatives and Republicans. When these two constituencies disagree, we know that one or both are not correctly assessing the presence of bias. Even if partisans agree, we cannot be sure that they are correct, although this inference is substantially stronger. Although these groups tend to diverge in their perceptions of media bias, I wondered whether some characteristics would reduce the gap in partisan assessments of bias. Here, I assess whether political knowledge helps partisans to reach a consensus about the presence and direction of bias.

Returning to the Knowledge Networks data, I analyzed what people think about partisan leanings in the media. In general, public assessments of news media bias match the categorizations that I made in chapter 3. People tend to label CNN, MSNBC, the *New York Times,* and National Public Radio as liberal, not conservative. They also tend to label Rush Limbaugh, Bill O'Reilly, the *Wall Street Journal,* and Fox News as conservative, not liberal. Though some do not perceive any partisan bias, respondents weighing in on the presence or absence of partisan bias most frequently indicated biases in line with these categorizations. Numerous other surveys yield similar evidence.[17] But are politically knowledgeable partisans more likely to perceive bias in these outlets? And do knowledgeable liberals and Democrats agree with knowledgeable conservatives and Republicans? The results of this analysis are shown in Figure 4.2.[18]

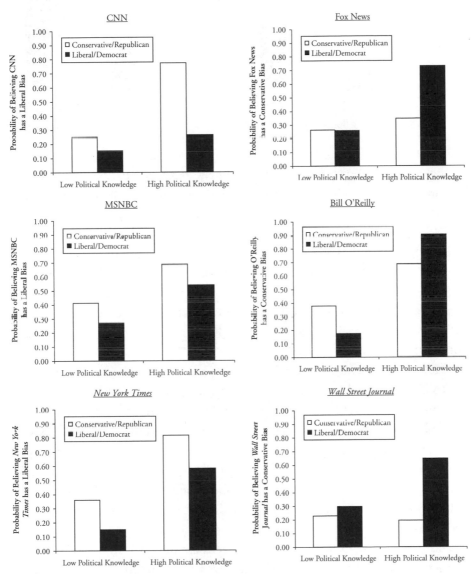

FIGURE 4.2 Perceptions of Media Bias by Political Knowledge and Ideology/Partisanship. Results based on logistic regression analyses predicting beliefs about media bias. Results are for respondents with an opinion about the presence or absence of bias in each outlet. Patterns of significance for political knowledge, ideology/partisanship, and the interaction between these variables vary and are included in the technical appendix. Analyses control for demographics, political orientations, and patterns of media use. Political knowledge and ideology/partisanship values are calculated using one standard deviation from the mean values. More details can be found in the technical appendix for this chapter.

Source: Data from the 2008 Knowledge Networks Study.

(Figure continues on following page)

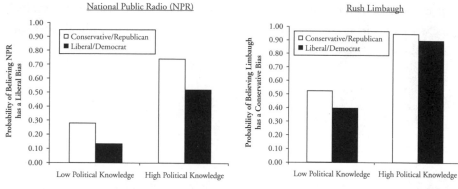

FIGURE 4.2 (Continued from previous page)

The politically knowledgeable are more likely to perceive partisan media biases. The sorts of media bias seen, however, depend on where people stand politically. Knowledgeable conservatives and Republicans are particularly likely to see CNN, MSNBC, the *New York Times,* and National Public Radio as liberally biased. Knowledgeable liberals and Democrats are particularly likely to see Bill O'Reilly, Fox News, and the *Wall Street Journal* as conservatively biased. There is some exception to this rule in the case Rush Limbaugh, where partisans on both sides of the political spectrum perceive a conservative bias. Yet political knowledge still matters—knowledgeable citizens are more likely to report that Limbaugh has a conservative bias.

Knowing more about politics rarely leads partisans to form a consensus about media bias. In several instances, political knowledge expands gaps in partisan perceptions of media bias. For CNN, Fox News, and the *Wall Street Journal,* large gaps in media bias perceptions appear only for those with higher levels of political knowledge. Partisans are quick to see hostile biases and somewhat less likely to perceive likeminded bias. And knowledgeable partisans, it seems, are especially likely to see media bias—especially in favor of the opposition.[19]

Other findings confirm that knowledge doesn't help partisans to agree on the presence of media bias. When evaluating television broadcast segments, as opposed to entire media outlets, knowledgeable citizens are more apt to see the programming as hostile to their partisan inclinations.[20] Further, political elites' statements about bias influence perceptions of media bias primarily among the politically knowledgeable. Knowledgeable partisans, however, respond selectively to the sentiments of political elites.[21] Political scientist Jonathan Ladd found that when Democratic leaders criticize the media, educated liberal Democrats follow suit and evaluate the media more negatively.[22] Conservative Republicans, however, are unmoved. When Republican leaders criticize the media, however, the opposite occurs: Educated conservative Republicans evaluate the media more negatively and liberal Democrats are unmoved.

Applying these results to the elite statements mentioned earlier, we would expect that knowledgeable Democrats would follow Obama and Clinton and believe that the *Chicago Tribune* and Fox News favor Republicans. Knowledgeable Republicans would follow Cheney and Schmidt and believe that CNN and MSNBC favor Democrats. As these examples illustrate, elite discussion of media bias follows a predictable pattern: Partisans accuse outlets of favoring the opposition. Other examples abound. Vice President Dick Cheney, for example, was quoted in the *Washington Post* on June 27, 2006, as saying, "Some of the press, in particular the *New York Times,* have made the job of defending against further terrorist attacks more difficult...." Although Cheney's statement aims to deter partisans of all stripes, his conservative ideology likely makes his statement particularly persuasive for those sharing his political views. From these sorts of statements, politically knowledgeable partisans can learn which outlets are hostile.

Political knowledge is supposed to help citizens sort through political facts and to possess a "[resistance] to biased information."[23] Recognizing that a bias exists, after all, should empower citizens to resist it. It is good news, then, that the politically knowledgeable are more likely to perceive biases in the news media. It is not so reassuring, however, that these citizens are likely to perceive bias favoring the *other side* but aren't as likely to find bias in their favor.

CHANGING PERCEPTIONS OF MEDIA BIAS

Given that political knowledge often does not lead partisans to agree on the presence of partisan media biases, perhaps there are ways to encourage citizens to cast aside their partisan inclinations and to reach more of a consensus about media bias. After all, the detection of bias is a popular curricular goal and a staple of critical thinking.[24] One text offering advice on how to critically assess the news media, for example, recommends being "sensitive to whether particular news vehicles present either a liberal or conservative bias."[25] To examine whether partisan reactions to the media can be influenced by prompts like these, I devised two studies.

In the first study, participants were asked to read and assess an article from the mainstream news media. The article described where the 2008 presidential nominees Barack Obama and John McCain stood on domestic and foreign policy issues. Before reading the article, participants were given instructions about the purpose of reading the article. A random half of the participants were instructed to think about bias. Before reading the article, they were told, "We are interested in your impressions about bias in the media. With this in mind, please read the article below. As you read, think about whether this article favors presumptive Democratic presidential nominee Barack Obama or favors presumptive Republican presidential nominee John McCain. When you finish reading, we will ask you about your thoughts on this matter." The other half of the respondents were instructed to focus on the clarity of the article: "We are interested in your impressions of whether the average American voter is able to read and understand news coverage. With this in mind, please read the article below. As you read, think about the article's grammar, format, and structure as well as how clearly the information is presented. When you finish reading, we will ask you about your thoughts on this matter." I was curious whether cuing people to think about bias might lead partisans to reach similar conclusions about the presence of bias in the article.

After reading the article, participants were asked about their impressions of the article. Regardless of whether they read the "bias instructions" or the "clarity instructions," participants reached similar conclusions about how readable, understandable, and well written the article was. When evaluating whether the article was biased, however, participants who read the "bias instructions" evaluated bias differently compared to those who read the "clarity instructions."

More people saw bias in the article when they were given the "bias instructions" compared to the "clarity instructions." Twenty-eight percent of respondents reading the clarity instructions condition reported bias in the article compared to 44 percent of respondents reading the bias instructions. Instructing people to approach an article differently, therefore, can influence perceptions about bias in the media.

How did asking people to think about bias change their impressions of bias? The results are shown in Figure 4.3. In the chart, a score of 3.0 indicates that on average, respondents did not perceive any partisan bias. Scores greater than 3.0 indicate that respondents believed that the coverage favored McCain, and scores less than 3.0 indicate that respondents believed that the coverage favored Obama.

As shown in Figure 4.3, perceptions of media bias are related to respondents' political perspectives. Conservatives and Republicans see a stronger pro-Obama bias than liberals and Democrats do. The instructions also are influential. After reading the bias instructions, conservatives and Republicans develop stronger impressions that the media coverage is hostile to their perspective. Liberals and Democrats perceive slightly more bias in favor of Obama, but their assessment of the article remains close to 3.0—neutral. Neither set of instructions led partisans to converge in their impressions about the presence of bias. The size of the partisan gap in assessments of the article was consistent irrespective of the instructions read.[26]

This study shows that perceptions of bias can be influenced. Yet it isn't possible to know whether the bias instructions *changed* perceptions of bias or whether the

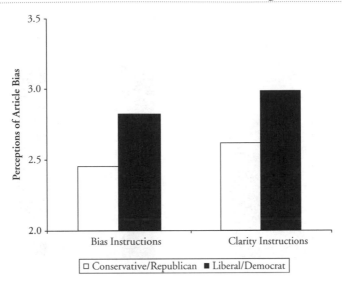

FIGURE 4.3 Perceptions of Media Bias by Political Leanings. Results based on a regression analysis predicting perceptions of bias in the article. Ideology/partisanship and instructions are significant. Ideology/partisanship values are calculated using one standard deviation from the mean values. More details can be found in the technical appendix for this chapter.

Source: Data from the 2008 Knowledge Networks Study.

clarity instructions *distracted* people from perceiving a bias that they otherwise would have. To evaluate whether the bias instructions, the clarity instructions, or both influenced perceptions of bias, I conducted a second study.

Three differences between the first and second studies are particularly noteworthy. First, I used a different news media article, again pulled from the mainstream media. This helps to assess whether the results from the prior study hold for different articles. The article used in this second study discussed differences between Democrats and Republicans regarding how to stimulate the economy during the economic downturn in early 2009.

The second difference between the first and second studies is that the second study included three conditions, as opposed to two in the prior study. A random third of participants were told, "We are interested in your impressions about bias in the media. With this in mind, please read the following article. As you read, think about whether this article favors Democrats or favors Republicans. When you finish reading, we will ask you about your thoughts on this matter." Another random third were told, "We are interested in your impressions of whether the average American voter is able to read and understand news coverage. With this in mind, please read the following article. As you read, think about the article's grammar, format, and structure as well as how clearly the information is presented. When you finish reading, we will ask you about your thoughts on this matter." The final third were

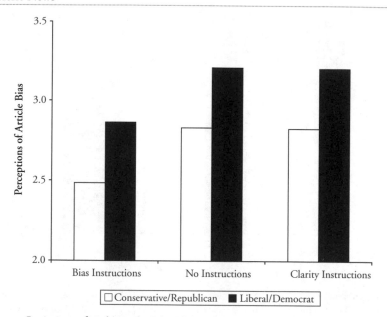

FIGURE 4.4 Perceptions of Media Bias by Political Leanings. Results based on a regression analysis predicting perceptions of bias in the article. Ideology/partisanship and bias instructions are significant. Ideology/partisanship values are calculated using one standard deviation from the mean values. More details can be found in the technical appendix for this chapter.

Source: Data from the 2009 Student Study.

told, "Please read the following article. When you finish reading, we will ask you what you think about this article." This third set of instructions allows me to evaluate whether the bias instructions, the clarity instructions, or both influence perceptions of the media.

The third change from the prior study is that participants in this second study were students from southwestern universities, as opposed to the general population sample in the first study. I analyzed the data from the first study to see if there were any differences in the effects based on the age or education level of respondents. There were no differences, providing some justification for proceeding with this alternative sample.

In this second study, a majority of respondents in all conditions saw bias in the article—irrespective of which instructions they read. The instructions did, however, influence the direction of bias perceived by respondents. The results are shown in Figure 4.4. As with Figure 4.3, a score of 3.0 signals that no bias was seen in the article. Higher scores indicate that on average, respondents believed that the article favored Republican views. Lower scores indicate that on average, respondents believed that the article favored Democratic views.

Like the previous study, perceptions of bias were related to political orientations. Instructions to look for clarity or no instructions at all produced very similar results.

Just as in the prior experiment, however, the bias cue led respondents to perceive that the article was more favorable toward Democrats. Although liberals and Democrats did not perceive much bias (the mean hovers around 3.0), conservatives and Republicans perceived a stronger liberal bias when instructed to pay attention to bias compared to those who did not receive this instruction.

People can be influenced in how they approach the media. Instructions to look for bias did influence perceptions of media bias. Interestingly, in both studies, respondents tended to see a stronger pro-Obama or pro-Democratic bias when instructed to look for bias. As a function of their partisanship, however, conservatives and Republicans see a stronger liberal bias than others when looking for bias. Liberals and Democrats see an article that is closer to neutral. This effect may be due to the intensity with which the "liberal media" claim had been made. In the 2008 election, for example, Republican vice presidential nominee Governor Sarah Palin frequently critiqued the "liberal media." And the public overwhelmingly believed that the media favored Democratic presidential candidate Barack Obama.[27] Based on this, the public may have been particularly likely to perceive a bias in favor of liberal views when instructed to look for bias. It simply isn't possible to tell from these two studies whether partisans always see more liberal bias when prompted to look for any signs of bias in the news media. And research showing that Democrats *and* Republicans can be influenced to see *hostile* biases confirms a need for caution in overgeneralizing these results.[28]

What we do know from these studies is that the instructions did not lead partisans to find common ground about media bias.[29] Democrats and Republicans and liberals and conservatives were equally divided in their impressions of bias in the articles irrespective of the instructions they received. They did not look past their partisanship to reach a consensus about the presence of partisan media bias. Without question, other instructions may produce different results. Figuring out what type of instructions help citizens to shake their partisan perceptions of bias is well worth more research. The instructions used here, however, reflect one way in which citizens are encouraged to critically use news media: to be on the lookout for signs of partisan bias. And instructing people to look for bias in this way, it seems, does not help people to see past their partisan inclinations when examining bias in the media.

PERCEPTIONS OF MEDIA BIAS AND PATTERNS OF MEDIA USE

Perceptions of media bias are critical to understanding partisan selective exposure for at least two reasons. First, citizens must recognize bias in order to discount biased information. Yet citizens do not uniformly detect bias. Factors that we might think would help people to detect bias fall short. Political knowledge and prompts to look for bias don't help partisans to agree on the presence and direction of bias. Consistently, in fact, partisans are more likely to see hostile biases than to see bias in their favor. For the study of partisan selective exposure, this means that the use of likeminded media has the potential to influence citizens at least in part because citizens do not always see likeminded information as biased information.

The second way in which perceptions are critical to understanding partisan selective exposure is that perceptions relate to media use. The relationship is peculiar, however. It isn't that using a particular media outlet helps citizens to carefully study and to recognize an outlet's partisan bent. Rather, perceptions seem to predict distinct patterns of media use.

Citizens aren't consistently able to detect partisan bias in the media that they use. This means that some citizens use likeminded media without even knowing it. According to one account, approximately half of the public can't accurately report the partisan leaning of the newspaper that they read.[30] When a newspaper's political leaning is more extreme, citizens are better able to detect the paper's leaning, but subtle leanings seem to escape public notice.[31]

There are many reasons that people may be unable, or unwilling, to report bias in the news media sources that they use. First, people may perceive that their chosen media outlets are unbiased. They may reason that they are unbiased news consumers and that their selected media outlets, therefore, must be unbiased. Second, those using likeminded outlets may believe that the outlets are objective because they don't perceive any biased content—likeminded views seem perfectly reasonable. Third, reporting unbiased news use could be the result of social desirability concerns. There is a cultural norm of valuing unbiased information seeking. People have an intuitive and ingrained understanding that "knowing both sides" is a good thing. When asked in a survey to say whether the media *that they choose* are biased, for example, people may be hesitant to do so. Fourth, some may sincerely believe that their political perspective diverges from the outlets that they view. Strong conservative Republicans, for example, truly may find Fox News liberal relative to their own political stance.[32] Fifth, citizens may recall the presentation of diverse viewpoints in media that they use and conclude that their chosen outlets aren't so biased. Based on their exposure, citizens may be able to name nonlikeminded hosts, guests, commentators, and ideas on their preferred news media outlets. They may not be able to do the same for nonlikeminded sources because they are not as familiar with these outlets. They may then fail to infer that the same diversity of opinion that they see in the sources that they use might exist in other sources. This very phenomenon occurs when people make judgments about in-groups and out-groups—in-groups are seen as more variable and out-groups more homogenous.[33] This could explain not only citizens' perceptions of less bias in the outlets that they use but also perceptions of stronger, and more hostile, biases in nonlikeminded media.

In sum, there are many reasons that perceptions of bias may not accurately reflect reality. Questions about perceptions, therefore, should be taken with a grain of salt. For example, the Pew Research Center reports that about a quarter of the public prefer getting news from sources sharing their political point of view and just over half report liking news sources sharing their political point of view.[34] These figures are conservative if people are reluctant to admit enjoying likeminded news or if they are unaware that their news selections are driven by partisanship.[35]

This does not mean that perceptions of bias are without value. On the contrary, perceptions are a key ingredient in understanding people's news media selections. First, cable news stations perceived as neutral are used more frequently. This is especially true for Fox News viewers. Based on the Knowledge Networks data, those believing that Fox News is a neutral news source watch the network more frequently.[36] Second, perceptions of bias *across* media outlets are related to media use. Citizens seeing some media outlets as hostile to their political perspective use more likeminded media. Those perceiving that the media environment contains a host of conservative outlets—a pattern more common among liberal Democrats— should be more likely to use the outlets classified in chapter 3 as liberal. And those who believe that the media environment is rife with liberal outlets would be expected to use more conservative outlets. The Knowledge Networks study provides evidence that this is the case. I examined whether perceiving more liberal sources (e.g., labeling

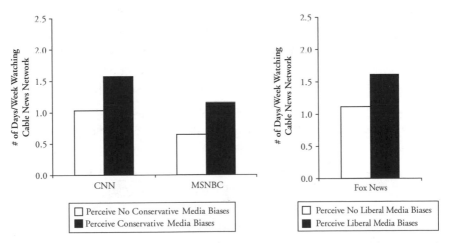

FIGURE 4.5 Use of Cable News Networks by Perceptions of Media Bias. Results based on regression analyses predicting media use. Analyses control for demographics and political orientations. Bias perceptions are significant in all displayed analyses. Perceptions of conservative and liberal biases are calculated using one standard deviation from the mean value. More details can be found in the technical appendix for this chapter.
Source: Data from the 2008 Knowledge Networks Study.

CNN, MSNBC, the *New York Times,* and/or NPR as liberally biased) or more conservative sources (e.g., labeling Fox News, Rush Limbaugh, Bill O'Reilly, and/or the *Wall Street Journal* as conservatively biased) relates to media use. The results are shown in Figure 4.5.

As suspected, those believing that there are more liberally biased outlets watch Fox News more frequently. In addition, those believing that there are more conservatively biased outlets watch CNN and MSNBC more frequently. Although these data do not show a causal relationship, they do indicate that perceptions of bias relate to media use.[37]

KNOWLEDGE, INTEREST, AND PARTISAN SELECTIVE EXPOSURE

Politically knowledgeable citizens find bias—particularly counterattitudinal bias—throughout the media. And perceptions of bias are related to likeminded media use, at least for cable news. Based on these two findings, it follows that knowledgeable partisans should be particularly likely to engage in partisan selective exposure.

At first glance, this may seem counterintuitive. Politically knowledgeable citizens shouldn't be more likely to use politically likeminded media; "well-educated, middle-class people should be less likely to ignore dissonant information—a rather primitive method of protecting oneself from it; rather, they should be more inclined to read and refute it."[38] Indeed, politically knowledgeable and curious citizens are information omnivores—they view more likeminded *and* contradictory political information compared to less knowledgeable and less curious citizens.[39] Yet even these citizens display a net preference for likeminded information.[40] The politically knowledgeable and interested are drawn toward information consistent with their beliefs on hot-button issues like gun control and affirmative action.[41] They also should gravitate toward likeminded outlets in terms of where they typically turn for news.

One reason that the politically interested and knowledgeable may seek likeminded media is that these citizens have little interest in hearing opposing arguments with which they are already familiar: "Selective exposure effects seem to be most apparent...when the audience is most familiar with the arguments on both sides of the issue."[42] If those high in political knowledge and interest are familiar, or believe that they are familiar, with opposing arguments, then this may lead them to likeminded media—why bother going to those hostile sources if you already have a pretty good idea of what they're going to say?

Another reason that politically interested and knowledgeable partisans may select likeminded media is that they tend to rely on their impressions of the media as heuristics. Political scientists Matthew Baum and Phil Gussin asked respondents to take a look at a transcript that was labeled as either from CNN or from Fox News.[43] Respondents then were asked whether the coverage was more favorable toward Democratic presidential nominee John Kerry or toward the Republican incumbent, President George Bush. Even though the story was *identical,* attributing it to a different source led partisans to reach different conclusions about whether the story was biased. Politically knowledgeable individuals were especially likely to find bias in the transcript in line with their prior beliefs about CNN and Fox News.[44] That is, knowledgeable respondents believing that a network was biased were particularly likely to perceive bias in that network's transcript. If perceptions of bias influence judgments about the media more so for the politically knowledgeable, perceptions of bias also may influence the selection of media more so for the politically knowledgeable.

To examine the relationship between political interest, knowledge, and partisan selective exposure, I turned to the NAES to evaluate whether those with higher levels of political knowledge and interest are more likely to use likeminded media. With respect to political knowledge, the results persist across various media types: Knowledgeable partisans make more likeminded media choices.[45] As there is consistent evidence that political knowledge is related to partisan media use, I used the liberal and conservative media use indices from chapter 3 to summarize the results in Figures 4.6 and 4.7.

As political knowledge increases, respondents are more likely to select media that match their political leanings and less likely to select media that contradict their leanings. Even after controlling for a host of other variables, the relationship persists. Though political interest does not explain perceptions of media bias, I examined whether interested partisans are more likely to use likeminded media. Here, those who are more politically interested are more likely to engage in partisan selective exposure, even after taking political knowledge into account. In sum, politically knowledgeable and interested citizens are more likely to use politically likeminded media.[46]

Cause or Consequence: Partisan Selective Exposure, Political Knowledge, and Political Interest

Thus far, we know that partisan selective exposure is related to political knowledge and interest. The causal direction of the relationship, however, requires more investigation. Does possessing political interest and knowledge *lead* partisans to select more likeminded media? Or does the use of likeminded media inspire political interest and generate political knowledge?

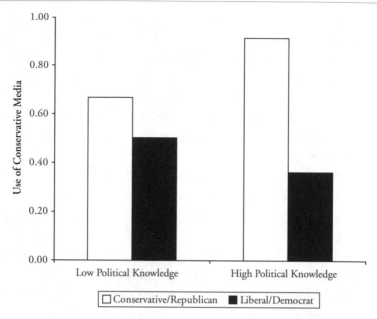

FIGURE 4.6 Conservative Media Use by Political Leanings and Political Knowledge. Results based on a regression analysis predicting media use. Analysis controls for demographics, political orientations, and patterns of media use. The interaction between ideology/partisanship and political knowledge is significant. Political knowledge and ideology/partisanship values are calculated using one standard deviation from the mean value. More details can be found in the technical appendix for this chapter.

Source: Data from the 2004 NAES RCS.

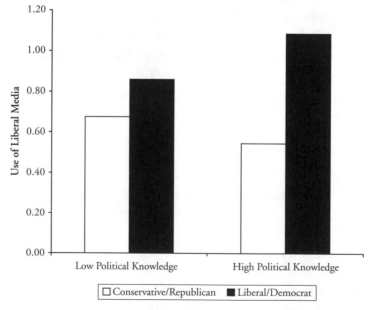

FIGURE 4.7 Liberal Media Use by Political Leanings and Political Knowledge. Analysis details are the same as those described below Figure 4.6.

Disentangling these relationships is important for understanding whether people's media selections influence their political beliefs and aptitudes or if people actively use media based on their political beliefs and aptitudes. There are several possibilities. First, it is possible that certain political attributes cause people to engage in selective exposure. Second, partisan selective exposure could cause audiences to change their political attitudes and behaviors. Third, certain political attributes could be both causes and consequences of selective exposure. If selective exposure leads to political knowledge, for example, and political knowledge motivates selective exposure, a spiral of knowledge and partisan selective exposure would result. Though there always will be counteracting forces present—if a person discusses politics with diverse others, the effects of partisan selective exposure may be dampened, for example—a spiral effect from partisan selective exposure could be particularly consequential.[47]

Considering the ambiguity surrounding the causes and consequences of selective exposure, few studies have attempted to sort out the relationships. Research by psychologists Paul Sweeney and Kathy Gruber represents a noteworthy exception.[48] These scholars surveyed people at several points in time during the 1973 Senate Watergate hearings. Each time they spoke to people, Sweeney and Gruber asked the study participants about their interest in politics, their attention to details about Watergate, and how frequently they discussed Watergate with others. Sweeney and Gruber also asked participants whether they would vote for a Republican, whether they believed that Nixon had lost his credibility, and whether they thought that Nixon should resign. Sweeney and Gruber wanted to know if exposure to information about Watergate influenced people's political beliefs or whether people's political beliefs influenced their exposure to information about Watergate. The results were revealing. Nixon supporters attended to Watergate information far less than others. And exposure to Watergate information strengthened beliefs about Nixon's culpability and reduced Republican vote intentions. Sweeney and Gruber's study provides a helpful starting point for assessing the causes and consequences of partisan selective exposure.

I examined whether political knowledge and interest precede or follow from partisan selective exposure using the four NAES panel surveys conducted around the conventions, debates, and general election. Panel surveys cannot provide unequivocal evidence of causal relationships. However, as reviewed in the previous chapter, they are a stronger test of the relationship between two variables and they can provide some insight into the causal direction of a relationship. For each of the panel surveys, I analyzed whether political knowledge and interest predict partisan media use over time. In five of eight cases, political knowledge significantly led to likeminded media use. Though not significant, the remaining cases are in the hypothesized direction. Politically knowledgeable conservative Republicans use more conservative media compared to other respondents. Politically knowledgeable liberal Democrats use more liberal media compared to other respondents. The magnitudes of these effects are not particularly strong. We are, after all, looking at habitual media use patterns at two points that differ by only a short period of time. For example, very knowledgeable, strong liberal Democrats watching one liberal media type before the debates reported watching, on average, 1.30 liberal media types afterward, holding all other factors constant. Very knowledgeable, strong conservative Republicans watching one liberal media type before the debates reported watching, on average, 0.64 liberal media types afterward, again holding all other factors constant. The overall pattern from the panel analyses, however, suggests that political knowledge leads to partisan selective exposure.

In examining whether politically interested partisans are more likely to select like-minded media, the results are more modest. In only two of eight cases does political interest relate significantly to partisan selective exposure—both occur in the panel survey conducted before and after the presidential election. This provides some evidence that political interest motivates partisans to use likeminded media.

The other possible causal direction is perhaps even more interesting. Instead of considering whether political knowledge and interest *predict* partisan selective exposure, I now turn to examining whether partisan selective exposure influences political knowledge and interest.

LEARNING FROM PARTISAN SELECTIVITY

In the summer of 2003, the situation in Iraq was at the top of the public agenda. Where were the weapons of mass destruction? Was there a link between Iraqi leader Saddam Hussein and the terrorist organization Al Qaeda? Though facts did not favor either of these contentious explanations for the invasion of Iraq, beliefs that Hussein had weapons and that he was linked to Al Qaeda persisted. Intriguingly, some Americans were more likely to express these beliefs than others. In particular, those viewing Fox News were more likely to believe in both the link and the weapons and those watching PBS and listening to NPR were less likely.[49] Although we don't know whether differences in how these outlets covered Iraq led to these different outlooks,[50] the potential implications of this finding are troubling: Different patterns of news exposure could lead people to develop different stores of knowledge about the world of politics.

To this point, I have examined whether politically knowledgeable and interested citizens use more politically likeminded media. Yet using likeminded media may influence political knowledge and interest. Receiving likeminded information from the media may help—or harm—political knowledge. And it could energize citizens, leading them to develop more interest in politics.

There is some debate about whether news media use in general enhances political knowledge and interest. Some find that political knowledge and interest are higher among those using the news media more frequently.[51] Others, however, conclude that the news media's effect on political knowledge and interest is minimal. After controlling for other factors that may explain the relationship, media use may not have a substantial influence on political knowledge or interest.[52] Education, for example, explains why some people use the news media and why they are politically knowledgeable and interested. Controlling for education reduces the relationship between news use, political knowledge, and political interest. Regardless of the news media's broad effects on political knowledge and interest, certain types of news media use may be more informative and inspiring than others. Here, I examine whether partisan media use uniquely contributes to political knowledge and interest.

Motivations to use media influence the media's effect. In his cognitive mediation model, for example, communication scholar William Eveland shows that motivations to use the media influence political knowledge.[53] When people want to know more about their environment, known as having a "surveillance motivation," they pay more attention to the news, elaborate more on the information that they receive from the news, and consequently, learn more. Those using media for entertainment purposes, however, have lower levels of political knowledge.[54] Using the media based on partisan inclinations, whether consciously or not, also may have unique effects.

Partisan selective exposure may increase political interest. In terms of cognitive dissonance theory, when dissonance is aroused by holding two conflicting cognitions—agreeing with a Democratic issue stance when identifying as a Republican, for example—there are numerous ways in which people can try to resolve this uncomfortable inconsistency. Selective exposure is one way. Another way is to minimize the *importance* of a conflicting cognition.[55] One can conclude that the contentious issue is relatively unimportant. Another solution would be to conclude that politics in its entirety is unimportant and uninteresting. Then encountering contradictory political views wouldn't be worrisome at all. If people decrease their interest in politics when faced with contradictory views, they may maintain or increase their interest when faced with likeminded views.

The relationship between encountering likeminded views in political discussion and political interest provides insight into the possible effect of encountering likeminded media. In particular, political interest is lower when people discuss politics with others holding different political opinions.[56] And political interest is highest among people surrounded by many discussion partners who favor the same political candidate.[57] Using likeminded—or contradictory—media may produce the same pattern. There is some evidence that the media may have a similarly inspiring effect. When asked to watch a news segment, for example, partisans find stories from likeminded sources more interesting than those from other sources.[58] Whether habitually watching likeminded news inspires more interest in politics overall, however, is unclear.

Turning to the NAES panel surveys, there is no evidence that partisan selective exposure influences political interest. Respondents to the panel surveys reported their level of political interest both in the prewave and in the postwave of the survey. I analyzed whether partisan selective exposure helped me to predict a person's political interest in the postwave of the survey after taking into account how politically interested people were in the prewave.[59] Analyzing the data gathered around the Republican and Democratic National Conventions, the debates, and the general election, those engaging in partisan selective exposure were no more—or less—politically interested in the postwave of the survey.

The possible effect of partisan selective exposure on political knowledge is another story. In particular, partisan selective exposure could *inhibit* political learning. Two processes may connect partisan selective exposure to lower political knowledge. First (and perhaps too obvious to state), the information provided by a media outlet determines what information people can learn from exposure. If partisan media outlets fail to provide audiences with adequate information, this could translate into lower political knowledge. Second, the way in which people process likeminded information may limit their ability to learn and to remember the details. Likeminded information is subject to less scrutiny than information contradicting one's beliefs.[60] It isn't necessary to counterargue or to think carefully about information with which we agree. As a consequence, likeminded information may be processed less systematically and long-term information gain may be hampered. Partisan selective exposure, therefore, could decrease political knowledge.

Support for the idea that exposure to likeminded information may reduce political knowledge also comes from studies investigating patterns of political discussion. Some research suggests that people who agree with their political discussion partners are less able to articulate points of view that differ from their own compared to those with more diverse discussion mates.[61] Though providing reasons for why others may disagree is not identical to political knowledge, the two are strongly related.[62] If exposure to likeminded *interpersonal* views can inhibit political knowledge, then exposure to likeminded *mediated* views also may inhibit political knowledge.

Yet the opposite remains a possibility. Specifically, partisan media outlets may *help* people to learn about politics. They may help people to make sense of a complex political environment by providing a way to organize political information: "To be sensible, political debate cannot be a set of simultaneous equations that only a computer could handle. It has to be a small set of identifiable branching alternatives that can be examined reasonably enough one at a time. The political party helped make that possible."[63] By promoting partisanship as an organizational scheme, partisan media may facilitate political learning. Likeminded media also may help people to learn about politics because they may provide more memorable information. People may remember likeminded information better than contradictory information "because of its superior fit with existing attitudes [and] its inherent pleasantness."[64]

I can draw from research on interpersonal political discussion to support this idea as well. As people have more and more likeminded discussion partners, they are able to give more comprehensive arguments in favor of their partisan beliefs. This isn't surprising—when discussing politics with fellow partisans, you tend to learn new reasons to support your point of view. Yet some research suggests that people with more likeminded discussion mates are *still* able to give reasons against their point of view. Discussing politics with more likeminded others may not reduce one's ability to come up with reasons supporting another point of view. Along these lines, likeminded media might not inhibit political knowledge; if anything, it could increase knowledge.[65]

Again turning to the NAES panel surveys, I analyzed whether partisan selective exposure influences political knowledge. Instead of measuring political knowledge using a quiz of basic political facts (e.g., the majority party in the House of Representatives, the branch of government deciding the constitutionality of laws, etc.), I measured political knowledge using a quiz about *contemporary* political facts. Respondents were asked questions such as, "Who favors allowing workers to invest some of their Social Security contributions in the stock market—George W. Bush, John Kerry, both, or neither?" I used these more contemporary questions because knowledge of basic political facts is unlikely to change over time; it tends to be a fairly stable indicator of political aptitude. Knowledge of contemporary political facts, however, does change. Citizens can—and do—learn about the presidential candidates from a barrage of media attention over the course of a campaign. Therefore, I analyzed whether partisan selective exposure influences political knowledge by looking at how many contemporary political knowledge questions respondents were able to answer correctly.

The results were clear: In no instance did the use of politically likeminded media depress political knowledge. And, in one case, partisan selective exposure predicted significantly *higher* levels of campaign knowledge. This result is shown in Figure 4.8.

After taking into account how much respondents knew before the Democratic National Convention, liberals and Democrats using likeminded media *knew more* after the convention.[66] In this instance, likeminded media use *enhanced* political

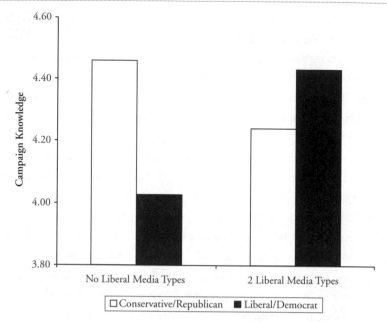

FIGURE 4.8 Campaign Knowledge by Media Use and Political Leanings. Results based on a regression analysis predicting campaign knowledge. Analysis controls for demographics, political orientations, patterns of media use, and the prewave value of campaign knowledge. The interaction between liberal media use and ideology/partisanship is significant. Ideology/partisanship values are calculated using one standard deviation from the mean value. More details can be found in the technical appendix for this chapter.
Source: Data from the 2004 NAES DNC Panel.

knowledge. It seems that partisan media outlets don't put citizens at a disadvantage in terms of learning contemporary political facts. The contemporary knowledge questions analyzed here, however, are fairly general. Respondents were asked about the candidates' positions on abortion, on allowing workers to invest some of their Social Security contributions in the stock market, and on funding for stem cell research, for example. Media outlets convey these facts irrespective of their leanings, thus enabling partisans to learn about candidates' issue stances. Beyond these types of undisputed facts, however, media outlets may vary in their coverage considerably. When facts are disputed, considerable differences may appear. Even if similar facts are conveyed, how these facts are framed can vary. They could be conveyed to audiences in a partisan way—is the candidate's position wise or unwise? Moral or immoral? Would the consequences be beneficial or detrimental? Even more, the *emphasis* placed on various issues and relevant facts may differ tremendously between partisan outlets and could influence citizens' attitudes and beliefs. I will return to these ideas in chapter 6. Based on the analysis to this point, however, we have every reason to conclude that partisan media use does not reduce knowledge of basic facts about presidential candidates.

SUMMARY

The aim of this chapter was to understand how people learn about and from partisan media. Citizens have numerous opportunities to form impressions about partisan bias—they can observe the media directly; they can rely on elite statements about media bias; they even can pay attention to references about bias in popular culture. With all of this discussion, citizens easily can learn to form impressions of the media on the basis of partisanship.

It is little wonder that citizens hold different beliefs about the presence of bias in the media. For any outlet, some perceive a liberal bias, some a conservative bias, and some no bias at all. In the aggregate, however, there is a strong correspondence between perceptions of media bias and the "liberal media" and "conservative media" categorizations described in the previous chapter. Variability in individual assessments of bias, however, signals a need for skepticism in relying on perceptions as accurately reflecting the reality of bias. It is difficult for citizens to evaluate the news media objectively. Partisans on different sides of the political spectrum differ in their perceptions of the media's leanings. And politically knowledgeable partisans are even more likely to disagree about the presence of bias. Although politically knowledgeable citizens tend to see more bias overall, they are especially likely to perceive biases favoring the opposition.

Understanding perceptions of media bias provides insight into partisan selective exposure. From chapter 3, we know that partisans are attracted to likeminded media content. In this chapter, we learn that this behavior is even more pronounced among politically knowledgeable and interested partisans. Perceptions also relate to media use. Seeing a media environment filled with hostile outlets—a perspective most frequent among the politically knowledgeable—corresponds with more likeminded media use.

It is interesting to observe that patterns of media use function as another indicator of one's political leaning. If a politically knowledgeable and interested partisan told me his stance on a controversial political issue (say, stem cell research), I could do a pretty good job of predicting the person's stance on other issues (say, government spending). If the person weren't as politically knowledgeable and interested, however, I would have a more difficult time predicting the person's stance on government spending after learning his stance on stem cell research. Media choices and perceptions are another way of signaling ideology and partisanship. If I know where you turn for news, I'll have a much better idea of your political leaning. My ability to make a correct inference about a person's political leaning from his news media habits, however, is heightened when the person is politically knowledgeable and interested.

This chapter also examined whether partisan selective exposure influences political knowledge or interest. Some normative concerns about partisan selective exposure, based on the results of this chapter, are unfounded. One often expressed concern is that those engaging in partisan selective exposure may not be adequately informed to perform their duties as citizens. There was no evidence that partisan selective exposure depresses political knowledge—in fact, some evidence suggests the reverse, namely, that partisan selective exposure enhances political knowledge. Further, there is no evidence that partisan selective exposure contributes to political interest. Instead, political knowledge and interest appear to be important prerequisites for partisan selective exposure.

Yet this chapter hints at the continued need for skepticism in evaluating partisan selective exposure. Citizens need to recognize bias in order to discount biased information. Clearly this is not easy for citizens to do. Citizens are more likely to see hostile biases than to see biases in their favor. Whether this is reason for concern, however, requires additional investigation. The next chapter looks at the relationship between partisan selective exposure and various forms of partisan involvement. Does partisan selective exposure affect political participation? The commitment to vote for a candidate? Polarization?

NOTES

1. Howard Kurtz, "Liberal Blogs Assail Anchor Changes; No Outside Pressure, Says MSNBC Head," *Washington Post,* September 9, 2008.

2. Mark Watts, David Domke, Dhavan Shah, and David Fan, "Elite Cues and Media Bias in Presidential Campaigns: Explaining Public Perceptions of a Liberal Press," *Communication Research* 26, 2 (1999): 144–75.

3. Glen R. Smith, "Politicians and the News Media: How Elite Attacks Influence Perceptions of Media Bias," *The International Journal of Press/Politics* 15, 3 (2010): 319–43.

4. Jodi Picoult, *Nineteen Minutes, A Novel* (New York: Atria Books, 2007): 335.

5. See the September 2008 edition of *Marie Claire.*

6. See the January 2009 edition of *Vogue.*

7. See, for example, discussions of detecting bias in John Barell, *Problem-Based Learning: An Inquiry Approach* (Thousand Oaks, CA: Corwin Press, 2007); Robert Postman, *How to Prepare for the CLAST: College Level Academic Skills Test,* 2nd ed. (Hauppauge, NY: Barron's Educational Series, 2003); W. James Potter, *Media Literacy,* 4th ed. (Thousand Oaks, CA: Sage, 2008).

8. Michael X. Delli Carpini and Scott Keeter, *What Americans Know about Politics and Why It Matters* (New Haven, CT: Yale University Press, 1996).

9. Vincent Price and John Zaller, "Who Gets the News? Alternative Measures of News Reception and Their Implications for Research," *Public Opinion Quarterly* 57, 2 (1993): 133–64.

10. Philip E. Converse, "The Nature of Belief Systems in Mass Publics," in *Ideology and Discontent,* edited by David F. Apter (New York: Free Press of Glencoe, 1964); M. Kent Jennings, "Ideological Thinking among Mass Publics and Political Elites," *Public Opinion Quarterly* 56, 4 (1992): 419–41; Milton Lodge and Ruth Hamill, "A Partisan Schema for Political Information Processing," *American Political Science Review* 80, 2 (1986): 505–20.

11. Michael G. Hagen and Kathleen Hall Jamieson, "Do Newspaper Endorsements Matter? Do Politicians Speak for Themselves in Newspapers and on Television?" in *Everything You Think*

You Know about Politics...And Why You're Wrong, edited by Kathleen Hall Jamieson (New York: Basic Books, 2000): 155–9.

12. Delli Carpini and Keeter, *What Americans Know about Politics*; Price and Zaller, "Who Gets the News?"; John Zaller, *Analysis of Information Items in the 1985 NES Pilot Study* (National Election Studies, 1986).

13. Zaller, *Analysis of Information Items in the 1985 NES Pilot Study*; Robert Luskin, "Explaining Political Sophistication," *Political Behavior* 12, 4 (1990): 331–61.

14. Robert P. Vallone, Lee Ross, and Mark R. Lepper, "The Hostile Media Phenomenon: Biased Perception and Perceptions of Media Bias in Coverage of the Beirut Massacre," *Journal of Personality and Social Psychology* 49, 3 (1985): 577–85. See also Russell J. Dalton, Paul A. Beck, and Robert Huckfeldt, "Partisan Cues and the Media: Information Flows in the 1992 Presidential Election," *American Political Science Review* 92, 1 (1998): 111–26.

15. See, for example, Albert C. Gunther, Cindy T. Christen, Janice L. Liebhart, and Stella Chih-Yun Chia, "Congenial Public, Contrary Press, and Biased Estimates of the Climate of Opinion," *Public Opinion Quarterly* 65, 3 (2001): 295–320; Kevin Coe, David Tewksbury, Bradley J. Bond, Kristin L. Drogos, Robert W. Porter, Ashley Yahn, and Yuanyuan Zhang, "Hostile News: Partisan Use and Perceptions of Cable News Programming," *Journal of Communication* 58 (2008): 201–19.

16. David O. Sears, "The Paradox of De Facto Selective Exposure without Preferences for Supportive Information," in *Theories of Cognitive Consistency: A Sourcebook,* edited by Robert P. Abelson, Elliot Aronson, William J. McGuire, Theodore M. Newcomb, Milton J. Rosenberg, and Percy H. Tannenbaum (Chicago: Rand McNally and Company, 1968): 785.

17. Rasmussen Reports, "Americans See Liberal Media Bias on TV news," July 13, 2007, http://www.rasmussenreports.com/public_content/politics/current_events/general_current_events/media/americans_see_liberal_media_bias_on_tv_news; PBS News, "PBS #1 in Public Trust for the Fifth Consecutive Year According to a National Roper Survey," June 10, 2008, http://www.pbs.org/aboutpbs/news/20080610_ropersurvey.html; Reuters, "Americans Slam News Media on Believability," January 8, 2008, http://www.reuters.com/article/pressRelease/idUS160770+08-Jan-2008+PRN20080108.

18. For each outlet, between 52 and 70 percent of respondents expressed an opinion about the presence or absence of bias. If those without an opinion about each outlet are included in the equations and coded as not seeing a bias, results are similar. See the technical appendix for more detail. When re-examining the data using political interest, as opposed to political knowledge, few significant differences appeared. Just as with the knowledge of which candidate one's newspaper endorsed, perceptions of bias seem to be far more influenced by political knowledge than by political interest. If I use dummy variables for ideology and partisanship, as opposed to the continuous measure employed in creating the chart, the same general patterns emerge.

19. This could explain why Dalton and colleagues found that those who are more politically attentive showed only modest gains in reporting the political leanings of newspapers. Dalton and colleagues asked people to report the leanings of the newspaper that people regularly read—which may minimize the detection of partisanship. Dalton, Beck, and Huckfeldt, "Partisan Cues and the Media."

20. Vallone, Ross, and Lepper, "The Hostile Media Phenomenon."

21. John R. Zaller, *The Nature and Origins of Mass Opinion* (New York: Cambridge University Press, 1992).

22. Although Ladd uses education as opposed to political knowledge, the two are significantly and positively correlated. Jonathan McDonald Ladd, "The Neglected Power of Elite Opinion Leadership to Produce Antipathy Toward the News Media: Evidence from a Survey Experiment," *Political Behavior* 32 (2010): 29–50.

23. Delli Carpini and Keeter, *What Americans Know about Politics*, 238.

24. See, for example, Barell, *Problem-Based Learning*; Postman, *How to Prepare for the CLAST*.

25. Potter, *Media Literacy*, 183.

26. If anything, the bias instructions increased gaps between partisans. Controlling for the presence or absence of a paragraph mentioning the candidates' issue strengths (described in the appendix) and the interaction between the issue strengths paragraph and the bias instructions, the interaction between the bias instructions and ideology/partisanship is marginally significant and in the direction of *increased* differences between partisans reading the bias instructions.

27. Pew Research Center for the People & the Press, *Most Voters Say News Media Wants Obama to Win* (Washington, DC, 2008).

28. Ladd, "The Neglected Power of Elite Opinion Leadership"; Smith, "Politicians and the News Media."

29. In the analysis, interactions between political leanings and the instructions read were not significant.

30. Robinson reported that just over half of his sample was able to detect the partisanship of the newspaper they read (newspaper partisanship was assessed using reports in *Editor & Publisher*). Using data that paired a content analysis of media leanings with public perceptions of media leanings, Mutz and Martin reported that only 48 percent of respondents correctly reported the presidential candidate favored by their newspaper. John P. Robinson, "Perceived Media Bias and the 1968 Vote: Can the Media Affect Behavior After All?" *Journalism Quarterly* 49 (1972): 239–46; Diana C. Mutz and Paul S. Martin, "Facilitating Communication across Lines of Political Difference: The Role of Mass Media," *American Political Science Review* 95, 1 (2001): 97–114.

31. Dalton, Beck, and Huckfeldt, "Partisan Cues and the Media."

32. In the Knowledge Networks Survey, conservative Republicans were more likely than liberal Democrats to label Fox News as liberal.

33. See, for example, Bernadette Park and Myron Rothbart, "Perception of Out-Group Homogeneity and Levels of Social Categorization: Memory for the Subordinate Attributes of In-Group and Out-Group Members," *Journal of Personality and Social Psychology* 42, 6 (1982): 1051–68.

34. Pew Research Center for the People & the Press, *Internet's Broader Role in Campaign 2008: Social Networking and Online Videos Take Off* (Washington, DC, 2008); Pew Research Center for the People & the Press, *Cable and Internet Loom Large in Fragmented Political News Universe: Perceptions of Partisan Bias Seen as Growing* (Washington, DC, 2004); Pew Research Center for the People & the Press, *How Young People View their Lives, Futures and Politics: A Portrait of "Generation Next"* (Washington, DC, 2007).

35. As Taber and Lodge point out, "people are largely unaware of the power of their priors" (p. 757), which could be reflected here. Charles S. Taber and Milton Lodge, "Motivated Skepticism in the Evaluation of Political Beliefs," *American Journal of Political Science,* 50, 3 (2006): 755–69.

36. Analysis predicting use of CNN, MSNBC, and Fox News finds that those perceiving no bias in an outlet use the outlet more frequently. Those perceiving no bias in MSNBC use Fox

News less frequently. If the analysis is conducted only for those who formed impressions of bias and not for those registering no opinion, the relationships remain for use of Fox News. Also confirming this pattern, Tsfati and Cappella find that those not trusting the media are more likely to use nonmainstream media sources. See Yariv Tsfati and Joseph N. Cappella, "Do People Watch What They Do Not Trust?" *Communication Research* 30, 5 (2003): 504–29.

37. If the analysis is run only among those registering an opinion about the presence and direction of bias, those seeing more liberal outlets are more likely to use Fox News.

38. Dorothy L. Barlett, Pamela B. Drew, Eleanor G. Fahle, and William A. Watts, "Selective Exposure to a Presidential Campaign Appeal," *Public Opinion Quarterly* 38 (1974): 269.

39. Barlett, Drew, Fahle, and Watts, "Selective Exposure to a Presidential Campaign Appeal"; Steven H. Chaffee, Melissa Nichols Saphir, Joseph Graf, Christian Sandvig, and Kyu Sup Hahn, "Attention to Counter-Attitudinal Messages in a State Election Campaign," *Political Communication* 18 (2001): 247–72.

40. Ibid.

41. Taber and Lodge, "Motivated Skepticism in the Evaluation of Political Beliefs"; Howard Lavine, Eugene Borgida, and John L. Sullivan, "On the Relationship between Attitude Involvement and Attitude Accessibility: Toward a Cognitive-Motivational Model of Political Information Processing," *Political Psychology* 21, 1 (2000): 81–106.

42. David O. Sears and Jonathan L. Freedman, "Effects of Expected Familiarity with Arguments upon Opinion Change and Selective Exposure," *Journal of Personality and Social Psychology* 2, 5 (1965): 421. Note, however, that the evidence supporting this proposition is limited. Two studies examining this question do not find that the anticipated novelty of arguments increased selective exposure. Yet both studies look at criminal legal proceedings—arguably quite different from the political contexts that prompted the hypotheses about familiarity. In addition to the Sears and Freedman article, see David O. Sears, "Biased Indoctrination and Selectivity of Exposure to New Information," *Sociometry* 28, 4 (1965): 363–76.

43. Matthew A. Baum and Phil Gussin, "In the Eye of the Beholder: How Information Shortcuts Shape Individual Perceptions of Bias in the Media," *Quarterly Journal of Political Science* 3, 1 (2008): 1–31. See also Joel Turner, "The Messenger Overwhelming the Message: Ideological Cues and Perceptions of Bias in Television News," *Political Behavior* 29 (2007): 441–64.

44. Baum and Gussin, "In the Eye of the Beholder."

45. In the outlet-by-outlet analysis, politically knowledgeable partisans were significantly more likely to use likeminded newspapers and to make cable news selections consistent with their political beliefs. The same trend appears for radio listening and liberal Web site use. The only exception is the analysis predicting use of conservative Web sites. Here, conservative Republicans are more likely to access conservative Web sites, but this behavior is unaffected by political knowledge, and the nonsignificant interaction between political knowledge and ideology/partisanship is negative.

46. Three-way interactions between ideology/partisanship, political knowledge, and political interest predicting the use of liberal media or the use of conservative media were significant and in the expected direction.

47. To see how interpersonal discussions could counteract the effects of partisan selective exposure, see Robert Huckfeldt and John Sprague, *Citizens, Politics, and Social Communication* (New York: Cambridge University Press, 1995); Mutz and Martin, "Facilitating Communication Across Lines of Political Difference." For more details on the potential for spirals in communica-

tion research, see Michael D. Slater, "Reinforcing Spirals: The Mutual Influence of Media Selectivity and Media Effects and Their Impact on Individual Behavior and Social Identity," *Communication Theory* 17, 3 (2007): 281–303.

48. Paul D. Sweeney and Kathy L. Gruber, "Selective Exposure: Voter Information Preferences and the Watergate Affair," *Journal of Personality and Social Psychology* 46, 6 (1984): 1208–21.

49. Steven Kull, Clay Ramsay, and Evan Lewis, "Misperceptions, the Media, and the Iraq War," *Political Science Quarterly* 118, 4 (2003–4): 569–98.

50. Turner, "The Messenger Overwhelming the Message."

51. Steven H. Chaffee and Joan Schleuder, "Measurement and Effects of Attention to Media News," *Human Communication Research* 13, 1 (1986): 76–107; William P. Eveland Jr., Andrew F. Hayes, Dhavan V. Shah, and Nojin Kwak, "Understanding the Relationship between Communication and Political Knowledge: A Model Comparison Approach using Panel Data," *Political Communication* 22 (2005): 423–46; John Horrigan, Kelly Garrett, and Paul Resnick, *The Internet and Democratic Debate,* Pew Internet & American Life Project (Washington, DC, 2004); Thomas J. Johnson and Barbara K. Kaye, "A Boost or Bust for Democracy? How the Web Influenced Political Attitudes and Behaviors in the 1996 and 2000 Presidential Elections," *The International Journal of Press/Politics* 8, 3 (2003): 9–34; Kate Kenski and Natalie Jomini Stroud, "Connections between Internet Use and Political Efficacy, Knowledge, and Participation," *Journal of Broadcasting and Electronic Media* 50, 2 (2006): 173–92; Jack M. McLeod, Dietram A. Scheufele, and Patricia Moy, "Community, Communication, and Participation: The Role of Mass Media and Interpersonal Discussion in Local Political Participation," *Political Communication* 16 (1999): 315–36.

52. Paul DiMaggio, Eszter Hargittai, W. Russell Neuman, and John P. Robinson, "Social Implications of the Internet," *Annual Review of Sociology* 27 (2001): 307–36; Thomas J. Johnson, Mahmoud A.M. Braima, and Jayanthi Sothirajah, "Doing the Traditional Media Sidestep: Comparing the Effects of the Internet and Other Nontraditional Media with Traditional Media in the 1996 Presidential Campaign," *Journalism & Mass Communication Quarterly* 76, 1 (1999): 99–123.

53. William P. Eveland Jr., "The Cognitive Mediation Model of Learning from the News: Evidence from Nonelection, Off-year Election, and Presidential Election Contexts," *Communication Research* 28, 5 (2001): 571–601; William P. Eveland Jr., Dhavan V. Shah, and Nojin Kwak, "Assessing Causality in the Cognitive Mediation Model: A Panel Study of Motivations, Information Processing, and Learning During Campaign 2000," *Communication Research* 30, 4 (2003): 359–86.

54. Markus Prior, *Post-Broadcast Democracy: How Media Choice Increases Inequality in Political Involvement and Polarizes Elections* (New York: Cambridge University Press, 2007); Dietram A. Scheufele and Matthew C. Nisbet, "Being a Citizen On-line: New Opportunities and Dead Ends," *The International Journal of Press/Politics* 7, 3 (2002): 53–73.

55. Leon Festinger, *A Theory of Cognitive Dissonance* (Stanford: Stanford University Press, 1957).

56. Robert Huckfeldt, Jeanette Morehouse Mendez, and Tracy Osborn, "Disagreement, Ambivalence, and Engagement: The Political Consequences of Heterogeneous Networks," *Political Psychology* 25, 1 (2004): 65–95.

57. Ibid.

58. Coe, Tewksbury, Bond, Drogos, Porter, Yahn, and Zhang, "Hostile News."

59. More details are available in appendix A, which describes the NAES and the general analysis strategy for the survey.

60. Kari Edwards and Edward E. Smith, "A Disconfirmation Bias in the Evaluation of Arguments," *Journal of Personality and Social Psychology* 71, 1 (1996): 5–24.

61. Diana C. Mutz, "Cross-Cutting Social Networks: Testing Democratic Theory in Practice," *American Political Science Review* 96, 1 (2002): 111–26; Vincent Price, Joseph N. Cappella, and Lilach Nir, "Does Disagreement Contribute to More Deliberative Opinion?" *Political Communication* 19 (2002): 95–112.

62. This is evident from the significant regression coefficients for political knowledge in predicting an awareness of similar views and opposing views in Mutz, "Cross-Cutting Social Networks," and in predicting reasons for one's own opinion and for why others might disagree in Price, Cappella, and Nir, "Does Disagreement Contribute to More Deliberative Opinion?"

63. Michael Schudson, *The Power of News* (Cambridge, MA: Harvard University Press, 1995): 200.

64. Alice H. Eagly, Patrick Kulesa, Serena Chen, and Shelly Chaiken, "Do Attitudes Affect Memory? Tests of the Congeniality Hypothesis," *Current Directions in Psychological Science* 10, 1 (2001): 7.

65. Huckfeldt, Morehouse Mendez, and Osborn, "Disagreement, Ambivalence, and Engagement."

66. I also examined the other causal direction—whether campaign 2004 knowledge contributed to partisan selective exposure. In three of eight cases, campaign 2004 knowledge and ideology/partisanship significantly interact in predicting partisan media use. These instances occur in the postelection and debate panels. Consistent with the findings described earlier in the chapter, conservative Republicans with higher levels of campaign 2004 knowledge consumed more conservative media outlets and liberal Democrats with higher levels of campaign 2004 knowledge consumed more liberal media outlets compared to other respondents.

5

PARTISAN INVOLVEMENT AND SELECTIVE EXPOSURE

IN 2008, MILLIONS of Americans had the opportunity to become secret agents. They could learn about mission objectives from their commander-in-chief through a password-protected Web site. They were directed about how to avoid detection while undercover—no showers, special clothing, the works. And they carried out their orders. One particularly grueling mission challenged agents to confront one of their deepest fears; they were directed to vote in the Democratic primary for Senator Hillary Clinton. This was all a part of Operation Chaos, carried out under the command of Commander-in-Chief Rush Limbaugh. The ultimate mission was to create chaos in the Democratic Party by exacerbating divides between Clinton voters and Obama voters.

There is no question that Limbaugh and Operation Chaos motivated some people to act. Callers were eager to report that they had successfully completed the mission: "Hey, Rush. Yeah, we went to vote for Hillary. I was a gun-toting evangelical clinging to those guns and clinging to my God. I went out and voted. They asked me on the way out, the pollsters asked me, 'Oh, were you one of the people who switched parties?' I said, 'Yeah, I switched parties.' 'So why did you do that?' I said, 'Because of Operation Chaosssss.'"

As Rush Limbaugh's Operation Chaos illustrates, partisan media can influence citizen behavior. Politically likeminded media can activate citizens and motivate political participation. Partisan selective exposure also can help citizens to decide for whom to vote earlier in an election season—even if it is to vote strategically for a candidate of another party. And partisan selective exposure can encourage the development of highly polarized attitudes toward political candidates. Though Operation Chaos was a one-time event, habitual use of likeminded media may influence political participation, the commitment to vote for a candidate, and polarization. This chapter is dedicated to examining the evidence for these effects.

Do partisan media, such as Limbaugh's show, lead people to develop more polarized attitudes, to participate in politics, and to reach a vote decision earlier? Or do these types of programs merely attract already polarized, participatory, and committed audiences? Or—of potentially even greater importance—is there a spiral, whereby partisan outlets both attract and create ever more polarized, participatory, and committed audiences?[1] These questions are particularly important because they directly relate to our understanding of the relationship between media effects and selective exposure.

Over the past half century, the relationship between media effects and selective exposure has undergone a transformation. Selective exposure made its debut as an explanation for why the media may have limited effects on people's beliefs. The logic was that if people were not exposed to information that conflicted with their beliefs, then they would have little impetus to change their beliefs.[2] Early researchers commonly investigated variables that would enhance or constrain people's tendency to engage in selective exposure. Concepts similar to polarization and commitment, for example, were investigated as reasons that people would seek out likeminded media.

Today, however, selective exposure is seen differently. Far from the preamble of a limited-effects perspective, selective exposure is seen as a reason to expect media effects. In his widely read *Republic.com*, for example, Cass Sunstein issued a strong warning about the consequences of exposure to likeminded views; with particular reference to the Internet, he cautioned that polarization and fragmentation could result, leading to less tolerance and ever more extreme views.[3] Others have posited that discussing politics with likeminded others encourages political participation—a similar relationship could appear between likeminded news use and participation.[4] Put bluntly, contemporary research no longer equates selective exposure with limited effects. This chapter returns to the tension between selective exposure and media effects to examine whether polarization, participation, and the commitment to vote for a candidate are causes, consequences, or both causes and consequences of partisan selective exposure.

PARTICIPATION AND PARTISAN SELECTIVE EXPOSURE

Political participation is an essential part of a democratic form of government. Without citizen participation, the government may not represent the interests of the citizenry. Equitable participation is of particular importance to ensure that many different groups are adequately represented by the government.[5] When some groups participate more than others, the views of less participatory groups may be under-represented. Though voting is the most obvious way in which citizens can partici-pate, other activities, such as working on a political campaign, also are valuable acts of political participation.

Given the importance of citizen involvement for a representative democracy, con-siderable time has been devoted to understanding what leads citizens to participate in politics. Though a number of demographic and political variables help to predict whether a citizen will participate, the communication environment also plays a role in promoting and deterring participation.[6] Being contacted by a political campaign or encouraged to vote by a neighbor, for example, increases the likelihood that a citizen will vote.[7] Who you visit with about politics also affects whether you partici-pate.[8] And of note for this chapter, the use of likeminded news media may influence political participation.

There is a strong historical precedent for expecting a partisan press to enhance citizen engagement. In the early 1800s, newspapers were fiercely partisan: "By 1810, when Isaiah Thomas published a list of American newspapers in his *History of Printing,* 86 percent of American newspapers had a clear party linkage."[9] Newspapers unabashedly affiliated themselves with popular political viewpoints of the day. Aligned with Alexander Hamilton, *The Gazette* competed with *The National Gazette,* a paper aligned with Thomas Jefferson. During a period of a rampantly partisan press, political participation in the United States flourished.[10] Yet was it merely a coinci-dence that high levels of political participation historically coincided with an era of partisan press? With the existence of partisan media today, we can return to this question and examine whether likeminded media use is related to participation.

We know that news media use in general is related to political participation.[11] The more people use the media to gather political information, the more they participate in politics. In an important project, Dhavan Shah and his colleagues used panel data to investigate this relationship.[12] They found evidence that seeking political information online leads to higher levels of political participation. Yet research to date has not inves-tigated whether *partisan* media use uniquely contributes to political participation.

To develop some expectations about how likeminded media might influence political participation, I turned to the research on how political discussion part-ners—be they likeminded or not—influence participation in politics. Unfortunately, the literature on how partisan discussion relates to political participation is mixed. Communication researcher Lilach Nir, for example, found that discussing politics with both politically similar and politically dissimilar others had *little effect* on political participation.[13] Yet fellow scholar Dietram Scheufele and his colleagues found that those discussing politics with diverse others—diverse in terms of politics, gender, and ethnicity—participated *more frequently*.[14] And yet another researcher, Diana Mutz, found that those discussing politics with people holding a different partisan affiliation participated *less frequently*.[15]

It is important to disentangle these results in light of the current project. Nir does not separately consider those who discuss politics with only likeminded others and those who discuss politics with only nonlikeminded others. Instead, her main focus is those who are pulled in two directions by their discussion partners. This is less applicable here, where I am interested in looking at those encountering likeminded views. The finding from Scheufele and his colleagues that discussing politics with diverse others increases political participation uses a broad measure of diversity; it includes both gender and ethnicity as markers of diversity. This is much broader than my focus on partisanship. Diana Mutz's results, however, are more directly applicable. She is interested in the amount of political disagreement encountered. More disagreement with political discussion mates depresses participation. The obverse of her results, therefore, may speak directly to the current project. Namely, exposure to *likeminded* views may encourage *more* participation.

Diana Mutz accounts for her findings by providing a social explanation. Interpersonal conflict can arise when discussing politics with others who disagree. In order to avoid interpersonal conflict, people develop more ambivalent attitudes toward politics and then participate less. Instead of disagreeing with one's discussion partners, a person withdraws from politics altogether. If the avoidance of interpersonal conflict explains why political participation is lower among those visiting about politics with non-likeminded others, why would exposure to likeminded *media* messages *encourage* participation? There are several possibilities. First, partisan selective exposure may *enable* participation by providing people with the requisite information for participation. Partisan media outlets may be particularly likely to give people information about participation—partisan Web sites, for example, often publicize partisan events and make it easy for people to donate money to a likeminded cause. When people agree with the cause, they arguably are more likely to take advantage of these mediated invitations for participation. Second, partisan selective exposure may *inspire* people to participate. When engaging in partisan selective exposure, people may feel more certain of the veracity of their political beliefs. This perception of being correct could propel people to feel not only more assured about participating but also more *obligated* to participate. In sum, partisan media exposure should motivate political participation.

To evaluate the relationship between partisan selective exposure and political participation, I turned to the National Annenberg Election Surveys (NAES). Early in the campaign season, when participants had limited opportunities for political participation, survey respondents were asked to report their *intentions* to participate in the presidential campaign. Intentions are a strong predictor of actually performing a behavior and hence serve as a good starting point for analyzing whether partisan selective exposure influences political participation.[16] In September, as the campaign went into full swing and opportunities for political participation increased, respondents were asked whether they had engaged in a number of campaign activities, such as attending political rallies or trying to convince others how to vote. I analyzed the data from the survey to understand whether the use of likeminded media is related to higher intentions to participate and to higher levels of actual political participation. The results are consistent. Liberals and Democrats who read newspapers endorsing Kerry, listen to liberal radio, watch CNN or MSNBC, or access liberal Web sites participate at higher rates compared to other liberal Democrats. Conservatives and Republicans who read newspapers endorsing Bush or watch Fox News participate at higher rates than other likeminded partisans. Though not significant, the same trends appear for conservatives and Republicans accessing conservative Web sites or listening to conservative talk radio. To summarize these results across the various media types, I used the indices of conservative and liberal media use described in chapter 3 to create Figure 5.1.

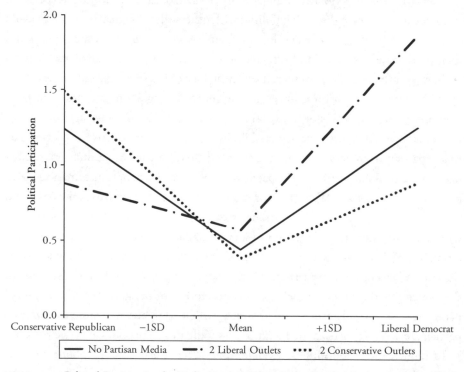

FIGURE 5.1 Political Participation by Media Use and Political Leanings. Results based on a regression analysis predicting political participation. Analysis controls for demographics, political orientations, and patterns of media use. The media use and ideology/partisanship interactions are significant. More details can be found in the technical appendix for this chapter.

Source: Data from the 2004 NAES RCS.

As shown in Figure 5.1, conservatives and Republicans using *conservative* media participate *more* and conservatives and Republicans using *liberal* media participate *less* compared to other likeminded partisans. The same general pattern appears for liberals and Democrats using partisan media. Results for intentions to participate are similar.[17] There may very well be something about likeminded media that motivates, activates, and enables political participation.

Yet does partisan selective exposure lead to political participation, or might political participation contribute to partisan selective exposure? The question of temporal order is pertinent here. Those participating in politics may find partisan media to be particularly useful. These individuals tend to be stronger partisans, and many opportunities for political participation tend to be partisan in nature—consider, for example, working for a candidate, donating money to a campaign, or wearing a campaign button.[18] In order for individuals to gain information useful for participation, they may be more apt to select media supportive of their political beliefs. A second, and related, rationale is that those with higher levels of political participation may be more motivated to recognize the political cues contained in partisan media compared to those who do not participate. Through their participation in partisan activities, they may be better trained to know which outlets are acceptable for people sharing their partisan leaning and which outlets are meant for people with the opposite political leaning. These people may be better, therefore, at picking up on and acting upon partisan cues about the news media. Given the possibility that political participation leads to the use of politically likeminded media, it is important to investigate the causal order of the relationship between political participation and partisan selective exposure.

As in chapters 3 and 4, I used data gathered from panel surveys to evaluate the relationship between partisan selective exposure and political participation further. The panel analyses help to provide information about the causal direction of the relationship. They cannot prove that the relationships are causal, but they are a more powerful test of a possible causal relationship between two variables. The NAES contacted the same people twice and asked about their political participation in two instances: before and after the presidential debates and during and after the general election. After taking into account how frequently people participated in politics earlier in the election, I looked at whether the extent of their partisan media use predicted how frequently they participated in politics later in the election.[19] Two other panel surveys were conducted, one around each of the national party conventions. Here, however, respondents were asked about their intentions to participate both before and after the conventions, rather than their actual participation.

Unfortunately, the panel surveys shed little light on the relationship between partisan selective exposure and participation. Weak evidence suggests that partisan selective exposure predicts participation as anticipated in only one instance. Data from the general election panel survey show that strong conservative Republicans using conservative media participate at higher rates than other strong conservative Republicans. The effect was marginally significant. Here, strong conservative Republicans who used two conservative media types and hadn't participated at all during the prewave reported participating in, on average, 0.35 political actions in the postwave. Strong conservative Republicans who did not use any conservative media engaged in only 0.25 political actions in the postwave. In a similar yet opposite pattern, strong liberal Democrats who hadn't participated at all during the prewave participated more frequently when they weren't using conservative media (0.61 political acts, on average) compared to when they did (0.15 political acts, on average). Further, there was an indication that participation contributed to partisan media use. In the Republican National Convention (RNC) panel, liberal Democrats who intended to participate in politics were more likely to use liberal media outlets. Despite some significant findings, evidence about the causal direction from these data is mixed and notably modest.

Why would the panel survey analyses provide only a limited indication of the causal direction despite the presence of clear relationships between partisan media use and participation, as shown in Figure 5.1? One possibility is that the amount of time that elapsed between the pre- and postwaves of the survey was simply too short to see effects—perhaps the relationship between partisan selective exposure and political participation develops over longer periods of time. As effort is involved in political participation—people must donate money to a campaign or purchase a bumper sticker for their car—more than a few weeks may need to elapse before people act based on their exposure to partisan media. To provide a preliminary test of this idea, I examined the responses of those respondents who both expressed their *intentions* to participate between July 16 and September 13 and those who reported the extent of their participation after the election had finished. This analysis is admittedly less stringent than looking at whether partisan media use predicts participation at a later point in time after taking into account *participation* at an earlier point in time. Here, I'm looking at whether participation as reported after the election can be predicted by partisan selective exposure after controlling for prewave *intentions* to participate.

In this analysis, there is support for the notion that partisan selective exposure leads to higher levels of participation. Liberals and Democrats using liberal media and conservatives and Republicans using conservative media had higher levels of participation relative to other likeminded partisans, controlling for their intentions to participate from earlier in the campaign. Among those both intending to partici-pate and using two conservative media types, strong conservative Republicans participated in an average of 1.53 political acts in the postwave and strong liberal Democrats participated in only 0.90 acts on average. When those intending to participate used two liberal media types, however, the pattern is reversed. Strong conservative Republicans participated in an average of 1.04 activities and strong liberal Democrats participated in an average of 1.59 activities.

There is also some indication that liberals and Democrats with higher intentions to participate used more liberal media outlets later in the campaign compared to other respondents—even after taking into account the number of liberal media outlets that they used earlier in the campaign. There is some evidence, therefore, that political participation intentions contribute to likeminded media exposure for liberals and Democrats. Strong liberal Democrats who used one liberal media type in the prewave used more liberal media in the postwave if they intended to participate (1.22 liberal media types on average) than if they did not (1.02 liberal media types on average). Strong conservative Republicans using one liberal media type in the prewave and intending to participate used fewer liberal media types on average in the postwave (0.50) compared to those not intending to participate (0.62).

In sum, political participation is related to partisan selective exposure. Few overtime results were significant, providing little guidance on the causal direction of the relationship between partisan selective exposure and participation. The analysis of the panel data with the largest time lapse between the pre- and postwave surveys suggests that likeminded media use can lead to higher levels of political participation and that, at least for liberal Democrats, an intention to participate inspires more partisan selective exposure.

COMMITMENT AND PARTISAN SELECTIVE EXPOSURE

One's time of decision—when, during a campaign, one decides for whom to vote—and how committed a person feels toward one's vote choice also may be influenced by partisan selective exposure. Specifically, partisan selective exposure may lead people to feel more committed to their vote choice and to decide for whom to vote earlier in a campaign.

Why should we expect this to be the case? Research on the effects of political discussion again provides some important insights. Those who discuss politics with others who do not share their political point of view are more likely to delay their presidential vote decision.[20] This is at least in part because people try to protect their social relationships—to avoid conflict with political discussion partners who disagree, people can delay deciding for whom to vote. This provides little information about why the *media* may influence when one decides for whom to vote, however.

The relationship between partisan media use and when one makes a vote choice likely has little to do with an individual's distaste for social conflict. As another explanation, partisan media may provide *information* that influences when people decide for whom to vote. Faced with contradictory media messages, people may rationally delay their vote decision in order to gather additional information. Alternatively, partisan selective exposure may help people to make their candidate choices earlier in a campaign because the media messages justify and confirm their candidate preference. Equipped with information largely agreeing with a candidate choice from the media, there is little reason to delay making a commitment to vote for a preferred candidate.

To investigate whether partisan selective exposure influences commitments to vote for a candidate, I contrast two different types of people—those who have reached a decision about their vote choice and those who remain undecided. People can signal that they have settled on their vote choice in two ways. Those who have already cast a ballot through early voting obviously have decided for whom they will vote. And those who have a vote preference and believe that it is very unlikely that they will change their mind also seem to have reached a decision. People can signal that they are undecided in two ways as well. People who think there's a good chance that they will change their mind about for whom to vote have not yet reached a decision. And those who don't have any idea for whom they will vote also clearly have not decided. I analyzed whether those engaging in partisan selective exposure are more likely to have settled on their vote choice. The results are consistent. Liberals and Democrats reading Kerry-endorsing newspapers, listening to liberal talk radio, or watching CNN or MSNBC are more likely to have decided for whom to vote than other liberal Democrats. Conservatives and Republicans listening to conservative talk radio, watching Fox News, or accessing conservative Web sites are more likely to have decided for whom to vote than other conservative Republicans. In Figure 5.2, I summarize the results using the indices of partisan media use.

Figure 5.2 documents that those with stronger partisan and ideological attachments are more likely to know for whom they will vote. And if they also use like-minded media, they are even more likely to say they are committed to their vote decision. Partisan selective exposure is related to a stronger commitment to vote for a specific candidate.

After the election, respondents were asked when they made up their mind about their presidential vote choice. Election day? The day before the election? During the summer? This measure is closely related to the commitment measure analyzed in Figure 5.2—those who reported that they were committed to their vote choice during the campaign also reported that on average, they had decided for whom to vote during the summer before the election. Those who were not committed to a

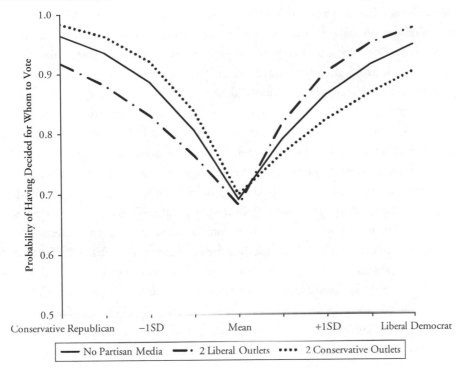

FIGURE 5.2 Commitment to Vote for a Candidate by Media Use and Political Leanings. Analysis details are the same as those described below Figure 5.1. Results based on a logistic regression analysis predicting commitment to vote for a candidate.

candidate during the campaign reported that, on average, they had reached a vote decision only during the last weeks of the campaign. As there was a significant relationship between commitment and partisan selective exposure, I anticipated that I would find the same relationship between time of decision and partisan selective exposure. And this is exactly what I found. The results closely mirror those shown in Figure 5.2. Liberal Democrats using liberal media decide for whom to vote earlier in the campaign than other liberal Democrats. And conservative Republicans using conservative media decide for whom to vote earlier in the campaign. Likeminded media seems to help citizens make up their mind about for whom to vote.

Though making a commitment to vote for a political candidate may be a consequence of selective exposure, there is a precedent for considering commitment as a cause of selective exposure. Early researchers debated whether or not people engage in selective exposure prior to making a decision.[21] Leon Festinger argued that people are unbiased in their information search before a decision is made; he wrote that "information seeking in the pre-decision period is not selective but is rather objective and impartial."[22] Cognitive dissonance theory maintains that dissonance is not aroused before a decision is reached and hence, people are not motivated to select likeminded information before they have reached a decision. In accordance with this idea, several early experimental results suggest that people engage in dissonance reduction strategies like selective exposure only *after* reaching a decision.[23] Reaching a decision, therefore, may motivate partisan selective exposure.

Both Festinger's contemporaries and more recent scholars have questioned whether *un*biased information search occurs prior to reaching a decision.[24] Psychologists Irving Janis and Leon Mann proposed that before reaching a decision, individuals feel conflict (as opposed to dissonance) between choosing one option as opposed to the other.[25] They suggest that selective exposure can occur prior to the moment of decision in order to avoid *pre*decisional conflict. In support of this idea, one study found that "*prior to a commitment* people who are certain that one alternative is best will avoid information favoring a different alternative."[26] Attempting to conduct a critical experiment to evaluate when selectivity starts, one of Festinger's students, Jon Jecker, found that those who had reached a decision preferred likeminded information more than those who hadn't yet reached a decision.[27] The relationship, however, was not statistically significant. Further, it isn't clear that those considered *pre*decisional hadn't made a choice. They were asked to rate their choices in a pretest—couldn't this be considered a type of decision making?

As Jecker's experiment shows, determining conclusively whether someone engages in predecisional versus postdecisional selectivity is not an easy task. How do you isolate a person's moment of decision? What does it mean to decide? Casting a ballot certainly represents a moment of decision, but people can decide for whom to vote long before they actually cast their ballots. Instead of attempting to isolate a moment of decision, one can evaluate a person's *commitment*—exactly the concept that I evaluated earlier. Commitment captures the strength of a citizen's intentions to vote for a specific candidate. As people develop a preference and become more committed to this preference, the logic goes, they may increasingly engage in selective exposure. An individual with little or no clear preference for any available alternative has very low commitment and little incentive to seek out likeminded perspectives. Alternatively, an individual who has indicated a more established candidate preference has a higher level of commitment and thus may be more likely to engage in selective exposure.

Political scientists Richard Lau and David Redlawsk conducted an experimental study with particular relevance to this discussion.[28] Subjects in their study participated in a computer simulation of a primary election where they could choose from bits of information crossing a computer screen. Their information selection during the simulated campaign was recorded. Lau and Redlawsk found that early in the primary, information exposure was nearly evenly divided between the hypothetical candidates. As the mock primary drew near, however, information exposure became more confined to the candidate the individual ultimately chose. These changes over the course of the campaign could be attributed to changes in commitment. As individuals became increasingly committed to their favored candidate over time, they engaged in more selective exposure. Since commitment may lead to selective exposure, it is important to analyze the causal direction of the relationship.

As with the relationship between participation and partisan selective exposure, I use data gathered from people at two points in time. For the panel surveys conducted around three major campaign events (the Democratic National Convention (DNC), the RNC, and the debates), I analyzed whether partisan selective exposure predicts a commitment to vote for a candidate after the event, taking into account how committed people were before the event. In only one instance does partisan selective exposure predict the commitment to vote for a candidate. In the DNC panel, liberal Democrats using liberal media outlets were more committed to their vote choice after the DNC compared to liberal Democrats who did not use liberal media outlets. Uncommitted, strong liberal Democrats using two liberal media types in the prewave were nearly universally committed in the postwave. Their probability of commitment in the postwave, given no commitment in the prewave, was 0.95. Those not using liberal media also became increasingly committed, but to a lesser extent (probability of 0.60). The opposite occurred for uncommitted strong conservative Republicans, where liberal media use was related to lower levels of commitment in the postwave compared to those not using liberal media (probability of 0.20 versus 0.60). One instance, however, supports the opposite causal relationship. In the RNC panel, committed liberal Democrats selected more liberal media after the convention. Here, committed strong liberal Democrats using no liberal media types before the RNC reported using an average of 0.55 liberal media types afterward. This is in contrast to committed, strong conservative Republicans, who reported using an average of only 0.18 liberal media types after the RNC.

In the general election panel, the measures of commitment differed between the pre- and postwaves of the survey. For the postwave of the survey, I have a measure of when people decided for whom to vote, and in the prewave of the survey, I have a measure of how committed people were about for whom to vote. This analysis is not an ideal way to test relationships over time because the measurement differs between the two survey waves. Yet it does allow for additional examination of the relationship between partisan selective exposure and commitment.

The results of the analysis provide additional information about the causal direction of the relationship between partisan selective exposure and commitment. The results show that committed liberal Democrats use more liberal media and committed conservative Republicans use more conservative media relative to other likeminded respondents. This suggests that commitment leads to partisan selective exposure. There also is some evidence of the opposite causal direction; namely, strong liberal Democrats using liberal media decided for whom they would vote earlier in the campaign compared to other liberal Democrats.

These findings document a relationship between the commitment to vote for a political candidate, when a person decides for whom to vote, and exposure to like-minded media. In two panel surveys, partisan media use contributed to higher levels of commitment and earlier decision times for liberal Democrats. Yet the panel surveys provide more evidence in favor of the opposite causal direction, namely, that commitment contributes to partisan media exposure. There is evidence that both committed liberal Democrats and committed conservative Republicans were more likely to use likeminded media.

POLARIZATION AND PARTISAN SELECTIVE EXPOSURE

There is little disagreement in the scholarly literature that political elites have become increasingly polarized in the past several decades.[29] In Congress, for example, we have seen an increasing ideological divide between the major political parties.[30] Whether patterns of polarization in the mass public resemble elite polarization, however, is an issue that truly polarizes academics.[31] Some argue that the public has become increasingly politically polarized, while others claim that it has not.[32] An analysis of the media may play an important role in mediating this debate, however. After all, the media are the primary way that elite polarization would be transmitted to the public. Those selecting media outlets that cohere with their political leanings may be particularly likely to adopt elites' polarized attitudes. Indeed, communication scholar Diana Mutz notes that although partisan selective exposure *should* lead partisans to "polarize further in the direction of their original views, this consequence is not yet well documented."[33] Accordingly, I turn to evaluating whether partisan selective exposure contributes to political polarization before turning to an evaluation of the reverse causal direction.

There are several reasons to anticipate that media consumers will develop more extreme and polarized attitudes when they are exposed to views that resonate with their own. Research on likeminded interpersonal groups provides important justification for a link between likeminded media use and polarization.[34] Those discussing politics with politically likeminded others have more polarized political attitudes compared to those discussing politics with others holding divergent political preferences.[35] This finding is arguably relevant to investigating the effects of exposure to likeminded media messages.

The two primary explanations that have been offered for why likeminded interpersonal groups develop more polarized attitudes should continue to apply in mediated contexts. The first, and stronger, mechanism is that polarization occurs because group members are exposed to persuasive arguments.[36] By hearing arguments that favor their side, group members are persuaded to develop more polarized attitudes in the direction of the group norm. In an identical process, likeminded partisan media could provide information supporting a preferred perspective and therefore, would be expected to produce polarization.

The second explanation for polarization is social comparison, whereby people want to be perceived well by their fellow group members and hence adjust their opinions toward a group mean that is perceived to be more extreme than their own.[37] Though this is not as easily transferred into a mediated context, there may be a social element to information selection as well. Those who discuss political campaigns more often are more likely to seek out partisan political information.[38] Polarized individuals not only may discuss politics with likeminded others more frequently, but also may seek more likeminded information because this type of information has social utility. They may want their discussion partners to think that they are well informed about partisan happenings. They also may feel that it is expected that they contribute to the group's argument pool. Research has shown that likeminded discussion groups prefer supportive over contradictory information to a degree larger than the preference for supportive information among individuals.[39] This supports the idea that there is a social element to information selection. By seeking and internalizing more favorable partisan information for social reasons, individuals may become more polarized. As this discussion demonstrates, the mechanisms proposed for why likeminded political discussion would lead to polarization also could explain why exposure to likeminded partisan media messages would lead to polarization.

Although there are theoretical reasons to predict a link between the selection of likeminded media outlets and polarized attitudes, current empirical evidence is inconclusive. Several studies have found evidence of a link between media exposure and polarization. Yet there are exceptions where scholars have found no evidence of polarization or where scholars have raised questions about whether *likeminded* media exposure enhances polarization.[40]

Several studies have examined whether a one-time media exposure, such as viewing a film, is related to polarization.[41] Research on the effects of exposure to discrete political media events yields mixed evidence as to whether selective exposure polarizes opinion. Media events can attract likeminded audiences and have little effect on their attitudes. For example, the film *Roots: The Next Generation* did not significantly affect audience attitudes after taking into account audience attitudes *before* viewing the film.[42] Partisan media also may not always have the intended effect. Boomerang effects (whereby attitude change occurs in the opposite direction of the intended message) can occur when, for example, the content of a media message is perceived to be offensive.[43] There is evidence, however, that partisan media can influence attitudes in the direction of the message. In a study of the film *The Right Stuff,* individuals who watched the pro-Glenn film had more favorable attitudes toward John Glenn, a candidate for the Democratic presidential nomination, after exposure to the film.[44] Further, the anti-Bush film described in chapter 3, *Fahrenheit 9/11,* influenced attitudes toward President Bush.[45] Those viewing the film held more negative attitudes toward President Bush compared to those who only intended to see the film. These studies suggest that there are some instances in which a one-time media exposure *can* lead to polarized attitudes. Yet it isn't guaranteed. Sometimes people rebel against the message. Other times, polarized attitudes can motivate exposure rather than the other way around.

Other studies have examined the relationship between polarization and exposure to a single media type, whether exposure to newspapers, Rush Limbaugh, or Web sites.[46] There is some evidence that these media types can influence audiences' political attitudes. Yet several of these studies have relied on data gathered at a single point in time, making it difficult to draw conclusions about the causal direction of a relationship between polarization and media use.[47] Further, no one has looked at the effect of people's media exposure diet on political polarization—what about newspaper, radio, cable news, *and* Web use? Here, I look at people's comprehensive media use and polarization over time to shed some light on the direction of the relationship.

To analyze whether patterns of partisan selective exposure are related to polarization, I follow the same strategy employed in the prior analyses. Though polarization could be assessed in numerous ways, I examined polarization by looking at how favorably or unfavorably people felt about the major party candidates in the 2004 presidential election. Respondents reported how favorably they felt toward Republican President Bush and how favorably they felt toward Democratic challenger Kerry. I combined these measures so that someone who rates the candidates very differently—someone who feels very favorably toward one candidate and very unfavorably toward the other candidate—is considered highly polarized. Someone who rates both candidates identically is not polarized at all. Similar measurement strategies have been used in the past.[48] I looked at whether there was a relationship between partisan selective exposure and polarized attitudes toward the candidates. The results are consistent. Whether I look at newspaper reading, radio listening, cable news viewing, or partisan Web site accessing, when people choose media more consistent with their partisan leanings, they hold more polarized attitudes than other likeminded partisans.[49] Rather than showing each media type individually, I use the indices to summarize the results in Figure 5.3.

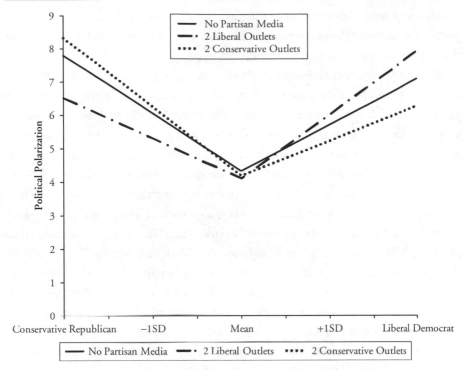

FIGURE 5.3 Political Polarization by Media Use and Political Leanings. Analysis details are the same as those described below Figure 5.1. Results based on a regression analysis predicting political polarization.

A now familiar pattern appears in this chart. Even after taking into account demographic differences, differences in political interest and knowledge, and differences in news media use, *partisan* media use significantly influences political polarization. Using likeminded media is related to higher levels of political polarization and using contradictory media is related to lower levels of political polarization. Put simply, likeminded news media audiences hold more polarized political views.

Though partisan selective exposure may increase polarization, it also is possible that polarized partisans pick more likeminded media outlets. It is an open question whether polarization enhances partisan selective exposure or partisan selective exposure enhances polarization. In fact, early literature on selective exposure proposed that concepts similar to polarization were not consequences, but predictors of selective exposure.

In the 1960s—the heyday of cognitive dissonance and selective exposure research—scholars thought that certainty and confidence might cause selective exposure. Certainty, or "the perceived probability that [one's choice] is better than the alternatives,"[50] and the related concept of confidence, or how assured one feels about one's perspective compared to others, have been investigated as causes of selective exposure.[51] As a part of cognitive dissonance theory, Festinger argued that people should avoid dissonant information only when they lack the confidence that they can counterargue the information.[52]

In research on selective exposure, the similarity between confidence, certainty, and polarization is striking. An individual who is extremely favorable toward their preferred candidate and extremely *un*favorable toward another candidate undoubtedly is confident, certain, and polarized. Further, the ways in which scholars have measured confidence, certainty, and polarization are similar. For example, communication scholar Dean Ziemke included a measure identical to polarization as an indicator of certainty.[53] Several experimental studies manipulated certainty by having subjects rate various products according to their desirability and then making them choose between either (a) similarly ranked products or (b) differently rated products.[54] This is quite similar to polarization. With two equally liked products, the choice is challenging and people would be less certain about which product to choose. With two differently liked products, the choice is far easier. Attitudes about the two products are starkly different and choosers would feel certain that they are selecting the superior product, just as voters would feel certain that they are selecting the superior candidate when they see immense differences between two candidates. These types of studies propose that certainty affects selective exposure.

Early theoretical work on the relationship between selective exposure and certainty/confidence surmised that the more confident or certain the individual, the less likely she would be to seek likeminded information. Given high levels of certainty or confidence, why not seek discrepant information? It shouldn't produce much of the psychological discomfort associated with cognitive dissonance. Instead of avoiding information, a confident and certain individual actually may seek discrepant information because of her confidence or certainty that she would be able to refute it. Alternatively, if a position is not held with certainty, an individual may seek confirmatory information in order to maintain the position. If this were in fact the case, then relationships between selective exposure and polarization in cross-sectional analysis may be *under*estimated because the positive (selective exposure → polarization) and negative (polarization → selective exposure) influences might cancel each other out.

Evidence supporting the theory that certainty and confidence reduce selective exposure is relatively weak. A series of experiments aiming to understand the conditions that motivate selective exposure were conducted in the 1960s. Though the use of experiments has the potential to clear up ambiguity in causal direction because the independent variable is under the control of the experimenter and is known to occur prior to the dependent variable, selective exposure experiments that have manipulated certainty and confidence have yielded conflicting results. Manipulating certainty by asking subjects to choose between either two products that were similarly attractive or two products that were differentially attractive, one study found that less certain individuals were *more* likely to seek supportive information.[55] Others, however, failed to replicate this finding.[56] Another series of experiments manipulated confidence by giving subjects feedback on their performance on several judgment tasks—some subjects were given positive feedback about their performance and others were given negative feedback. Those receiving negative feedback were less confident than those receiving positive feedback. After receiving this feedback, subjects were asked to make a preliminary judgment on another similar task and then were given the opportunity to read additional information before making a final judgment. Some of the additional information choices confirmed the subject's preliminary judgment on the task. Other choices countered the subject's preliminary judgment on the task. Their information selection was recorded and used to measure selective exposure. Though there was some evidence that confidence was related to selective exposure, others using similar designs failed to replicate the findings.[57] In another study, the authors attempted to manipulate certainty by telling people who had made a decision that others who had been interviewed for the study tended to either agree or disagree with their decision. Yet those who were told that others tended to agree were no more or less certain than those who were told that others tended to disagree.[58] Self-reported certainty was measured, however, and more certain participants preferred likeminded information—at least among those who weren't expecting to make a public statement about their views. A more recent study found that those with higher levels of confidence were more likely to select *non*likeminded information.[59] Despite extensive research attention, evidence that certainty *discourages* selective exposure is decidedly mixed.

Quite the opposite, certainty may *encourage* selective exposure. Communication scholar Dean Ziemke proposed that those who are more certain about their political leanings should engage in more selective exposure. He examined whether politically certain citizens were more selective in watching the national conventions, watching candidate speeches, watching candidate ads, tuning in to the news, and reading candidate pamphlets.[60] He found that "the more certain [the voters] are, the more they select information supportive *of their candidate*."[61] Building on Ziemke, other studies also suggest that certainty is positively related to partisan selective exposure.[62]

In sum, partisan selective exposure may increase polarized attitudes. When people use likeminded media, they may develop more extreme views of political candidates. But the other causal direction could be occurring as well. Those with polarized attitudes may seek likeminded media. Feeling certain and confident that a favored candidate is the far-superior choice in an election may inspire people to engage in partisan selective exposure.

To examine the evidence, I again used panel data to analyze the relationship between partisan selective exposure and polarization. The results provide good evidence that partisan selective exposure contributes to polarization. In most cases, likeminded media use predicts polarization above what is accounted for by polarization measured at an earlier point in time. One exception to this pattern occurs in the panel survey conducted around the presidential and vice presidential debates where partisan selective exposure does not significantly predict polarization. Throughout the other panels, however, evidence points in a consistent direction: Audiences for likeminded media develop more polarized views about politics. As an example, in the general election panel, liberal Democrats with a medium degree of polarization—scoring a five on the polarization measure—in the prewave had an average postwave polarization score of 4.39 if they used two conservative media types. Conservative Republicans using two conservative media types, however, had an average polarization score of 5.47 in the postwave.

Not only does partisan selective exposure feed polarized political attitudes, but there also is evidence for the opposite causal direction. More polarized partisans select more likeminded political media compared to those holding less polarized views. In the general election panel, polarized partisans selected more likeminded media after the election, even after controlling for their media selections before the election. Maximally polarized strong liberal Democrats using one liberal media type in the prewave used, on average, 1.14 liberal media types in the postwave. Alternatively, maximally polarized strong conservative Republicans who used one liberal media type reduced their use of liberal media types to, on average, 0.55 in the postwave. There is some evidence, therefore, for a spiral effect. Holding polarized attitudes leads to partisan selective exposure. And partisan selective exposure leads to more polarized political attitudes.

Summary

Partisan selective exposure is far from inconsequential. This chapter documents that partisan selective exposure is related to all sorts of important political outcomes. Partisan selective exposure predicts political participation, the commitment to vote for a candidate, and political polarization. Though selective exposure may be a component of the "limited media effects tradition," it does seem to have an effect. When citizens select news media sharing their political leanings, these outlets motivate citizens to participate in politics and to intensify their political attitudes. At the same time, those who are committed to voting for a candidate early in the campaign and those who hold polarized political attitudes are attracted to likeminded media outlets. There also is evidence that for some, likeminded media use can lead to a stronger commitment to vote for a candidate and that political participation can inspire likeminded media use. These patterns signal the presence of spirals. Using likeminded news media inspires certain political attitudes and behaviors. And several political attitudes and behaviors then inspire even more likeminded news media use. Although the data from this chapter cannot conclusively prove that the relationships are causal, they are in line with this conclusion.

Returning to the beginning of this chapter, partisan media—like Rush Limbaugh—have important effects on citizens. Whether encouraging people to contact their representatives or donate money to a political cause, creating a secret operation to vote strategically, or lambasting the opposition, partisan media outlets have great power to invoke political reactions among their loyal and likeminded audiences. But do these outlets also influence what citizens believe about the world in which we live? Do partisan media outlets influence citizen conceptions about the most important issues facing the nation? The next chapter turns to answering these questions.

NOTES

1. Michael D. Slater, "Reinforcing Spirals: The Mutual Influence of Media Selectivity and Media Effects and Their Impact on Individual Behavior and Social Identity," *Communication Theory* 17 (2007): 281–303.

2. Joseph T. Klapper, *The Effects of Mass Communication* (Glencoe, IL: The Free Press, 1960).

3. Cass Sunstein, *Republic.com* (Princeton: Princeton University Press, 2001); Cass Sunstein, *Republic.com 2.0* (Princeton: Princeton University Press, 2007).

4. Diana C. Mutz, "The Consequences of Cross-Cutting Networks for Political Participation," *American Journal of Political Science* 46, 4 (2002): 838–55.

5. Steven J. Rosenstone and John Mark Hansen, *Mobilization, Participation, and Democracy in America* (New York: Pearson Education, 2003).

6. William P. Eveland Jr. and Dietram A. Scheufele, "Connecting News Media Use with Gaps in Knowledge and Participation," *Political Communication* 17 (2000): 215–37; Kate Kenski and Natalie Jomini Stroud, "Connections Between Internet Use and Political Efficacy, Knowledge, and Participation," *Journal of Broadcasting and Electronic Media* 50, 2 (2006): 173–92; Jack M. McLeod, Dietram A. Scheufele, and Patricia Moy, "Community, Communication, and Participation: The Role of Mass Media and Interpersonal Discussion in Local Political Participation," *Political Communication* 16 (1999): 315–36; Rosenstone and Hansen, *Mobilization, Participation, and Democracy in America*; Dhavan V. Shah, Jaeho Cho, William P. Eveland Jr., and Nojin Kwak, "Information and Expression in a Digital Age: Modeling Internet Effects on Civic Participation," *Communication Research* 32, 5 (2005): 1–35.

7. Donald P. Green and Alan S. Gerbner, *Get Out the Vote! How to Increase Voter Turnout* (Washington, DC: Brookings Institution Press, 2004); Rosenstone and Hansen, *Mobilization, Participation, and Democracy in America*.

8. Mutz, "The Consequences of Cross-Cutting Networks."

9. Darrell M. West, *The Rise and Fall of the Media Establishment* (Belmont, CA: Wadsworth/Thomson Learning, 2001).

10. Michael Schudson, *The Power of News* (Cambridge, MA: Harvard University Press, 1995).

11. Eveland and Scheufele, "Connecting News Media Use"; Kenski and Stroud, "Connections Between Internet Use"; McLeod, Scheufele, and Moy, "Community, Communication, and Participation."

12. Shah, Cho, Eveland, and Kwak, "Information and Expression in a Digital Age."

13. Lilach Nir, "Ambivalent Social Networks and Their Consequences for Participation," *International Journal of Public Opinion Research* 17, 4 (2005): 422–42.

14. Dietram A. Scheufele, Matthew C. Nisbet, Dominique Brossard, and Erik C. Nisbet, "Social Structure and Citizenship: Examining the Impacts of Social Setting, Network Heterogeneity, and Informational Variables on Political Participation," *Political Communication* 21 (2004): 315–38.

15. Mutz, "The Consequences of Cross-Cutting Networks."

16. Icek Ajzen, "The Theory of Planned Behavior," *Organizational Behavior and Human Decision Processes* 50 (1991): 179–211; Icek Ajzen and Martin Fishbein, *Understanding Attitudes and Predicting Social Behavior* (Englewood Cliffs, NJ: Prentice-Hall, 1980); Martin Fishbein and Icek Ajzen, *Belief, Attitude, Intention, and Behavior: An Introduction to Theory and Research* (Reading, MA: Addison-Wesley, 1975); Martin Fishbein and Marco Yzer, "Using Theory to Design Effective Health Behavior Interventions," *Communication Theory* 13, 2 (2003): 164–83.

17. The interactions between ideology/partisanship and the indices of media use were significant and followed the general pattern shown in Figure 5.1.

18. Rosenstone and Hansen, *Mobilization, Participation, and Democracy in America.*

19. For the RNC and DNC panels, participation was measured using the item asking respondents to identify their intentions to participate. For the general election and debate panels, participation was measured using the index of political participation activities.

20. Nir found that individuals with *high* levels of individual ambivalence who were imbedded within an ambivalent network took a *long* time to decide for whom they would vote. Individuals with *low* levels of individual ambivalence who were imbedded within an ambivalent network took a comparatively *short* time to decide for whom they would vote. As discussed in the section on participation, however, Nir's operational definition of network ambivalence makes it difficult to translate her findings to the current study. See Nir, "Ambivalent Social Networks."

21. Leon Festinger, *A Theory of Cognitive Dissonance* (Stanford: Stanford University Press, 1957). Irving L. Janis and Leon Mann, "A Conflict-Theory Approach to Attitude Change and Decision Making," in *Psychological Foundations of Attitudes,* edited by Anthony G. Greewald, Timothy C. Brock, and Thomas M. Ostrom (New York: Academic Press, 1968): 327–60.

22. Leon Festinger, *Conflict, Decision, and Dissonance* (Stanford: Stanford University Press, 1964): 95–6; Festinger, *A Theory of Cognitive Dissonance.*

23. Jon R. Davidson and Sara B. Kiesler, "Cognitive Behavior Before and After Decisions," in *Conflict, Decision, and Dissonance,* edited by Leon Festinger (Stanford: Stanford University Press, 1964): 10–19; Jon D. Jecker, "The Cognitive Effects of Conflict and Dissonance," in *Conflict, Decision, and Dissonance,* edited by Leon Festinger (Stanford: Stanford University Press, 1964): 21–30.

24. Janis and Mann, "A Conflict-Theory Approach"; Aaron L. Brownstein, "Biased Predecision Processing," *Psychological Bulletin* 129, 4 (2003): 545–68; Jusdon Mills, "Improving the 1957 Version of Dissonance Theory," in *Cognitive Dissonance: Progress on a Pivotal Theory in Social Psychology*, edited by Eddie Harmon-Jones and Judson Mills (Washington, DC: American Psychological Association, 1999): 25–42; Tadeusz Tyszka, "Information and Evaluation Processes in Decision Making: The Role of Familiarity," in *New Directions in Research on Decision Making*, edited by Berndt Brehmer, Helmut Jungerman, Peter Lourens, and Guje Sevon (North Holland, the Netherlands: Elsevier Science, 1986): 151–61.

25. Janis and Mann, "A Conflict-Theory Approach."

26. Judson Mills and Jerald M. Jellison, "Avoidance of Discrepant Information Prior to Commitment," *Journal of Personality and Social Psychology* 8 (1968): 61, emphasis added.

27. Jon D. Jecker, "Selective Exposure to New Information," in *Conflict, Decision, and Dissonance*, edited by Leon Festinger (Stanford: Stanford University Press, 1964): 65–81.

28. Richard L. Lau and David P. Redlawsk, *How Voters Decide: Information Processing During Election Campaigns* (New York: Cambridge University Press, 2006).

29. Morris P. Fiorina with Samuel J. Abrams and Jeremy C. Pope, *Culture War? The Myth of a Polarized America* (New York: Pearson Longman, 2005); Gary C. Jacobson, "Partisan Polarization in Presidential Support: The Electoral Connection," *Congress & the Presidency* 30, 1 (2003): 1–37.

30. Jacobson, "Partisan Polarization in Presidential Support," 2.

31. Pietro S. Nivola and David W. Brady, *Red and Blue Nation? Characteristics and Causes of America's Polarized Politics* (Stanford: Hoover Institution on War, Revolution and Peace, and Washington, DC: Brookings Institution Press, 2006), 1.

32. See, for example, Jacobson, "Partisan Polarization in Presidential Support"; Fiorina, Abrams, and Pope, *Culture War?*

33. Diana C. Mutz, "How the Mass Media Divide Us," in *Red and Blue Nation? Characteristics and Causes of America's Polarized Politics*, edited by Pietro S. Nivola and David W. Brady (Stanford: Hoover Institution on War, Revolution and Peace, and Washington, DC: Brookings Institution Press, 2006), 1: 227.

34. David A Jones, "The Polarizing Effect of New Media Messages," *International Journal of Public Opinion Research* 14, 2 (2002): 158–74; Natalie Jomini Stroud, "Media Effects, Selective Exposure, & *Fahrenheit 9/11*," *Political Communication* 24, 4 (2007): 415–32; Sunstein, *Republic.com*; Sunstein, *Republic.com 2.0*.

35. Robert Huckfeldt, Jeanette Morehouse Mendez, and Tracy Osborn, "Disagreement, Ambivalence, and Engagement: The Electoral Consequences of Heterogeneous Networks," *Political Psychology* 25, 1 (2004): 65–95.

36. Daniel J. Isenberg, "Group Polarization: A Critical Review and Meta-Analysis," *Journal of Personality and Social Psychology* 50, 6 (1986): 1141–51.

37. Ibid.

38. Steven H. Chaffee and Jack M. McLeod, "Individuals vs. Social Predictors of Information Seeking," *Journalism Quarterly* 50 (1973): 237–45.

39. Stefan Schulz-Hardt, Dieter Frey, Carsten Lüthgens, and Serge Moscovici, "Biased Information Search in Group Decision Making," *Journal of Personality and Social Psychology* 78 (2000): 655–69.

40. For evidence of polarization, see William C. Adams, Allison Salzman, William Vantine, Leslie Suelter, Anne Baker, Lucille Bonvouloir, Barbara Brenner, Margaret Ely, Jean Feldman, and Ron Ziegel, "The Power of 'The Right Stuff': A Quasi-Experimental Field Test of the Docudrama Hypothesis," *Public Opinion Quarterly* 49 (1985): 330–39; Bruce Bimber and Richard Davis, *Campaigning Online: The Internet in U.S. Elections* (New York: Oxford University Press, 2003); Jamie N. Druckman and Michael Parkin, "The Impact of Media Bias: How Editorial Slant Affects Voters," *Journal of Politics* 67 (2005): 1030–49; Jones, "The Polarizing Effect of New Media Messages"; Howard Lavine, Eugene Borgida, and John L. Sullivan, "On the Relationship Between Attitude Involvement and Attitude Accessibility: Toward a Cognitive-Motivational Model of Political Information Processing," *Political Psychology* 21 (2000): 81–106; Matthew Mendelsohn and Richard Nadeau, "The Magnification and Minimization of Social Cleavages by the Broadcast and Narrowcast News Media," *International Journal of Public Opinion Research* 8 (1996): 374–90; Stroud, "Media Effects, Selective Exposure, & *Fahrenheit 9/11*"; Charles S. Taber and Milton Lodge, "Motivated Skepticism in the Evaluation of Political Beliefs," *American Journal of Political Science* 50 (2006): 755–69. For exceptions, see Sandra J. Ball-Rokeach, Joel W. Grube, and Milton Rokeach, "'Roots: The Next Generation': Who Watched and With What Effect?" *Public Opinion Quarterly* 45, 1 (1981): 58–68; David L. Paletz, Judith Koon, Elizabeth Whitehead, and Richard B. Hagens, "Selective Exposure: The Potential Boomerang Effect," *Journal of Communication* 22, 1 (1972): 48–53. For questions about whether *likeminded* media exposure enhances polarization, see Michael F. Meffert, Sungeun Chung, Amber J. Joiner, Leah Waks, and Jennifer Garst, "The Effects of Negativity and Motivated Information Processing During a Political Campaign," *Journal of Communication* 56, 1 (2006): 27–51.

41. Adams, Salzman, Vantine, Suelter, Baker, Bonvouloir, Brenner, Ely, Feldman, and Ziegel, "The Power of 'The Right Stuff'"; Ball-Rokeach, Grube, and Rokeach, "'Roots: The Next Generation': Who Watched and With What Effect?"; Bimber and Davis, *Campaigning Online*; Lavine, Borgida, and Sullivan, "On the Relationship Between Attitude Involvement and Attitude Accessibility"; Paletz, Koon, Whitehead, and Hagens, "Selective Exposure: The Potential Boomerang Effect"; Stroud, "Media Effects, Selective Exposure, & *Fahrenheit 9/11*"; Taber and Lodge, "Motivated Skepticism in the Evaluation of Political Beliefs."

42. Ball-Rokeach, Grube, and Rokeach, "'Roots: The Next Generation': Who Watched and With What Effect?"

43. Paletz, Koon, Whitehead, and Hagens, "Selective Exposure: The Potential Boomerang Effect."

44. Adams, Salzman, Vantine, Suelter, Baker, Bonvouloir, Brenner, Ely, Feldman, and Ziegel, "The Power of 'The Right Stuff.'"

45. Stroud, "Media Effects, Selective Exposure, & *Fahrenheit 9/11*."

46. See, for example, Druckman and Parkin, "The Impact of Media Bias"; Jones, "The Polarizing Effect of New Media Messages"; Bimber and Davis, *Campaigning Online*.

47. See, for example, Lavine, Borgida, and Sullivan, "On the Relationship Between Attitude Involvement and Attitude Accessibility"; Mendelsohn and Nadeau, "The Magnification and Minimization of Social Cleavages."

48. See, for example, Fiorina, Abrams, and Pope, *Culture War?*; Mutz, "The Consequences of Cross-Cutting Networks"; Ryan K. Beasley and Mark J. Joslyn, "Cognitive Dissonance and Post-Decision Attitude Change in Six Presidential Elections," *Political Psychology* 22, 3 (2002): 521–40.

49. The interactions between ideology/partisanship and media use were in the expected direction for all media use variables and were significant in all instances but one—using liberal Internet.

50. Judson Mills and Abraham Ross, "Effects of Commitment and Certainty Upon Interest in Supporting Information," *Journal of Abnormal Psychology* 68, 5 (1964): 552.

51. Though certainty and confidence are treated separately in the empirical literature on selective exposure, they are related concepts. For example, in attitude research, certainty and confidence measurements are highly related and have been combined for analysis purposes. See, for example, Ida E. Berger and Andrew A. Mitchell, "The Effect of Advertising on Attitude Accessibility, Attitude Confidence, and the Attitude-Behavior Relationship," *Journal of Consumer Research* 16, 3 (1989): 269–79.

52. Festinger, *Conflict, Decision, and Dissonance.*

53. Dean A. Ziemke, "Selective Exposure in a Presidential Campaign Contingent on Certainty and Salience," in *Communication Yearbook,* edited by Dan Nimmo (New Brunswick, NJ: Transaction Books, 1980), 4: 497–511.

54. See, for example, Judson Mills, "The Effect of Certainty on Exposure to Information Prior to Commitment," *Journal of Experimental Social Psychology* 1 (1965): 348–55.

55. Mills, "The Effect of Certainty on Exposure to Information Prior to Commitment."

56. Stephen Thayer, "Confidence and Postjudgment Exposure to Consonant and Dissonant Information in a Free-Choice Situation," *Journal of Social Psychology* 77 (1969): 113–20.

57. See evidence in Lance Kirkpatrick Canon, "Self-Confidence and Selective Exposure to Information," in *Conflict, Decision, and Dissonance,* edited by Leon Festinger (Stanford: Stanford University Press, 1964): 83–95. See replications: Jonathan L. Freedman, "Confidence, Utility, and Selective Exposure: A Partial Replication," *Journal of Personality and Social Psychology* 2, 5 (1965): 778–80; Aaron Lowin, "Further Evidence for an Approach-Avoidance Interpretation for Selective Exposure," *Journal of Experimental Social Psychology* 5 (1969): 265–71; Charles B. Schultz, "The Effect of Confidence on Selective Exposure: An Unresolved Dilemma," *Journal of Social Psychology* 94 (1974): 65–9.

58. Mills and Ross, "Effects of Commitment and Certainty."

59. Note that the authors examine defense confidence, or one's "perceived defense ability." This seems quite related to confidence in one's attitude in general. See Dolores Albarracín and Amy L. Mitchell, "The Role of Defensive Confidence in Preference for Proattitudinal Information: How Believing That One Is Strong Can Sometimes Be a Defensive Weakness," *Personality and Social Psychology Bulletin* 30 (2004): 1566.

60. Ziemke, "Selective Exposure in a Presidential Campaign."

61. Ibid, 505, italics from original source. Note that the cases where Ziemke found no evidence of a relationship don't hamper the conclusion that certainty relates to selective exposure because it would have been challenging for citizens to selectively seek or avoid these media types. It would have been more challenging to find only likeminded news and advertising during the 1976 election.

62. Knobloch and Meng found that certain individuals select fewer counterattitudinal articles. Silvia Knobloch-Westerwick and Jingbo Meng, "Looking the Other Way: Selective Exposure to Attitude-Consistent and Counter-Attitudinal Political Information," *Communication Research* 36, 3 (2009): 426–48.

6

THE HEART OF THE ISSUE

Partisan Media and the Problems Facing the Nation

IN 1914, FRENCH, English, and German residents of an isolated island depended on an infrequent British mail steamer to deliver news from the mainland. When fighting broke out between the countries, it took six weeks for the island residents to hear the news. Imagine their surprise to learn that their actions—treating fellow islanders as friends—had been wholly inconsistent with the actions of their fellow countrymen. This was the example that Walter Lippmann used to open his book *Public Opinion.*[1] He lamented the media's ability to direct public attention. Media, he reasoned, are wholly incapable of enabling the public to carry out their duties as citizens in a democracy because the media cover only some issues while ignoring others.

Recasting this example in contemporary times, the situation surely would be different. Certainly the French and Germans wouldn't rely on reports from the "biased" British mail steamer. Perhaps a French CNN, a German Fox News, and a British MSNBC would deliver the news. And these three sources likely wouldn't have the same thing to say. Who started the fighting, the rationale for the fighting, the implications of the fighting—each nation's media might tell a very different story. And the picture of the world that formed in the heads of each nation's citizens might be quite different.

In a similar way, partisan media outlets may present different versions of the world in which we live. If partisan media outlets emphasize different issues, then audiences may develop different impressions of which issues are important. Liberal media outlets may leave audiences with different perceptions of the most important issues facing the country compared to conservative media outlets.

Lippmann's contemporary, philosopher John Dewey, wrote extensively about the features of civic life that promote a healthy democracy.[2] He argued that democracy functions best when citizens have common goals and interests. Yet the onslaught of partisan media may undercut the development of common goals. Without a shared issue agenda, how does a community, a state, or a nation allocate limited resources? Which issues should receive monetary support? Which issues should be tackled by the legislature first? Partisan selective exposure may stunt the ability of government officials to create policies that are responsive to the public's needs if the public increasingly makes competing demands. Further, the public may increasingly question the political legitimacy of public figures not sharing their issue priorities. Others echo this concern:

> The traditional mass media are in decline as audiences shift to more individualized media, and, partially as a result, the ability of leaders to hold large social systems together is also in decline because citizens are as likely to seek out messages from other individuals or groups who think like themselves as they are to remain committed to messages that represent the entire group.[3]

Given these possible dangers, it is important to examine the empirical evidence. This chapter evaluates the relationship between patterns of partisan selective exposure and the issues that are seen as most important. When people use partisan media, do they develop divergent impressions of which issues are important? Do various media outlets cover issues differently, thus leading the public to different conclusions about issue priorities? What is it about media coverage that could have this effect? These questions probe whether partisan media are fragmenting public opinion and jeopardizing the ability to achieve consensus. After providing some background on these questions, I turn to the evidence.

AGENDA SETTING

Agenda-setting research investigates the relationship between coverage of an issue in the media and the salience of the issue in the public.[4] As the media devote more attention to an issue, agenda setting proposes, the public should increasingly see the issue as important. Research on agenda setting provides extensive support for this idea: "The mass media influence the public agenda. This proposition…has been generally supported by evidence from most public agenda setting investigations, which cover a very wide range of agenda items, types of publics, and points in time."[5] Though the evidence is persuasive that the media set the public agenda, it is an open question whether liberal and conservative media set *different* agendas. If this is the case, partisan selective exposure may have a divisive effect.

Exploring both agenda setting and selectivity is not a new idea. In fact, the original agenda-setting article by Maxwell McCombs and Donald Shaw juxtaposed agenda setting and selective perception.[6] McCombs and Shaw reasoned that if selective perception occurs, people should be more likely to follow their preferred candidate's issue agenda as presented in the media as opposed to the media agenda across candidates. Selectivity would lead people to focus on their preferred candidate's issue agenda and adopt it as their own while ignoring the issue agendas of other candidates. To test this idea, McCombs and Shaw examined (1) the comprehensive issue agenda as presented in the media, irrespective of candidate, and (2) each candidate's individual issue agenda as presented by the media. They found that the voters' issue agendas were more strongly related to media coverage *in general,* as opposed to media coverage of their *preferred candidate.* Based on this, McCombs and Shaw concluded that the phenomenon they were describing was "better explained by the agenda-setting function of the mass media than by selective perception."[7]

Several caveats about this original finding are warranted, however. Recall that the results of this initial study were based on a sample of *undecided* voters. These individuals are less likely to have the strong partisan and political affiliations that inspire selectivity. Furthermore, McCombs and Shaw did not investigate the different partisan leanings of various media outlets. Partisan media outlets may cover issues differently and produce different effects. Though agenda setting was a better explanation than selective perception in the original agenda-setting study, partisan media may inspire divergent impressions of the most important issues facing the nation.

Agenda Setting and Partisan Media

With the explosion of niche news media, it is important to revisit traditional assumptions about agenda setting. Do the media transmit a *single* agenda that influences the public *at large*? Or might audiences form fragmented issue agendas based on different patterns of media use? The idea that the media's agenda-setting power differs in the contemporary media environment, McCombs argues, is based on two assumptions. The first assumption is that "audiences will fragment and avail themselves of vastly different media agendas."[8] Chapter 3 presented a good deal of evidence that media exposure patterns do vary based on partisanship. The second assumption is that "the redundancy across outlets that has characterized mass communication for many decades will be greatly reduced as niche media offer very different agendas."[9] As this second assumption demonstrates, agenda setting traditionally refers to the transmission of a *single* agenda from the media to the audience.

In their original article about agenda setting, McCombs and Shaw content analyzed popular newspapers, magazines, and television evening news broadcasts.[10] Each media outlet was treated as an imperfect indicator of the media's issue priorities. McCombs and Shaw noted, "The political world is reproduced imperfectly by individual news media."[11] Indeed, McCombs and Shaw did find that the amount of attention an issue received was similar across various news outlets. Many later investigations of agenda setting make this assumption. Rather than analyzing the content of multiple media outlets, researchers analyze the content of a few outlets and assume that other outlets' coverage is approximately the same. For example, in defending a content analysis of the *New York Times,* the authors of one study noted, "It was thought that *Times* coverage would be indicative of national media coverage."[12] Summarizing the research on agenda setting, communication scholars James Dearing and Everett Rogers stated that "at a given point, or over a certain period of time, different media place a similar salience on a set of issues" and that "in general, the media tend to agree in the number of, or the proportion of, news stories that they devote to a particular issue."[13]

Both theoretical work and the empirical techniques used in agenda-setting research have contributed to the notion that the media cover issues similarly. Theoretical work on what establishes the media's agenda suggests that the media transmit a relatively uniform agenda because of the uniformity with which journalists are trained. Characteristics of the journalistic industry, such as high mobility and the fact that journalists receive similar education, give rise to a "similarity of professional values."[14] If all journalists are trained similarly, then one should expect that journalists would cover similar issues and transmit similar agendas through the media. And if the media transmit a similar agenda, then irrespective of the outlet to which people attend, they should form similar impressions of which issues are most important. Though it may have been true at some point that the mainstream media all transmitted nearly identical information, media messages arguably are far more diverse today.

Part of the contention that the media transmit a homogeneous agenda to the public also may be due to the empirical techniques that have been used in this area of research. Many agenda-setting studies have been conducted using an aggregate level of analysis—the rank ordering of important issues covered in the media is correlated with the rank ordering of important issues named by the public. It is possible, however, that this aggregate level of analysis hides important distinctions between individuals; individual agendas may be influenced by the types of media used, for example.[15] And, important for this chapter, individual agendas may be influenced by patterns of partisan media use.

Although it typically is presumed that exposure to the news media in general will lead to the adoption of a similar set of issue priorities, it is clear that agenda setting occurs because people are exposed to specific media content. For example, social scientists Shanto Iyengar and Donald Kinder found that subjects in their experiments changed their opinions about the most important problems facing the nation based on exposure to media.[16] Their results offered resounding support for the agenda-setting potential of the media. Those viewing news media about defense issues found defense issues to be increasingly important. Those viewing news media about unemployment found unemployment to be increasingly important. And these effects happen outside of the laboratory. Political scientist Fay Lomax Cook and her colleagues conducted a creative study that also demonstrated that agenda-setting effects are due to exposure to specific content.[17] Cook and colleagues had insider knowledge that an investigative report on fraud and abuse in home health care was going to be aired on the news. They found that viewing the broadcast led to changes in the perceived importance of health care as a problem. In sum, exposure to specific content influences the judgments that people make about which issues are important. If two groups were exposed to different content, one would anticipate that the two groups would develop different impressions of which issues are the most important. So, if partisan media cover some issues more intensely than others, the public may develop fragmented issue agendas. To the extent that this does occur, the concept of agenda setting would gain new importance by helping us to understand how various outlets influence their audiences' issue agendas.

Partisan media outlets may be particularly powerful agenda-setting agents. This would be the case because trusted media produce stronger agenda-setting effects.[18] From chapter 2, it just so happens that people tend to trust *likeminded* information more.[19] And from chapter 3, people tend to select likeminded sources. And from chapter 4, people do not always discount information from likeminded sources because they do not perceive any bias. These trusted sources then are in a privileged position to influence public perceptions of important issues. Adding more weight to this argument, *knowledgeable* citizens who trust the media are particularly likely to display agenda-setting effects.[20] Given that knowledgeable citizens also are more likely to engage in partisan selective exposure (see chapter 4), the agenda-setting potential of partisan media seems quite pronounced.

Putting together the two propositions developed to this point, namely, (1) content differences lead to agenda-setting differences and (2) trustworthy media lead to stronger agenda-setting effects, partisan outlets may be better able to define the important issues for their audience. Which issues might partisan media outlets hype and which issues might they hide? Partisan outlets could set an agenda that takes advantage of their party's issue strengths. This is particularly worrisome—partisan media outlets would be able to fragment the public's agenda in such a way as to benefit preferred causes and candidates. Citizens, then, increasingly may view the political world differently depending on their political leanings.

ISSUE AGENDAS IN PRESIDENTIAL CAMPAIGNS

An ideal method for evaluating the relationship between a media outlet's issue agenda and the audience's issue agenda would be to content analyze each media outlet and compare the results to a measure of which issues the audience perceives as most important. Yet conducting a content analysis of thousands of newspapers, radio stations, cable news stations, and Internet Web sites is not possible. Based on the literature, however, there is a compelling and much more manageable proxy.

Agenda-setting researchers have investigated how issues are selected for media coverage—how is it determined which issues receive media attention and which do not? Without question, the president and presidential candidates are sources of the media's agenda.[21] When a president or presidential candidate emphasizes an issue, this can translate into media coverage of the issue, which, based on agenda setting, can lead to more public attention. Speeches and political advertising, for example, are ways in which candidates can highlight issues, generate press coverage, and attract public attention.[22]

Political parties and candidates do not give equal attention to all issues. The issues receiving priority are partially dependent on the party's and the candidate's issue strengths. Democratic presidential contenders tend to emphasize traditionally Democratic issues (e.g., civil liberties) and Republican presidential contenders tend to emphasize traditionally Republican issues (e.g., addressing big government).[23] To the extent that partisan media outlets preferentially cover the issue agendas of like-minded candidates, therefore, media audiences may develop different impressions of the most important issues facing the country.

So far, I have argued that presidential candidates can influence the media's agenda and that candidates offer distinct issue agendas. Understanding the presidential candidates' agendas, therefore, could provide insight into which issues may be emphasized by partisan media *outlets* and which issues partisan media *audiences* should see as most pressing. I probe this claim in three ways. First, I evaluate candidate issue agendas in order to develop hypotheses about which issues partisan outlets will emphasize. I suspect that partisan outlets will hype the issue agendas of likeminded candidates. Second, I examine whether partisan media audiences are especially likely to adopt the candidates' issue priorities. If I am correct, those using liberal media should be more likely to adopt the issue priorities of Democratic candidates and those using conservative media should tend to adopt the issue priorities of Republican candidates. Third, I explicitly evaluate the claim that partisan outlets preferentially cover the issue agendas of likeminded candidates. I look at a subset of media content to evaluate whether partisan media actually do convey different issue priorities to the public.

In 2004, two of the most frequently discussed problems facing the nation were terrorism and Iraq. As it was the first presidential election after the terrorist attacks on September 11, 2001, citizens were concerned about the implications of the presidential election for homeland security. And since military action in Iraq had begun in 2003, President Bush's administration faced increasing scrutiny about the country's foreign policy actions. These issues were a central part of the campaigns of both presidential candidates. Yet there were important differences in how each campaign discussed these issues. The Bush campaign and the Republican Party emphasized the war on terror and de-emphasized Iraq by conceiving of military action in Iraq as a part of the larger war on terror. For example, in the Republican Party platform, the first, and longest, section of the platform was entitled, "Winning the war on terror." Iraq was discussed within this broader category. In contrast, the Democratic Party platform discussed Iraq as distinct from the war on terror; in one location, the platform reads, "this Administration badly exaggerated its case, particularly with respect to weapons of mass destruction and the connection between Saddam's government and al Qaeda."[24]

To establish that these issue priorities were apparent throughout the 2004 campaign, I analyzed campaign rhetoric from the two main party candidates, George W. Bush and John Kerry, to investigate the candidates' agendas during the 2004 presidential election. I used several sources to establish the candidates' agendas. First, the party platforms and candidate convention speeches were gathered and analyzed. Second, Kerry and Bush advertisements gathered by the Campaign Media Analysis Group were reviewed.[25] Third, candidate speeches made during the last week of the 2004 election campaign were analyzed. Use of these multiple sources representing different points during the campaign allowed for an investigation of the consistency and development of the candidates' agendas over time. For each of these sources, a team of coders and I evaluated the number of mentions of Iraq or terrorism. More details about the coding procedure are available in the technical appendix. The results of our examination are shown in Table 6.1.

Across all campaign components, the candidates placed at least some emphasis on each of the two main issues under investigation. Yet there are notable differences between the Bush and Kerry campaigns in terms of their relative emphases on Iraq and terrorism. Across all of the campaign rhetoric measures, the Bush campaign emphasized terrorism more than Iraq. Similarly, terrorism received more emphasis than Iraq in the Democratic platform. In Kerry's convention speech and in the Kerry

TABLE 6.1

Issue Emphasis in Campaign Rhetoric

	Party Platforms (% of total sentences)	Candidate Convention Speeches (% of total sentences)	Candidate Ads (% of total ads)	Candidate Speeches, Last Week of Campaign (% of total sentences)
Bush/Republican				
Iraq	4%	12%	6%	7%
Terrorism	11%	16%	39%	12%
Total	1,866	295	67	9,559
Kerry/Democrat				
Iraq	7%	5%	15%	26%
Terrorism	15%	5%	15%	22%
Total	957	309	156	523

Data from content analysis of campaign rhetoric. More details can be found in the technical appendix for this chapter.

advertising, however, Iraq and terrorism received similar amounts of attention. In the final week of the campaign, Kerry emphasized Iraq more than terrorism in his campaign speeches.

A content analysis of campaign direct mail provides further evidence for these issue emphases. Analyzing over 19,000 pieces of direct mail from the 2004 presidential campaign, political scientists D. Sunshine Hillygus and Todd Shields reported that 21 percent of Bush direct mail discussed terrorism, while 10 percent discussed Iraq.[26] For Kerry, 23 percent of his campaign's direct mail discussed Iraq, while only 13 percent discussed terrorism. In general, the Kerry campaign placed more emphasis on Iraq, while the Bush campaign placed more emphasis on terrorism.

Assuming that partisan outlets are more sympathetic toward likeminded candidates in their coverage of issues (a proposition I will evaluate explicitly later in this chapter), these observations allow for predictions about the relationship between partisan media use and issues named as the most important. Specifically, I anticipated that conservatives and Republicans using conservative media would be less likely to name Iraq as the most important problem facing the country and would be more likely to name terrorism. Further, liberals and Democrats using liberal media would be more likely to name Iraq as the most important problem facing the country and less likely to name terrorism. I explore the relationship between partisan media use and agenda setting in the next section.

MOST IMPORTANT PROBLEMS

To analyze differences in the most important problems named by respondents, I turned to the National Annenberg Election Surveys (NAES). To capture individual impressions of issue importance, respondents were asked, "In your opinion, what is the most important problem facing our country today?" Respondents were permitted to give any response to this open-ended question. Responses were sorted into categories. In total, 19 percent of respondents named terrorism or national security and 20 percent of respondents named Iraq as the most important problem facing the country.

But does the use of partisan media influence whether audiences thought that Iraq or terrorism was the most important problem facing the nation? Those using conservative radio, conservative Web sites, or Fox News were less likely to name Iraq as an important issue compared to others. Those using CNN or MSNBC were more likely to name Iraq as an important issue compared to others. Though not significant, those using newspapers endorsing Kerry also followed this pattern.

For terrorism, all of the media types were related to naming terrorism in the expected way and five of eight were significant. Those using conservative media outlets were more likely to name terrorism as an important problem, and those using liberal media outlets were less likely compared to other respondents. I summarize these results using the indices in Figures 6.1 and 6.2.

As shown in Figures 6.1 and 6.2, partisans' assessments of important issues followed the rhetoric of the presidential candidates. Conservatives and Republicans, coinciding with the Bush campaign, were more likely to report that terrorism was the most important problem facing the nation. To a somewhat lesser degree, though still in the expected direction, liberals and Democrats followed the Kerry campaign and tended to report that Iraq was the most important problem facing the nation.

Partisan media use also was related to which issue was reported as the most important. Conservative media use, in particular, corresponded with different impressions of the most important issues. Those using conservative media were slightly less likely to name Iraq as the most important problem. They were notably more likely than others to name terrorism as the most important problem. Partisan media appear to affect perceptions of important issues. When partisans consume likeminded media,

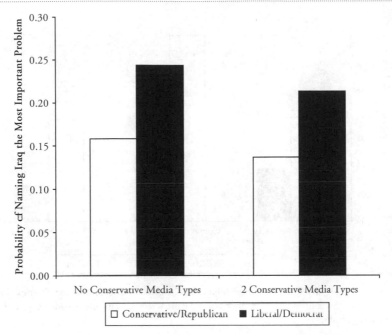

FIGURE 6.1 Naming Iraq the Most Important Problem by Media Use and Political Leanings. Results based on a logistic regression analysis predicting naming Iraq as the most important problem. Analysis controls for demographics, political orientations, and patterns of media use. The main effects of conservative media and ideology/partisanship are significant. Ideology/partisanship values are calculated using one standard deviation from the mean value. More details can be found in the technical appendix for this chapter. *Source*: Data from the 2004 NAES RCS.

the effects are stronger in some instances. Conservative Republicans using conservative media were particularly likely to report that terrorism was the most important problem facing the nation.

These results document that patterns of partisan media use are related to the issues believed to be most important. What is unclear is whether exposure to partisan media *precedes* naming an issue as the most important. Perhaps conservative Republicans viewing conservative media outlets already believe that terrorism is the most important problem and their patterns of media exposure do not influence their perceptions. In fact, their belief that this issue is important may make conservative outlets more attractive to them. I turned to an examination of panel data to evaluate whether the use of partisan media helps to predict which issues people name as most important at a later point in time.

For naming Iraq the most important issue, the expected relationship emerges in only one instance. Those viewing more conservative media outlets before the Republican National Convention (RNC) were less likely to name Iraq as the most important problem after the RNC. Participants naming Iraq as most important

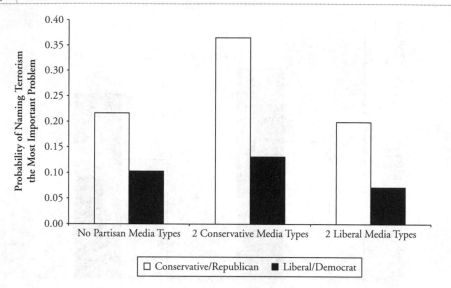

FIGURE 6.2. Naming Terrorism the Most Important Problem by Media Use and Political Leanings. Analysis details are the same as those described below Figure 6.1. The media use and ideology/partisanship interaction is significant.

before the RNC named Iraq as most important again after the RNC with a probability of 0.43 if they didn't use any conservative media types. If they used two conservative media types, they named Iraq again in the postwave with only a 0.10 probability, holding all else constant. The other panel analyses provide little evidence that partisan selective exposure influences whether people name Iraq as the most important problem.[27]

Evidence of a relationship between partisan media use and naming terrorism as the most important problem is stronger. Conservative Republicans using conservative media before the Democratic National Convention (DNC), for example, were more likely than other respondents to name terrorism as the most important problem after the DNC.[28] Those using liberal media before the RNC were less likely to name terrorism as an important issue after the RNC. Over the course of the campaign season, those using liberal media were *less* likely than other respondents to name terrorism as the most important problem, and those using conservative media were *more* likely than other respondents to name terrorism as the most important problem. The effect of media use was not influenced by the respondents' political leanings. For example, those using no liberal media who named terrorism as the most important issue facing the nation before the general election named terrorism again after the election with a probability of 0.51. Those using two liberal outlets, however, named terrorism again with a probability of 0.38. Overall, the use of conservative media prompted respondents to name terrorism at higher rates and the use of liberal media prompted respondents to name terrorism at lower rates than if they used other media sources.[29]

To this point, we know that partisan selective exposure is related to perceptions of issue importance. The analysis revealed that the use of liberal media was related to naming Iraq as the most important problem and the use of conservative media was related to naming terrorism as the most important problem. Some evidence also supports the idea that conservative Republicans using conservative media were particularly likely to name terrorism as the most important issue facing the nation. The panel data provide evidence that the use of partisan media leads to impressions of the most important issues, consistent with what agenda setting would predict.

Yet the manner in which the partisan media agenda was determined was admittedly indirect. A content analysis of each outlet was not conducted in order to establish its issue agenda. Instead, it was presumed that the candidate agendas were a good proxy for the agendas of liberal and conservative media outlets. Though there is a strong rationale for making this assumption, a content analysis could help to verify it. To what degree is there support for this idea?

Some evidence suggests that there are similarities between how left-leaning and right-leaning media outlets present issue agendas.[30] Political scientist Russell Dalton and his colleagues, for example, found few differences between the issue focus of newspapers endorsing Bill Clinton and the issue focus of newspapers endorsing George H. W. Bush.[31] If issue agendas are consistent across various outlets, it would be challenging to argue that media *content* is responsible for the aforementioned findings.

Yet other evidence suggests that left-leaning and right-leaning media outlets present issue agendas differently.[32] One example of research in this area is a historical analysis of Franklin Roosevelt's ability to obtain preferential media coverage for his pet issues conducted by communication scholar Tom Johnson and his colleagues.[33] It turns out that Roosevelt was more effective in obtaining coverage of his issue agenda in likeminded newspapers than in more critical newspapers. In the same way, modern candidates and political parties might be able to transmit their issue agenda more effectively through likeminded media outlets.

What are we to make of these apparently conflicting findings? Are there few differences in the issue priorities of partisan media outlets or significant differences? One difference between these studies seems particularly instructive. In the Clinton and Bush analysis, the issues under investigation were far less nuanced than the issues under investigation in the Roosevelt analysis. When examining the differences between newspapers endorsing Clinton and newspapers endorsing Bush, the issues under investigation included economic issues, budget and finance, and foreign policy. In the Roosevelt analysis, however, the issues included justification of New Deal policies, success of the National Industrial Recovery Act, and success of the Economy Act. In the Roosevelt analysis, issues are not only more specific but also have a valence (e.g., *success* of the National Industrial Recovery Act versus the economy). It may be that partisan media convey issue priorities to the public not by covering some issues *more* than others, but instead by the *manner* in which they describe various issues.

This discussion coincides with what various theories have to say about how the media influence the public agenda. First-level agenda setting presumes that the more frequently an issue is covered, the more the public will name the issue as most important. Instead of differences in *how often* issues are covered, it is possible that differences in *how* issues are covered explain the findings. For example, although Kerry placed more emphasis on Iraq than Bush, the candidates also spoke about Iraq differently. Bush, for example, highlighted the improvements in Iraq ("There will be presidential elections in Iraq in January. Think how far that country has come from the days of torture chambers and mass graves. Freedom is on the march, and we're more secure for it"). Kerry, on the other hand, frequently criticized the situation in Iraq ("[Bush] failed to secure Iraq and keep it from becoming what it is today—a haven for terrorists"). Studies on framing and second-level agenda setting suggest that differences in *how* an issue is presented can influence perceptions of an issue.[34] Two possibilities, therefore, could explain why the public reaches different conclusions about important issues based on their use of partisan media: There could be differences in *how frequently* outlets discuss Iraq and terrorism (first-level agenda setting) or in *how* they discuss Iraq and terrorism (second-level agenda setting or framing).

Media Coverage of Iraq and Terrorism

To examine whether differences in media content can explain different perceptions of the most important issues facing the country, a content analysis was conducted. Articles from four newspapers that endorsed Kerry in 2004 (the *New York Times, Washington Post, San Francisco Chronicle,* and *Boston Globe*) and four newspapers that endorsed Bush in 2004 (*Chicago Tribune, New York Daily News, New York Post,* and *Houston Chronicle*) from the week before the 2004 election were analyzed. Broadcast transcripts for Fox News and CNN also were coded. Kristin Stimpson, a team of coders, and I evaluated the content of the articles and transcripts. One important feature of our analysis is that all transcripts and articles were completely blinded before they were coded. Any mention of hosts, stations, programs, locations—anything that could allow a coder to identify the source of an article or transcript—was removed. Coders' perceptions about the outlets, therefore, could not influence their coding decisions. We first looked at whether the articles and transcripts mentioned Iraq or terrorism to investigate a first-level agenda-setting explanation.

A first-level agenda-setting explanation would mean that CNN and Kerry-endorsing newspapers should cover Iraq more than terrorism and that Fox News and Bush-endorsing newspapers should cover terrorism more than Iraq. This is not the case, however. CNN, Fox News, Kerry-endorsing newspapers, and Bush-endorsing newspapers all covered Iraq more than terrorism. It is noteworthy, however, that the ratio of Iraq coverage to terrorism coverage was higher for CNN and Kerry-endorsing newspapers compared to Fox News and Bush-endorsing newspapers. For each terrorism story, there were 2.25 Iraq stories on CNN and 2.29 Iraq stories in Kerry-endorsing newspapers. In contrast, Fox News aired 1.47 Iraq stories for every one terrorism story and Bush-endorsing newspapers printed 1.61 Iraq stories for every one terrorism story. This provides modest support for the idea that partisan media sources may set different agendas by covering issues with different intensities.

To evaluate whether the articles discussed these issues differently, we looked for the presence or absence of claims about Iraq and terrorism. For each claim, it was possible to compare (1) coverage in newspapers endorsing Kerry, (2) coverage in newspapers endorsing Bush, (3) coverage on CNN, and (4) coverage on Fox News. The results of this analysis allow me to look at *relative* differences in how the issues were covered.[35] If coverage in Kerry-endorsing newspapers and on CNN tends to support the conclusion that Iraq is a more important issue than terrorism and coverage in Bush-endorsing newspapers and on Fox News tends to support the conclusion that terrorism is a more important issue than Iraq, then I am on to something. Specifically, if these differences are apparent, then I have a stronger case that partisan media use leads people to reach different conclusions about the most important issues facing the nation.

The coders and I examined claims that could lead viewers and readers to conclude that Iraq or terrorism were important problems. For example, we analyzed the frequency of claims that Iraq *was* a part of the war on terror and claims that Iraq *was not* part of the war on terror. Believing that Iraq was part of the war on terror leads to the conclusion that the war on terror—and not Iraq—should be given more weight as the most important problem. The frequency with which various claims appeared in the media outlets are shown in Table 6.2.

TABLE 6.2

Content Analysis of Newspaper and Cable Coverage of Iraq and the War on Terrorism Percent of articles / transcripts analyzed

	Cable		Newspaper	
	CNN	Fox News	Kerry-endorsing	Bush-endorsing
Leads to inference that Iraq *is* a problem				
Iraqi civilian casualties	28%	5%	8%	16%
US civilian casualties in Iraq	2%	0%	3%	1%
US military casualties in Iraq	37%	9%	19%	17%
Iraq damaged US int'l relationships	17%	5%	6%	4%
War in Iraq increased danger	19%	9%	12%	3%
Leads to inference that Iraq *is not an integral part of* the war on terrorism				
No links between Iraq and terror	6%	9%	4%	2%
Iraq diverted from war on terror	42%	33%	13%	6%

Iraq increased threat of terrorism	21%	0%	6%	0%
Leads to inference that Iraq *was* a problem / is *no longer* a problem				
Iraq *was* a threat to the US	7%	23%	3%	2%
Diplomacy *was not* working	4%	14%	1%	1%
Saddam *was* a brutal dictator	0%	9%	3%	6%
Leads to inference that Iraq *is an integral part of* the war on terrorism				
Iraq success helps in war on terror	4%	7%	1%	0%
Iraq linked to war on terror	17%	7%	4%	2%
Iraq *was* a safe haven for terrorists	2%	5%	1%	2%

Data from content analysis of media coverage of Iraq and terrorism. More details can be found in the technical appendix for this chapter.

A framing, or second-level agenda-setting, explanation of the relationship between partisan media use and the issues seen as important holds that when issues are covered differently, people form different impressions of the issues. The evidence does suggest that various outlets covered these issues differently. I roughly organized the various claims that were coded into four different inferences. The first two inferences support a liberal perspective: Iraq is a problem and Iraq is separate from the war on terrorism. Almost always, CNN and newspapers endorsing Kerry mentioned these claims more frequently than Fox News and newspapers endorsing Bush. The second two inferences support a conservative perspective: Iraq was a problem in the past and Iraq is an integral part of the war on terrorism. Though weaker, the expected pattern appears. Fox News in particular was more likely to make these claims compared to CNN. These claims were less consistently made in Bush- and Kerry-endorsing newspapers.[36]

Most important here, newspaper and cable news coverage of Iraq and terrorism can help to explain why partisan media use influences perceptions of the most important issues facing the nation. Those using newspapers endorsing Kerry and CNN would have heard more frequently that Iraq was a problem distinct from the war on terrorism. Those using newspapers endorsing Bush and Fox News would have heard that the Iraq War was helping to address problems in Iraq and that Iraq was part of the larger war on terrorism. Hearing these messages could have led partisan media audiences—irrespective of their political leanings—to reach different conclusions about how important these issues were to the nation.

Yet we have some evidence that conservatives using conservative media were particularly likely to name terrorism as the most important problem. Why would this happen? Why conservatives? Why terrorism? There are at least two possibilities. First, terrorism may be a particularly potent issue for conservatives—media coverage of this issue may be particularly likely to have an agenda-setting influence. And since conservative media seem to have emphasized this issue, conservatives using conservative media may be especially likely to see terrorism as important. Psychologist John Jost and colleagues found that "fear and threat are...related to political conservatism."[37] Perhaps conservatives and Republicans are likely to name terrorism as the most important issue because media messages about terrorism comport well with being sensitive to fear and threat. This confluence of individual predisposition, campaign strategy, and partisan media coverage may be powerful in creating terrorism agenda-setting effects.

Second, another feature of the coverage may have inspired conservative Republicans to name terrorism as the most important problem. We know that Republicans typically are considered to be strong on defense-related issues.[38] And, as I discuss in more detail in the next section, media coverage in 2004 repeatedly highlighted Republican ownership of the terrorism issue.

The Influence of Claims of Issue Ownership

In examining the media content, the coders and I kept running across a particularly intriguing claim. Here are some examples:

- "But a continuing problem for [Kerry], at least according to the latest polls, he has not narrowed the nearly 20 point gap between himself and the president when voters are asked who would do a better job handling terrorism." (CNN, October 30, 2004)
- "In all the polls, virtually all the polls, when the American public is asked who do you think can do a better job in the war on terror, Bush scores better than Kerry, as you will concede." (CNN, October 29, 2004)
- "In all—in every poll out, Bush leads big in terror effectiveness." (Fox News, October 29, 2004)
- "Bush leads in the polls on terrorism. That's Bush's strong suit. Everyone knows that." (Fox News, October 29, 2004)
- "But the fact of the matter is, is that our poll, and consistently this is the case, shows that on the issue of terrorism, Bush leads by a mile. I mean our latest poll at 61 to 28 that Bush leads on the issue of terrorism." (Fox News, October 29, 2004)
- "The polls show that the American people think President Bush will do a better job in the war on terror than John Kerry." (*New York Post*, November 1, 2004)
- "[Bin Laden's tape] also refocused the nation on terrorism, which polls show helps Bush." (*New York Daily News*, October 30, 2004)
- "Last March, Americans preferred Bush over Kerry in fighting terrorism by 60 percent to 33 percent, according to the Gallup Poll. Now, after a furious campaign and months of criticism, that number is unchanged. Bush is untouched on this issue." (*New York Times*, October 30, 2004)
- "Bush wants the focus on national security, calculating that if voters cast ballots based on who will keep them safest, he's more likely to win." (*Boston Globe*, October 31, 2004)

Over and over again, the media let the public know that *terrorism* was Bush's signature issue. The coders and I didn't find the same thing with respect to Iraq, however. In fact, we found conflicting claims about which candidate was seen as better on Iraq. We wondered if statements about issue ownership might provide some insight into our findings. After all, beliefs that terrorism was an important issue were more consistently related to partisan media use than beliefs that Iraq was an important issue. And conservative Republicans using conservative media were particularly likely to nominate terrorism as an important problem. Perhaps these types of claims influenced conservatives in particular to name terrorism as an important issue facing the nation.

These types of statements were not unique to the 2004 presidential election. A similar thing happened in 2008. Media coverage informed the public that Democratic nominee Obama was a leader on domestic issues and that Republican nominee McCain was a leader on national security and foreign policy issues. Here are some examples.

Obama on domestic issues:

- "The poll found Obama was seen as a better steward of the economy than McCain, leading 48 percent to 39 percent." (Reuters, May 21, 2008)
- "In a recent Pew Research Center poll, 51 percent of voters said they saw [Obama] as best able to improve the economy, compared with 36 percent for McCain." (*Christian Science Monitor,* June 10, 2008)
- "Barack Obama has a slight edge over presidential rival John McCain on the economy, according to a poll of registered voters released Thursday." (CNN, June 12, 2008)
- "Obama would be better at dealing with healthcare, 54% to 25%." (*Los Angeles Times,* September 25, 2008)
- "Obama continues to hold an edge over McCain on many domestic policy areas." (*Washington Post,* July 16, 2008)

McCain on national security and foreign policy issues:

- "The dust-up played out on the trail as Rasmussen Reports released a new national poll showing more voters trust Mr. McCain than Mr. Obama on national security and Iraq. The poll of 1,200 likely Republican, Democrat and independent voters showed the Arizona senator leading Mr. Obama on trust in national security 55–30, and had Mr. McCain on top as more trustworthy on Iraq 49 to 39 for Mr. Obama." (*Washington Times,* February 27, 2008)
- "Polls show that Mr. McCain has an advantage over Mr. Obama on the questions of who has the most experience and who would be the most effective in dealing with terrorism." (*New York Times,* June 3, 2008)
- "Polls show that voters favor Obama's positions over McCain's on the economy, health care and other domestic issues but that they view McCain as the stronger candidate for combating terrorism." (*Washington Post,* June 8, 2008)
- "Our latest FOX poll shows that a majority trusts McCain over Obama on the issue of Iraq and terrorism." (Fox News, July 1, 2008)

These statements were a feature of campaign media coverage—reports that McCain polled better on foreign affairs and Obama polled better on domestic issues could be found throughout media coverage of the election. Could these statements help to explain why partisan selective exposure leads to different impressions of the most important issues?

I suspected that these statements also might hold an important key to understanding partisan selective exposure more broadly. To explain why, let me pause for a moment to take stock of what has been uncovered to this point. Chapter 3 revealed that partisanship consistently motivates exposure. We know from chapter 4 that those who engage in partisan selective exposure are politically knowledgeable and interested. These individuals use partisan cues when thinking about the news, much like they organize other political information based on partisanship. The inclination to use partisan cues also may explain the relationships between likeminded news media use, participation, and polarization as discovered in chapter 5. The same citizens who are attuned to which media sources are appropriate for their partisan inclinations may be attuned to polarizing information—they may be particularly effective at recognizing claims from the media that then strengthen their favorable or unfavorable impressions of political candidates. Those using likeminded media also may act on information about opportunities for partisan participation in much the same way that they already acted based on partisan cues when deciding which media outlet to use.

Many findings to this point, therefore, could be due to the same underlying cause: Some citizens are excellent at picking up on partisan cues. They are experts at detecting cues in line with their partisanship. They pick up on cues about hostile media bias. They pick up on cues about opportunities for political participation. They pick up on cues about favored and disliked political candidates. They use their political knowledge and interest to organize their attitudes, beliefs, and behaviors into partisan categories. If this is true, then it would be expected that these same partisans also would be more likely to pick up on partisan cues about important issues from the media. Statements about which candidate can handle an issue better would instruct these partisans about the issues that they *should* say when asked about the most important issues facing the nation.

To find out if I was on to something, I conducted an experiment to see if statements about which candidate is better equipped to handle an issue affected the issues people found to be most important. In my Knowledge Networks study, respondents read a newspaper article about where McCain and Obama stood with respect to the economy and foreign policy. For a random half of participants, I included a paragraph in the newspaper article reminding voters that polls showed that voters preferred Obama on the economy and McCain on national security and

foreign policy. With the exception of that paragraph, the rest of the article was identical and described the candidates' positions on these issues.

I wanted to know if including a paragraph about the candidates' issue strengths
would influence which issues respondents considered most important. After reading
the article, respondents clicked to another Web page and were asked a number of
questions about the article content. Respondents then clicked to a subsequent Web
page where they were told that the researcher was interested in obtaining some additional information about the people participating in this study. Only then were they
asked to name the most important issues facing the nation. I analyzed whether the
presence of the paragraph describing the candidates' issue strengths influenced people's impressions of these important problems.

The results for mentions of domestic issues as most important only partially confirm my expectations. Liberal Democrats *were* more likely than conservative
Republicans to mention the domestic issues as most important. Yet the paragraph of
candidate strengths stating that polls showed Obama as better able to handle
domestic affairs didn't affect whether people mentioned domestic affairs as most
important. Overall, around three-fourths of respondents named domestic issues as
the most important problem. Considering that the economy was on the verge of a
dramatic downturn when this study was conducted, it may not have been possible to
sway people's impressions of the importance of these issues.

For mentions of foreign policy, however, there was evidence that the paragraph of
candidate issue strengths influenced the issues that people named as most important. The results are shown in Figure 6.3.

The results shown in Figure 6.3 are in line with my expectations. When conservative Republicans are told that foreign policy is McCain's strong suit, they are more
likely to name foreign policy issues as the most important issues facing the nation. Yet
when liberal Democrats are told that foreign policy issues are McCain's strength, they
mention foreign policy less frequently. The differences are not particularly large, but
they do appear after exposure to a single paragraph embedded in an article.

If it is true that some people are simply more sensitive to partisan cues that comport with their partisan identity, then those individuals who tend to see hostile partisan biases in the media should be particularly likely to name important issues that
correspond with their political predispositions. Those with a propensity to see liberal
biases in the media also should respond to the cue that foreign policy was an issue
strength for the Republican candidate. I therefore examine whether those perceiving
many liberal-biased outlets also tend to name foreign policy as most important. In
Figure 6.4, I evaluate whether people who report that CNN, MSNBC, the *New
York Times,* and National Public Radio (NPR) are liberally biased are even more
responsive to the paragraph about candidate strengths.

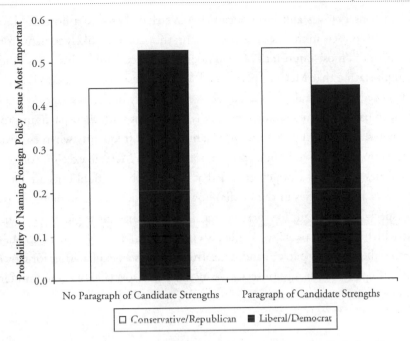

FIGURE 6.3 Probability of Naming Foreign Policy as Most Important by Political Beliefs and Paragraph of Candidate Strengths. Results based on a logistic regression analysis predicting naming foreign policy most important. The interaction between ideology/partisanship and the paragraph of candidate strengths is marginally significant. After controlling for perceptions of media bias (Figure 6.4), the result is significant. Ideology/partisanship values are calculated using one standard deviation from the mean value. More details can be found in the technical appendix for this chapter.

Source: Data from the 2008 Knowledge Networks Study.

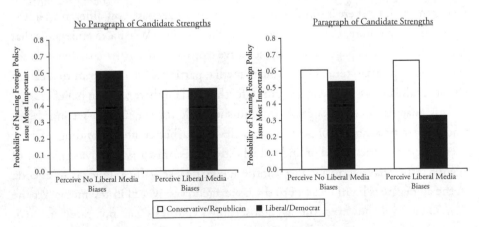

FIGURE 6.4 Probability of Naming Foreign Policy as Most Important by Political Beliefs and Perceptions of Liberal Biases in the Media. Analysis details are the same as those described below Figure 6.3. Perceptions of liberal bias are calculated using one standard deviation from the mean value. Interactions between perceptions of liberal bias and ideology/partisanship are significant. More details are available in the technical appendix.

When conservatives and Republicans believe that there are a host of liberally-biased media outlets in the media environment, they are more likely to name foreign policy issues as most important. This tendency is exacerbated when they read the paragraph stating that McCain performed well on these issues. Liberal Democrats who believed that several of these outlets were liberally biased respond to the issue ownership paragraph in a manner decidedly consistent with their partisan proclivities. They name foreign policy an important issue less frequently when confronted with the information that public opinion polls showed McCain excelling on foreign policy issues. We know from chapter 4 that conservative Republicans are far more likely to see liberal biases in the media, however, making the aforementioned patterns especially important for these citizens. It seems that those picking up on cues about which media outlets are hostile also pick up on cues about which issues are better handled by their party's candidate. This provides an explanation for why conservative Republicans using conservative media were especially likely to find terrorism an important issue in 2004.

Summary

This chapter documents that partisan media use is related to different perceptions of the most important issues facing the nation. This arguably represents an important change in the agenda-setting function of the mass media. In a fragmented media system characterized by many diverse sources of news and information, different media audiences can develop divergent impressions of the most important problems facing the nation. There is some evidence that this occurs based on differences in the issue emphases and reporting in partisan media coverage. What also emerges is that those people who engage in partisan selective exposure are particularly likely to see the world in partisan terms—to evaluate media, participation opportunities, claims about candidates, issue strengths, and so forth based on their partisan beliefs.

This analysis does not suggest a diminished role for the agenda-setting thesis. Rather, it represents an opportunity to develop a better understanding of how agenda setting varies based on individual differences. Historically, investigations of agenda setting have performed well at the aggregate level—the public's issue agenda in the aggregate is highly related to the issue agenda conveyed in the media. At the individual level, however, the agenda-setting hypothesis has not fared as well; researchers have encountered difficulty in predicting individual-level issue agendas. By looking specifically at individual patterns of consumption and whether individuals process incoming information in partisan terms, we are better able to predict individual-level issue agendas.

Given the presence of partisan media outlets and a documented propensity for people to prefer news media expressing beliefs that match their partisan inclinations, this chapter proposes that patterns of partisan selective exposure may further divide people into different publics by encouraging partisans to adopt different issue priorities based on candidate strengths. The fragmentation of issue agendas has arguable consequences not only in terms of social cohesion but also in terms of the development of public opinion and beliefs of political legitimacy. Although the fragmentation of audiences and media content is incomplete, trends of partisan selectivity and differences in perceptions of important issues can make finding common ground more challenging.

Returning to the modernized version of Lippmann's example from the beginning of this chapter, it may be that the French CNN, the German Fox News, and the British MSNBC would have provided different coverage. They may have led audiences to see different aspects of the conflict between the nations. And the fact that a French CNN, a German Fox News, and a British MSNBC even exist may lead some to reason that since the *media* is divided by country, *information* must be divided by country. And processing information based on national identity may follow easily from consuming media based on national identity. Each nation's citizens may be attuned to information that supports their nation's role in the conflict. They may be quick to latch on to aspects of the conflict that support their nation's righteous cause. And the pictures that form in the minds of each nation's citizens may rip the social fabric of the isolated island.

NOTES

1. Walter Lippmann, *Public Opinion* (New York: Free Press, 1922/1997).

2. John Dewey, *Democracy and Education* (Carbondale: Southern Illinois University Press, 1916/1985); John Dewey, *The Public and Its Problems* (Chicago: Swallow Press, 1927).

3. Donald L. Shaw and Bradley J. Hamm, "Agendas for a Public Union or for Private Communities? How Individuals Are Using Media to Reshape American Society," in *Communication and Democracy: Exploring the Intellectual Frontiers in Agenda-Setting Theory,* edited by Maxwell E. McCombs, Donald L. Shaw, and David H. Weaver (Mahwah, NJ: Lawrence Erlbaum Associates, 1997): 210.

4. Maxwell E. McCombs and Donald L. Shaw, "The Agenda-Setting Function of Mass Media," *Public Opinion Quarterly* 36, 2 (1972): 176–87.

5. Everett M. Rogers and James W. Dearing, "Agenda-Setting Research: Where Has It Been, Where Is It Going?" in *Communication Yearbook,* edited by James A. Anderson (Newbury Park, CA: Sage, 1988), 11: 579; see also Wayne Wanta and Salma Ghanem, "Effects of Agenda Setting," in *Mass Media Effects Research: Advances through Meta-Analysis,* edited by Raymond W. Preiss, Barbara Mae Gayle, Nancy Burrell, Mike Allen, and Jennings Bryant (Mahwah, NJ: Lawrence Erlbaum Associates, 2007).

6. McCombs and Shaw, "The Agenda-Setting Function of Mass Media."

7. Ibid, 182.

8. Maxwell McCombs, *Setting the Agenda: The Mass Media and Public Opinion* (Cambridge: Polity Press, 2004): 147.

9. Ibid.

10. McCombs and Shaw, "The Agenda-Setting Function of Mass Media."

11. Ibid, 184.

12. James P. Winter and Chaim H. Eyal, "Agenda-Setting for the Civil Rights Issue," *Public Opinion Quarterly* 45, 3 (1981): 379.

13. James W. Dearing and Everett M. Rogers, *Agenda-Setting* (Thousand Oaks, CA: Sage, 1996): 90, italics removed.

14. Ibid, 35.

15. Ibid.

16. Shanto Iyengar and Donald R. Kinder, *News That Matters* (Chicago: University of Chicago Press, 1987).

17. Fay Lomax Cook, Tom R. Tyler, Edward G. Goetz, Margaret T. Gordon, David Protess, Donna R. Leff, and Harvey L. Molotch, "Media and Agenda Setting: Effects on the Public, Interest Group Leaders, Policy Makers, and Policy," *Public Opinion Quarterly* 47, 1 (1983): 16–35.

18. Shanto Iyengar, "New Directions of Agenda-Setting Research," in *Communication Yearbook,* edited by James A. Anderson (Newbury Park, CA: Sage, 1988), 11; Iyengar and Kinder, *News That Matters*; Yariv Tsfati, "Does Audience Skepticism of the Media Matter in Agenda Setting?" *Journal of Broadcasting & Electronic Media* 47, 2 (2003): 157–76; Wayne Wanta, *The Public and the National Agenda: How People Learn about Important Issues* (Mahwah, NJ: Lawrence Erlbaum Associates, 1997).

19. David O. Sears, "The Paradox of De Facto Selective Exposure Without Preferences for Supportive Information," in *Theories of Cognitive Consistency: A Sourcebook,* edited by Robert P. Abelson, Elliot Aronson, William J. McGuire, Theodore M. Newcomb, Milton J. Rosenberg, and Percy H. Tannenbaum (Chicago: Rand McNally and Company, 1968), 785; Charles G. Lord, Lee Ross, and Mark R. Lepper, "Biased Assimilation and Attitude Polarization: The Effects of Prior Theories on Subsequently Considered Evidence," *Journal of Personality and Social Psychology* 37, 11 (1979): 2098–109; Arthur G. Miller, John W. McHoskey, Cynthia M. Bane, and Timothy G. Dowd, "The Attitude Polarization Phenomenon: Role of Response Measure, Attitude Extremity, and Behavioral Consequences of Reported Attitude Change," *Journal of Personality and Social Psychology* 64, 4 (1993): 561–74.

20. Joanne M. Miller and Jon A. Krosnick, "News Media Impact on the Ingredients of Presidential Evaluations: Politically Knowledgeable Citizens Are Guided by a Trusted Source," *American Journal of Political Science* 44, 2 (2000): 295–309.

21. Catherine Cassara, "US Newspaper Coverage of Human Rights in Latin America, 1975–1982: Exploring President Carter's Agenda-Building Influence," *Journalism & Mass Communication Quarterly* 75, 3 (1998): 478–86; Sheldon Gilberg, Chaim Eyal, Maxwell McCombs, and David Nicholas, "The State of the Union Address and the Press Agenda," *Journalism Quarterly* 57 (1989): 584–88; Randy E. Miller and Wayne Wanta, "Sources of the Public Agenda: The President-Press-Public Relationship," *International Journal of Public Opinion Research* 8, 4 (1996): 390–402; Marilyn Roberts, "Political Advertising's Influence on News, the Public, and Their Behavior," in *Communication and Democracy: Exploring the Intellectual Frontiers in Agenda-Setting Theory,* edited by Maxwell E. McCombs, Donald L. Shaw, and David H. Weaver (Mahwah, NJ: Lawrence

Erlbaum Associates, 1997); Wayne Wanta, Mary Ann Stephenson, Judy VanSlyke Turk, and Maxwell E. McCombs, "How President's State of Union Talk Influenced News Media Agendas," *Journalism Quarterly* 66 (1989): 537–41.

22. Roy L. Behr and Shanto Iyengar, "Television News, Real-World Cues, and Changes in the Public Agenda," *Public Opinion Quarterly* 49, 1 (1985): 38–57; Jeffrey E. Cohen, "Presidential Rhetoric and the Public Agenda," *American Journal of Political Science* 39, 1 (1995): 87–107; Roberts, "Political Advertising's Influence on News, the Public, and Their Behavior."

23. John R. Petrocik, "Issue Ownership in Presidential Elections, With a 1980 Case Study," *American Journal of Political Science* 40, 3 (1996): 825–50.

24. *Strong at Home, Respected in the World: The 2004 Democratic National Platform for America,* http://www.democrats.org/pdfs/2004platform.pdf, 8.

25. See details in Ken Goldstein and Paul Freedman, "Lessons Learned: Campaign Advertising in the 2000 Elections," *Political Communication* 19 (2002): 5–28.

26. D. Sunshine Hillygus and Todd G. Shields, *The Persuadable Voter: Wedge Issues in Presidential Campaigns* (Princeton: Princeton University Press, 2008): 168.

27. There was little evidence favoring the other possible causal direction, namely, that beliefs about Iraq's importance influenced media use. Only in the general election panel was there evidence that liberal Democrats thinking Iraq was the most important issue were more likely to use liberal media in the postwave compared to others.

28. As there is a significant interaction between ideology/partisanship and conservative media use in the DNC panel, the results are more complicated than the other results (where only a main effect of media use was found). Here, strong conservative Republicans naming terrorism in the prewave are very likely to do so again in the postwave. If they used two conservative media types, they named terrorism again with a probability of 0.94. They are only somewhat less likely to do so if they don't use any conservative media types (probability of 0.71). Contrary to expectations, strong liberal Democrats using two conservative media types are less likely to rename terrorism (0.15) compared to those not using any conservative media (0.66).

29. Looking at the opposite causal direction, finding terrorism the most important problem predicted greater use of conservative media in the debate and general election panels and less use of liberal media in the general election panel.

30. Russell J. Dalton, Paul Allen Beck, Robert Huckfeldt, and William Koetzle, "A Test of Media-Centered Agenda Setting: Newspaper Content and Public Interests in a Presidential Election," *Political Communication* 15, 4 (1998): 463–81; Jae Kook Lee, "The Effect of the Internet on Homogeneity of the Media Agenda: A Test of the Fragmentation Thesis," *Journalism & Mass Communication Quarterly* 84, 4 (2007): 745–60.

31. Dalton, Beck, Huckfeldt, and Koetzle, "A Test of Media-Centered Agenda Setting."

32. Thomas J. Johnson and Wayne Wanta, with John T. Byrd and Cindy Lee, "Exploring FDR's Relationship with the Press: A Historical Agenda-Setting Study," *Political Communication* 12 (1995): 157–72; Matthew A. Baum and Tim Groeling, "New Media and the Polarization of American Political Discourse," *Political Communication* 25 (2008): 345–65.

33. Johnson and Wanta, with Byrd and Lee, "Exploring FDR's Relationship with the Press."

34. See, for example, Maxwell E. McCombs and Hendry F. Schulte, "Expanding the Domain of the Agenda-Setting Function of Mass Communication," World Association for Public Opinion Research (Montreaux, Switzerland, 1974); Maxwell McCombs, Esteban Lopez-Escobar, and Juan Pablo Llamas, "Setting the Agenda of Attributes in the 1996 Spanish General Election," *Journal of*

Communication 50, 2 (2000): 77–92; Spiro Kiousis, "Compelling Arguments and Attitude Strength: Exploring the Impact of Second-Level Agenda Setting on Public Opinion of Presidential Campaign Images," *The International Journal of Press/Politics* 10, 2 (2005): 3–27; Vincent Price, David Tewksbury, and Elizabeth Powers, "Switching Trains of Thought: The Impact of News Frames on Readers' Cognitive Responses," *Communication Research* 24 (1997): 481–506.

35. Note that the results of this analysis do not enable me to evaluate whether media outlets are biased because I don't have a fixed neutral point to use as a basis for comparison.

36. The differences in coverage were more pronounced in cable news than in newspapers. One take on this finding is that cable news is more biased than newspapers. Economic models suggest that news organizations will bias their content to cater toward the predispositions of their audience. See, for example, Matthew Gentzkow and Jesse M. Shapiro, "Media Bias and Reputation," *Journal of Political Economy* 114, 2 (2006): 280–316. If newspapers aim to attract a broader audience than cable news networks, then their coverage may be less biased. Yet newspapers cater to very different audiences—in some locations, differences in coverage may be larger. Although some evidence to support this claim may be found in the content analysis results, it isn't clear whether the same relationship would be found with respect to other issues or other claims or with more newspapers. Even though coverage differences were not as clear for newspapers, they were still apparent.

37. John T. Jost, Jack Glaser, Arie W. Kruglanski, and Frank J. Sulloway, "Political Conservatism as Motivated Social Cognition," *Psychological Bulletin* 129, 3 (2003), 362.

38. Petrocik, "Issue Ownership in Presidential Elections."

7

PARTISANSHIP AND NICHE NEWS

NOT EVERYONE SEEKS out political information from the media. There are undoubtedly people who opt out of politics and avoid news media content altogether. And not everyone who seeks out political information from the media gravitates toward news sharing their political perspective. Political predispositions are, however, an important predictor of where people turn for news. Conservatives and Republicans are more likely to read newspapers endorsing a Republican presidential candidate, browse conservative-leaning magazines, listen to conservative talk radio, watch Fox News, and access conservative Web sites. Liberals and Democrats are more likely to read newspapers endorsing a Democratic presidential candidate, subscribe to liberal-leaning magazines, listen to liberal talk radio, watch CNN or MSNBC, and access liberal Web sites. There is consistent evidence that people's political leanings motivate them to select likeminded partisan media.

With an explosion of available news sources, citizens have ample options in terms of where to get their news: newspapers, radio, magazines, television, the Internet. And for each of these media types, the number of news options is staggering. *Austin American Statesman* or *Wall Street Journal*. Randi Rhodes or Rush Limbaugh. *The Nation* or the *National Review*. MSNBC or Fox News. Moveon.org or Townhall.com. The list could go on endlessly. The amount of choice is consequential in terms of selective exposure. Why? When confronted with numerous choices, we must develop strategies for sorting through them. Consider an everyday purchase decision and your rationale for your preference. Why pick the Kleenex brand over the Scotties brand of tissues? We likely have a rationale for our choice: price, convenience, softness, and so forth. The same holds true when we make news choices. But it just so happens that we think about our news choices through the lens of partisanship. Ask people the difference between the cable news networks, for example, and those with only a smidgen of political knowledge likely will mention partisanship as a difference. Just as softness is a criterion that we employ for tissue decisions, partisanship is a criterion that we employ for news decisions. It really needn't be this way—we could evaluate tissues based on fabric density and news based on issue density. But partisanship is the way in which we increasingly organize our news world. When confronted with lots of choice and a heuristic for navigating the choices, partisan differences make news selections a bit easier.

Those who traditionally excel at using political heuristics are the same people who tend to see partisan media biases and to make news selections consistent with their political leanings. In assessing partisan media biases, politically knowledgeable partisans seem to engage in forms of selective perception and retention. They are particularly attuned to cues of hostile partisan biases in the media. And politically knowledgeable and interested partisans tend to select likeminded media outlets. It seems that the characteristics that facilitate political learning—ability and motivation—also are prerequisites for partisan selective exposure.

But what effect does the use of likeminded media have? Partisan selective exposure does not make people more interested in politics. Nor does it depress knowledge about presidential candidates—if anything, it may increase it. There are strong relationships between partisan selective exposure and political participation, the commitment to vote for a particular candidate, and political polarization. The direction of the relationships indicates the presence of spirals—partisan selective exposure affects how citizens approach politics and how citizens approach politics can influence partisan selective exposure. There is some evidence that partisan selective exposure leads people to settle on their presidential vote choice earlier in the campaign season. Evidence for the opposite causal direction is even stronger—committed partisans tend to select politically likeminded media. Further, partisan selective exposure can lead people to participate in politics. Again, there also is an indication of the reverse causal direction, namely, that participation in politics can lead people to seek out likeminded media. Finally, partisan selective exposure contributes to higher levels of political polarization. As people consume partisan media that match their political predispositions, they develop more polarized attitudes. These polarized political attitudes, in turn, lead people to seek out partisan media.

Partisan media use also influences the issues people find to be most important. In particular, people develop different impressions of which issues facing the nation are most important depending on the news outlets they use. And there seems to be something about the *content* of media coverage that contributes to these differences. In 2004, for example, conservative outlets emphasized Iraq as a part of the larger war on terror. Liberal outlets, on the other hand, highlighted problems with the Iraq War. Corresponding to these differences in media content, those using conservative media tended to name terrorism as an important issue. Those using liberal media tended to name Iraq as an important issue. Another aspect of media coverage also helps to explain why partisan selective exposure leads audiences to different conclusions about the most important issues facing the nation: Media outlets explicitly cover the issue strengths of various presidential candidates. Public opinion about which candidate is better suited to handle an issue is a feature of media coverage. Experimental evidence suggests that this coverage leads people to report important issues that coincide with the issue strengths of likeminded candidates. Those who see hostile media biases are particularly likely to name likeminded candidates' issue strengths as important issues facing the nation. In sum, the evidence is substantial that partisan selective exposure is consequential.

The picture that emerges should give us pause. When people perceive media bias and use media in accordance with their partisanship, they develop more polarized political attitudes, participate more, and focus more on issues on which their candidate performs better. And the people most likely to engage in this behavior are those that we typically herald as good citizens: the politically knowledgeable, interested, and participatory. What do these findings imply for research on political communication? How do these findings square with historical trends and, more important, for the practice of democracy? I turn to each of these questions in turn.

PARTISAN SELECTIVE EXPOSURE AND POLITICAL COMMUNICATION RESEARCH

The study of partisan selective exposure has much to contribute to the study of political communication. Three specific contributions are discussed here. First, this research and its findings challenge the common assumption that selective exposure corresponds to a conception of limited media effects. Instead, this project finds that partisan selective exposure can have important political consequences. Second, the effects of partisan selective exposure call into question the treatment of (1) the media as undifferentiated transmitters of messages and (2) the audience as undifferentiated recipients of messages. Third, the study of partisan media exposure can inform future research regarding the relationship between the effects of the media and interpersonal communication.

The study of selective exposure has a long history. In early research and theory, selective exposure was proposed as a rationale behind limited media effects.[1] For example, in their ambitious overview of findings regarding human behavior, scholars Bernard Berelson and Gary Albert Steiner noted that "people tend to see and hear communications that are favorable or congenial to their predispositions; they are more likely to see and hear congenial communications than neutral or hostile ones."[2] This correspondence can translate into a limited media effects perspective because people would have no reason to change their beliefs. Though I broadly agree that selective exposure is a "handmaiden of reinforcement" and a "protector of predispositions,"[3] this project significantly parts ways with the limited effects perspective. As a handmaiden of reinforcement, the media do not fail to influence the public. Instead, partisan selective exposure affects the strength of preexisting beliefs, intensifying them in their original direction. Partisan selective exposure produces more polarized attitudes, higher levels of political participation, and differences in which issues are judged to be most important.

Second, several research traditions assume that the media convey homogeneous messages to the public. Research in agenda setting, for example, often assumes that different media outlets devote approximately equal amounts of attention to various political issues. As another example, cultivation research often assumes that media exposure, irrespective of media content, leads people to adopt the media's portrayal of reality.[4] I am not the first to question this assumption. Others have shown that paying attention to *which* outlets are used can help in understanding agenda-setting and cultivation effects.[5] Following along these lines, this book questions the notion that the media transmit a single agenda. If the media were transmitting the same issue agenda, for example, then one would *not* expect to find that different patterns of media exposure are related to different issues being named as the most important. Yet this is precisely what I find.

Not only does this research call into question the assumption that media *content* is homogeneous, but it also reminds us that media *audiences* are not homogeneous. This idea has roots in the uses and gratifications tradition. This tradition assumes that people actively seek out media content to fulfill their needs.[6] Because people have different motivations for consuming media, the influence of the media may not be the same for all respondents. Similarly, I evaluated whether people's political leanings would amplify or diminish the influence of partisan media use. Following research documenting that motivations for viewing media contribute to what people take from media, I find that that people's political leanings both motivate media exposure *and* moderate the influence of partisan media outlets.[7] In doing so, this analysis adds to the conception of media effects as moderated by individual motivations and predispositions.

Third, a tradition of research in political communication contrasts the effects of the media with the effects of interpersonal communication. Do people encounter more diverse views in the media compared to their interpersonal interactions?[8] Does interpersonal communication enhance the media's effect?[9] Can interpersonal communication motivate people's media exposure?[10] I drew from research on the effects of exposure to interpersonal networks to understand the effects of likeminded media use. In several cases, the effects of partisan media exposure parallel the effects of discussion with likeminded others. For example, just as visiting with likeminded others is related to participating in politics, use of likeminded media is related to participating in politics. In other cases, the results presented here about the effects of exposure to likeminded media now need to be examined in interpersonal contexts. Given that likeminded media use influences the issues people consider most important, can the same be said for discussing politics with likeminded others? This book also goes beyond many studies of political discussion by delving into questions about the causal direction of relationships between likeminded media use and political outcomes. Are the relationships similar for likeminded discussions?

Questions about the relative influence of interpersonal networks and media and the ways that they may interact also provide an important avenue for additional research. Do interpersonal contacts influence people's political attitudes and behaviors more so than the media? Does the composition of one's interpersonal network moderate the influence of partisan media use and vice versa? Future research into these issues would provide important insights into the media's political role and give us a more refined understanding of the overall effects of partisan information exposure.

As this discussion aims to establish, the study of partisan selective exposure has much to offer to a more general understanding of political communication and media effects. The study of partisan selective exposure in our contemporary media environment also can contribute to our understanding of how a partisan press may have functioned historically, which I turn to next.

A PARTISAN PRESS

Whether Federalist versus Anti-Federalist, Whig versus Democrat, North versus South, or Democrat versus Republican, partisan rancor in the media has been a staple for centuries. Consider the following quotations, each from the media about a different president or presidential hopeful spanning over two centuries:

- "The man who is the source of all the misfortunes of our country is this day reduced to a level with his fellow citizens, and is no longer possessed of powers to multiply evils upon the United States."[11]

- "He carries with him the near-universal opprobrium of the permanent class that inhabits our nation's capital."[12]
- "Weak, vain old man" who was "called into public service by family influence."[13]
- "An indecisive, impractical and impulsive challenger whose radical views, wild accusations and ever-changing positions inspire no confidence that he would be capable of leading the nation."[14]
- "A characterless candidate, supported by an aimless party."[15]
- "As earnestly and passionately as Hitler once did, [he] assails our own capitalist system."[16]

(The subject of each quotation can be found in the endnotes if you're curious.)

As these quotations show, political figures have taken jabs from the press. And, not surprisingly, the press has taken jabs from political figures. As we've seen, citizens can learn from political elites' statements about the media. They learn to connect their news use with their partisan beliefs.

Although eras can be characterized as having stronger and weaker connections between partisanship and the news, I'd be hard pressed to identify any point in time where the link was entirely absent. In the early days of the United States, a newspaper *without* a partisan stance was considered morally repugnant, a sign of a printer devoid of principle. Accordingly, many newspapers published during the nineteenth century openly favored—and, in fact, were sponsored by—political parties. Faithful partisan newspaper printers were rewarded with lucrative governmental printing contracts or appointed to government offices by appreciative presidents. Critical newspapers maneuvered to avoid legal sanctions and to stay in print with the support of the loyal opposition. Party loyalists considered subscriptions to likeminded newspapers an important duty. Coinciding with the presence of a partisan press was a strong uptick in political involvement among the citizenry; Michael Schudson noted that political participation skyrocketed during an era of partisan press: "The press of the heyday of American political participation, from the 1840 to 1900, was…typically loyal to political parties; [the press] served as information promoting boosters of a particular political organization."[17]

Partisan rallying was slowly replaced by the ideas of objectivity and balanced reporting, emerging in the early twentieth century.[18] Editorial and news content were separated in many of the major newspapers in the United States. Newspapers increasingly became entities separate from political parties, dependent more on advertising revenue than government contracts and overseen by powerful editors rather than partisan loyalists. Although newspapers were no longer dependent on party patronage, to say that newspapers were devoid of partisan sentiment certainly would be an overstatement. As historian Si Sheppard notes,

[Objectivity] may reflect the stated policy of the industry, and does contain an element of truth in that the template of objectivity was widely adopted as an industry standard, the better to maximize sales, in reality editors manipulated the shell of objectivity to serve as a Trojan Horse, the ideal mechanism with which to wage ideological warfare—for what argument is more persuasive than one developed in a detached style by credible sources in an authoritative forum? Behind the façade—the professional journalistic standards, the foreign correspondents, the impersonal and anonymous wire stories, the carefully seg-regated news and op-ed pages—objectivity stretched no further than disinter-estedly reporting precisely those issues about which management had no previously determined opinion.[19]

Despite questions about the extent to which objectivity characterized the news, formal training programs for journalists stressed balanced reporting and taught journalists to avoid privileging perspectives in their news decisions.

Today, partisanship in the media arguably is becoming more blatant.[20] We may not have an openly partisan press in quite the same way we did in the 1800s, but the link between partisanship and the news is resurging. The citizenry is repeatedly instructed—by the media, by political figures, and by popular culture—to make news choices based on partisanship. And citizens *are* making news choices based on their political beliefs. The effects of these choices lend insight not only into contem-porary media effects, but also into the historical role of partisan media. The observa-tion that participation rose with a partisan press in the past receives support with data from contemporary times. The documented increases in polarization and in diverging impressions of important issues today also may have characterized the attitudes and beliefs of those using partisan papers in earlier times. As these exam-ples suggest, the choice of likeminded partisan media can have important implica-tions for the functioning of our democratic system, and so I now turn to these implications.

PARTISAN SELECTIVE EXPOSURE, CITIZENS, AND DEMOCRACY

Freedom of the press is an important part of a democratic system. In the United States, for example, the press's freedom is enshrined in the Bill of Rights. As a commercial enterprise, however, the media are subject to market pressures. As more media options become available to consumers, each media outlet competes for a smaller niche audience. If political partisanship persists as a viable segmentation strategy, news outlets may increasingly target their news to attract audiences with specific political leanings. If the market demands partisan news, the media will supply partisan news. My research here suggests that there is indeed demand for this type of media targeting: There are quite clear relationships between the political leanings expressed by media outlets and the political leanings of the audience.

Increasing use of likeminded political media, whether or not it represents a commercial feat of effective segmentation, should not be greeted as an unalloyed good. It should, at a minimum, raise the eyebrows of those concerned with the non-commercial role of the news media in our democratic system, their role in providing the public with the tools to be good citizens. Can partisan media fulfill this role?

As with most puzzles garnering sustained attention, the answer to this question is not readily apparent. Though a partisan media system can exacerbate social divides and cleavages, it also can invigorate citizens and assist voters trying to make sense of a complex political world.

Partisan media contribute to a democratic system by providing an impetus for political participation. As a frequently employed benchmark, political participation is an important component of a properly functioning democracy. By providing information and motivation, partisan media encourage political participation. This research finds that likeminded media exposure contributes to political participation. Partisans using likeminded media are simply more active in politics. They seem to be motivated and energized by partisan media.

Partisan media also can help citizens to make sense of politics by highlighting partisanship as an organizational scheme. With a working knowledge of political parties, citizens can use partisanship as a political heuristic and as a basis for categorizing political information.[21] In discussing politics using partisan terms, partisan media outlets may help people to develop partisan schemas. Consistent with this idea, I found no evidence that partisan media exposure reduces political knowledge. On the contrary, there is some evidence that likeminded media use may increase political knowledge. Based in part on this rationale, one may encourage media coverage of political parties and point to the benefits of emphasizing partisanship in the media.[22]

Theories about the possible dangers of the partisan media provide a stark contrast to these optimistic treatments. Specifically, concern has been voiced that partisan selective exposure exacerbates divides in who participates in politics and impedes the development of common goals and interests.

Though partisan selective exposure increases political participation, not everyone consumes partisan media. A fractured media system permits not only partisan selective exposure but also political avoidance. Those uninterested in politics can avoid political content. When those with a preference for entertainment have more media options, they are less politically engaged.[23] The combination of enhanced engagement among those using partisan media and depressed engagement among those using nonpolitical media is troubling because people's political interests may not be equitably represented. Those engaging in partisan selective exposure may have their political interests overrepresented in comparison to those avoiding politics. An explosion of both partisan and nonpolitical media, therefore, may in tandem compound gaps in citizen participation.

Partisan selective exposure also works against the development of shared interests. Philosopher John Dewey argued that a properly functioning democracy is characterized by common goals and interests.[24] As people develop different issue agendas fed by their media exposure patterns, they may increasingly fail to share such a common agenda. This consequently may impede the creation of broadly supported public policies and the ability of diverse interests to achieve consensus and rally around important social issues. As the findings here indicate, partisan selective exposure contributes not only to differences in the political issues perceived to be most important but also to more polarized attitudes. More polarization may lead citizens to have less tolerance for people with other political perspectives, an effect that could confound efforts to reach social consensus and solve important social issues.

People engaging in partisan selective exposure also may not be adequately informed to perform their duties as citizens. In the present study, there is no evidence that partisan selective exposure depresses political knowledge. On the other hand, the examination of knowledge, in particular the *types* of knowledge evaluated, was necessarily limited in this research. Normative prescriptions contend that good citizens should employ rational criteria in reaching political decisions. Whether partisan selective exposure meets this objective is questionable. Partisan media may not always provide news coverage that assists audiences in understanding multiple political perspectives. A constant barrage of partisan talking points surely doesn't help audiences to develop their critical thinking skills. Perhaps it does help audiences perfect their ability to defend their own political perspective, but partisan media coverage is far from providing compassionate, civil, and comprehensive knowledge about our political world.

Patterns of selective exposure have implications for governance as well. Political figures can use a fractured media system to their advantage. Instead of facing a divided or critical audience, it is strategic to deliver certain messages to likeminded audiences. Consider, for example, Vice President Dick Cheney's exclusive Fox News interview after he accidentally shot hunting partner Harry Whittington. Some messages that may engender animosity in an uncongenial audience can inspire congenial audiences, and savvy politicians can take advantage of partisan selective exposure to target political messages. Without the loyal opposition or a nonpartisan entity checking and counterarguing a partisan version of reality, politicians may more readily get away with distortions of the truth. This creates a type of partisan *selective production* whereby political officials can differentially grant interviews and differentially convey information depending on the political leanings of the media outlet. In accordance with this view, media outlets then become, perhaps hopelessly, confounded with political parties.

How do we reconcile these two divergent views of the role of partisan media in a democratic system? Should we bemoan or celebrate partisan media? Though undoubtedly anticlimactic, it seems that the most satisfying response to this question is: It depends.

A desirable media system would maximize the benefits of partisan media exposure while minimizing the consequences. If everyone engaged in partisan selective exposure, the consequences of partisan selective exposure would be *maximized*. People would increasingly fragment into different groups and develop different goals, attitudes, and perceptions. Alternatively, if no one engaged in partisan selective exposure, the benefits of partisan selective exposure would be *minimized*. Political participation would not be encouraged and political media coverage may be less effective in helping people to understand politics. Hence, neither extreme yields a desirable system.

These extremes are reflected well in communication scholar James Carey's description of two forces at work in the media environment.[25] He labels media targeting broad national audiences a *centripetal* force and media targeting small segments of the population a *centrifugal* force. As any introductory physics book would explain, equilibrium is reached when centripetal and centrifugal forces are balanced. Accordingly, a system where people use both partisan media outlets *and* outlets catering to more politically diverse audiences yields equilibrium. As communication scholar Elihu Katz notes, "If one were designing a participatory democracy, one would make provision for a central space in which all citizens could gather together and for dispersed spaces in which they could meet in smaller, more homogeneous groups."[26] If centrifugal forces dominate, the system must bolster centripetal forces to regain equilibrium. If centripetal forces dominate, the system must bolster centrifugal forces to regain equilibrium.

Today, the centrifugal force of partisan selective exposure is gaining strength. There is something compelling about contemporary partisan media that attracts likeminded audiences. Perhaps partisan media provide a refreshing contrast to the "fiercely dull" news coverage of putatively nonpartisan outlets.[27] The day may soon come—some might well argue that it has already arrived—when the media no longer help to unify the public. The high levels of partisan media exposure, attitude polarization, and divergences in public agendas documented here certainly can be read as disconcerting. As such, the challenge becomes figuring out how to balance a drive for partisan information with the need for a united citizenry.

In the following section, I lay out several directions that solutions could take and consider both the promises and perils of these ideas. These ideas are not meant as a call to eliminate all partisan programming. Not only is that unrealistic, but it is also undesirable unless we can figure out ways to obtain the same benefits as partisan media without the drawbacks. This is a formidable challenge, and one that would require much experimentation. Rather than an endpoint, this discussion is meant as a starting point for thinking about how to present the news, how to use the news, and how to discuss the news.

New Ways of Judging the News

One way of counteracting the detrimental effects of partisan selective exposure would be to encourage citizens to employ different criteria for judging and for selecting news media. Without question, citizens need decision criteria to help them sort through all of the available news media options. Numerous criteria are possible: completeness of coverage, clarity of coverage, density or depth of informational content, and so forth. Could we reduce the reliance on partisanship as a criterion?

This is a formidable challenge. Judgments of the news are not independent from one's political leaning. Typically, an informative and trustworthy source also is a likeminded source. Asking citizens to focus on how *informative* the news is, therefore, may have no effect at all. Or, even more upsetting, the effect may be to reinforce partisan patterns of news use. Even standard ways of encouraging citizens to think critically about arguments, such as teaching them to identify logical fallacies, may be ineffective if citizens are empowered only to identify logical fallacies from the side with which they disagree. News media literacy initiatives advising citizens to be skeptical when encountering information in the news media also may not be effective if they motivate *partisan* skepticism, whereby people only increase their skepticism of the other side's claims. Indeed, chapter 4 shows that partisans came no closer to agreeing on the partisan bent of a news article when prompted to look for signs of bias. Asking people to stop using partisanship as a criterion for news choice also is difficult because a significant percentage of the public presently perceive partisan leanings in the media. Changing established perceptions is not an easy task.

Despite these difficulties, this strategy is worth considering. It could have substantial payoffs in terms of helping to shift the public's focus away from partisanship when assessing the news media. Though not everyone sees bias in the news media, those who do are precisely the people who matter both to the news media and to the practice of democracy more generally: the politically involved, interested, and knowledgeable. These people are the quintessential news consumers. Advertisers pay good money to reach these citizens via ads during the news. As such, news programs are beholden to these audiences. These also are the people who vote, who serve in government, and who act as a check on government by monitoring governmental affairs. In an audience-driven news market, citizens are empowered. Through their consumption patterns, citizens *have* control of the news. If citizens begin making news selections using criteria other than partisanship, then there is additional pressure on news programming to cater to the audience. Rather than focusing on partisanship, news outlets could compete to provide engaging, clear, and complete coverage of issues.

Diverse News Exposure

Given the challenge of encouraging citizens to judge media using a new standard, perhaps the solution could be simplified. Perhaps citizens could be encouraged to diversify their news exposure. This would help people to encounter diverse views and to reduce their reliance on likeminded sources of information. Consider the following from *New York Times* columnist Nicholas Kristof:

> So what's the solution? Tax breaks for liberals who watch Bill O'Reilly or conservatives who watch Keith Olbermann? No, until President Obama brings us universal health care, we can't risk the surge in heart attacks. So perhaps the only way forward is for each of us to struggle on our own to work out intellectually with sparring partners whose views we deplore. Think of it as a daily mental workout analogous to a trip to the gym; if you don't work up a sweat, it doesn't count. Now excuse me while I go and read The Wall Street Journal's editorial page.

By itself, however, this solution is unlikely to produce significant amounts of change. If people watch diverse news programs but spend their time analyzing hostile biases, then watching diverse outlets may only reinforce the effects of partisan selective exposure. Citizens would not only need to change where they turn for news, but also would need to change the manner in which they approach the news media. Instead of approaching diverse outlets prepared to look for signs of bias, citizens need to view diverse news outlets with a different perspective. We need to adjust our motivations. Before using another source of news, perhaps we could tell ourselves that the purpose of this exercise is to obtain new information and to try to understand, as best we can, how others think. This is not to say that we should view other outlets passively. Rather, this is to say that when we view the news, we should actively try to understand the arguments we encounter—both those with which we agree and those with which we disagree.

Again, this is not an easy charge. It is natural for citizens to develop news use habits. It isn't particularly efficient to continually look at multiple news sources. And for many, it is second nature to look for signs of media bias. The extent to which citizens are willing and able to take up these charges is an important question.

New News Formats

The first two potential solutions ask much of citizens. But the news media also can work to counteract the less desirable effects of partisan selective exposure. In particular, the news media could be more reflective about how they present the news. Partisan media often are compelling—audiences turn to this form of news in droves. A different type of reporting, such as a technical, detailed, and balanced report of the day's facts, may fail to capture an audience. Yet there must be a middle ground. Philosopher John Dewey recognized this in the early 1900s.[28] He challenged the news media to devise artful ways of presenting the news that would draw an audience. The challenge remains today. We should use all of the ingenuity that goes into the latest reality programming to develop news media products that inform, motivate, and attract audiences.

Communication research has much to offer news organizations seeking to develop innovative programs with new formats, new hosts, and new production techniques. For example, we know that tabloid news formats are seen as less objective, but that they can help citizens remember certain types of news.[29] We know that students are seen as less biased than professional news anchors.[30] We know that production techniques showing Democrats and Republicans reacting negatively to each other can promote polarization.[31] News programs can draw from this pool of research to create programs that engage and inform audiences. Not everything will be successful, to be sure. But without sustained efforts to find out what *does* work, there is little reason for optimism that something besides partisanship will rise to govern the news media.

Speaking about Media Partisanship

In much the same way that citizens learn about candidates in an election season, citizens learn about media bias. By discussing partisan media bias, therefore, we—academics, the news media, citizens—are training others to see the news in partisan terms. We may be encouraging people to seek political information in ways consistent with their partisanship. There is evidence that people can be trained to see partisanship in the media. Merely mentioning that some people believe that the media are biased changes how people approach the media. The main message from the news media and popular culture seems clear: Be vigilant in the search for lurking partisanship in the media.

When opinion leaders focus on partisan biases in the media, therefore, they add fuel to the fire of partisan selective exposure. Extensive coverage of accusations of media bias, such as the examples in chapter 1, likely reinforces partisan perceptions of media bias. In terms of promoting the news, I suspect that catchy slogans including any reference to partisanship (e.g., "No Bias, No Bull"; "Fair and Balanced"; "A Fuller Spectrum of News") get us nowhere. They serve only to remind audiences to focus on partisanship. This, in turn, serves only to exacerbate partisan selective exposure. Instead of telling the audience about nonpartisanship, the news media must think of ways to break out of the left-right continuum altogether. Obviously, this is easier said than done, but we should be wary of the potential democratic consequences of these types of statements.

By discussing the media using *other* attributes, we may be able to reduce the link between partisanship and the news media. This is not to say that opinion leaders should keep silent about partisan biases in the news media. Rather, it is to advocate that opinion leaders should be cognizant of behaviors that amplify partisan selective exposure. If the focus could be placed on other attributes of the media, opinion leaders should consider doing so.

Political campaigns also should be cautious about using accusations of media bias as campaign strategy. Accusing an outlet of bias may minimize the outlet's impact on voters, which may seem like a good strategy in the short run. Even more, those who see hostile biases in the media are more likely to pick up on other partisan cues. And this can be used to a campaign's advantage. Seeing partisanship in the media facilitates learning about the party's issue strengths. If partisans know the issues on which their preferred candidate performs best, they can promote these issues. These issues can be discussed at social gatherings and communicated through social networks. This could amplify a campaign's message and help to direct the electorate to focus on issues that advantage one candidate over the other. In sum, encouraging people to see the world in partisan terms may help candidates win elections. In the long run, however, a government crippled by partisan divides will be unsuccessful in the process of governance. Compromise, shared objectives, and thoughtfully hearing the other side have been, and must continue to be, valued in our society. Using accusations of partisan media bias merely as campaign strategy undermines these democratic goals. The only victory a politician in this political context can achieve is getting elected, not making accomplishments in governance.

CONCLUSION

It is true that we cannot totally separate partisanship from the news. Partisan conflict is a feature of our political system, and it is important that the news media cover the activities of the government. Even if we could separate partisanship and the news, I am not convinced that we should. Partisan media have a place in a democracy. They can unite likeminded individuals, help them to organize their political thinking, and motivate them to participate. These outcomes are not too shabby when evaluated in terms of ideals in a democracy.

Though partisan media may play an important role in a democracy, they cannot do it all. Unchecked, partisan media create and inflate gaps in the citizenry: gaps between those with partisan inclinations and those without, gaps between those who participate in politics and those who do not, gaps between those who affiliate with the political left and those who affiliate with the political right. It is for this reason that we must work toward counteracting these gaps and limiting spirals of partisan selective exposure that could undermine the workings of society.

This book began with Bill Clinton labeling Fox News as conservative and Lynne Cheney labeling CNN as liberal. On one hand, these cues are helpful. They convey information about partisanship in the media. On the other hand, these cues are not helpful. They remind citizens of a black-and-white political world where the news media and the government can be sorted into two groups: us...and them.

It is perhaps a great irony that in discussing partisanship as a criterion for news use, this book may encourage patterns of partisan selective exposure. Partisan-warped habits of judgment are easy to invoke. I hope that this is not the case. Instead, I hope that this project inspires critical reflection about where each of us turns for news. It would be even more desirable if this project started a conversation about how we teach others to critically think and judge the news media. Even if it is the case that this project encourages partisan selective exposure, however, the alternative is more troubling. Failing to critically examine partisan selective exposure would be a far graver form of selective exposure.

NOTES

1. Joseph T. Klapper, *The Effects of Mass Communication* (Glencoe, IL: The Free Press, 1960).

2. Bernard Berelson and Gary Albert Steiner, *Human Behavior: An Inventory of Scientific Findings* (New York: Harcourt, Brace & World, 1964): 529.

3. Klapper, *The Effects of Mass Communication*, 64.

4. See, for example, George Gerbner, Larry Gross, Michael Morgan, Nancy Signorielli, and James Shanahan, "Growing Up with Television: Cultivation Processes," in *Media Effects: Advances in Theory and Research*, edited by Jennings Bryant and Dolf Zillmann (Mahwah, NJ: Lawrence Erlbaum Associates, 2002), 2: 43–67.

5. Robert P. Hawkins and Suzanne Pingree, "Uniform Content and Habitual Viewing: Unnecessary Assumptions in Social Reality Effects," *Human Communication Research* 7, 4 (1981): 291–301; R. Andrew Holbrook and Timothy G. Hill, "Agenda-Setting and Priming in Prime Time Television: Crime Dramas as Political Cues," *Political Communication* 22, 3 (2005): 277–95.

6. See Elihu Katz, Jay G. Blumler, and Michael Gurevitch, "Uses and Gratifications Research," *Public Opinion Quarterly* 37, 4 (1973): 509–23.

7. William P. Eveland Jr., "The Cognitive Mediation Model of Learning from the News: Evidence from Nonelection, Off-Year Election, and Presidential Election Contexts," *Communication Research* 28, 5 (2001): 571–601; William P. Eveland Jr., Dhavan V. Shah, and Nojin Kwak, "Assessing Causality in the Cognitive Mediation Model: A Panel Study of Motivations, Information Processing, and Learning During Campaign 2000," *Communication Research* 30, 4 (2003): 359–86.

8. Diana C. Mutz and Paul S. Martin, "Facilitating Communication Across Lines of Political Difference: The Role of Mass Media," *American Political Science Review* 95, 1 (2001): 97–114.

9. Bruce W. Hardy and Dietram A. Scheufele, "Examining Differential Gains from Internet Use: Comparing the Moderating Role of Talk and Online Interactions," *Journal of Communication* 55 (2005): 71–84; Dietram A. Scheufele, "Examining Differential Gains from Mass Media and their Implications for Participatory Behavior," *Communication Research* 29, 1 (2002): 46–65.

10. Steven H. Chaffee and Jack M. McLeod, "Individuals vs. Social Predictors of Information Seeking," *Journalism Quarterly* 50 (1973): 237–45.

11. Quotation in reference to President George Washington, originally published in the *Aurora*. Si Sheppard, *The Partisan Press: A History of Media Bias in the United States,* (Jefferson, NC: McFarland & Company, 2008): 32.

12. Quotation in reference to President George W. Bush. Note that the remainder of the article offered a positive review of Bush's handling of Iraq, displaying a positive—albeit partisan—political assessment. William McGurn, "Bush's Real Sin Was Winning in Iraq," *Wall Street Journal,* January 20, 2009.

13. Quotation in reference to President William Harrison, originally published in the *Washington Globe.* Sheppard, *The Partisan Press,* 109.

14. Quotation in reference to presidential candidate George McGovern, originally published in the *Boston Herald.* Ibid., 276.

15. Quotation in reference to President Abraham Lincoln, originally published in *Vanity Fair.* Ibid., 136.

16. Quotation in reference to President Franklin Roosevelt, originally published in the *Omaha World-Herald.* Ibid., 237.

17. Michael Schudson, *The Power of News* (Cambridge, MA: Harvard University Press, 1995): 199.

18. Michael Schudson, "The Objectivity Norm in American Journalism," *Journalism,* 2, 2 (2001): 149–70.

19. Si Sheppard, *The Partisan Press: A History of Media Bias in the United States,* 198.

20. Daniel C. Hallin, "Not the End of Journalism History," *Journalism* 13, 3 (2009): 332–4.

21. Richard R. Lau and David P. Redlawsk, "Advantages and Disadvantages of Cognitive Heuristics in Political Decision Making," *American Journal of Political Science* 45, 4 (2001): 951–71; Milton Lodge and Ruth Hamill, "A Partisan Schema for Political Information Processing," *American Political Science Review* 80, 2 (1986): 505–20.

22. Schudson, *The Power of News.*

23. Markus Prior, *Post-Broadcast Democracy: How Media Choice Increases Inequality in Political Involvement and Polarizes Elections* (New York: Cambridge University Press, 2007).

24. John Dewey, *Democracy and Education* (Carbondale: Southern Illinois University Press, 1916/1985); John Dewey, *The Public and Its Problems* (Chicago: Swallow Press, 1927).

25. James Carey, "The Communications Revolution and the Professional Communicator," in *James Carey: A Critical Reader,* edited by Eve Stryker Munson and Catherine A. Warren (Minneapolis: University of Minnesota Press, 1969/1997): 128–43.

26. Elihu Katz, "And Deliver Us from Segmentation," *Annals of the American Association of Political and Social Sciences* 546, 1 (1996): 23.

27. Kevin G. Barnhurst and Diana C. Mutz, "The New Long Journalism: The Decline of Event-Centered Coverage in American Newspapers," *Journal of Communication* 47 (1997): 27–53.

28. Dewey, *The Public and Its Problems.*

29. Maria Elizabeth Grabe, Annie Lang, and Xiaoquan Zhao, "News Content and Form: Implications for Memory and Audience Evaluations," *Communication Research* 30, 4 (2003): 387–413.

30. Albert C. Gunther and Janice L. Liebhart, "Broad Reach or Biased Source? Decomposing the Hostile Media Effect," *Journal of Communication* 56, 3(2006): 449–66.

31. Dietram A. Scheufele, Eunkyung Kim, and Dominique Brossard, "My Friend's Enemy: How Split-Screen Debate Coverage Influences Evaluation of Presidential Candidates," *Communication Research* 34, 1 (2007): 3–24.

Appendix A: The National Annenberg Election Surveys

The technical appendices provide additional information about the datasets and analyses. Even more analysis information is available in a Web appendix at http://commstudies.utexas.edu/nichenews/. I first review the two main datasets used, the National Annenberg Election Surveys (appendix A) and the Knowledge Networks Study (appendix B). The subsequent appendices review the analyses and datasets from chapters 3 through 6 (appendices C through F).

The National Annenberg Election Surveys (NAES) were conducted during the 2000, 2004, and 2008 presidential primary and general election campaigns. Data for all three campaign seasons were collected using a random-digit-dial telephone survey. Two types of data are analyzed in this book. First, the NAES employed a rolling cross-sectional (RCS) design. In this design, a fresh set of telephone numbers that have not been dialed previously are released into the field each day of interviewing. In addition, telephone numbers where a respondent has not completed the survey are redialed. Using this method, data from each day of interviewing includes both those respondents who were reached on the first dial and those who required more dials before completing the survey. This design yields daily random cross-sections of the population. The response rate was 25 percent for the 2000 RCS (calculated using the RR1 formula from the American Association for Public Opinion Researchers), 22 percent for the 2004 RCS, and 19 percent for the 2008 RCS. Note that this computation of the response rate is strict in that all instances where contact was not made are counted as eligible.

Second, the 2004 NAES included a number of panel surveys conducted at various points during the election season. Panels were conducted around the Democratic National Convention (prewave 7/16–7/25/04, postwave 7/30–8/8/04, recontact rate 42 percent), the Republican National Convention (prewave 8/20–8/29/04, postwave 9/3–9/13/04, recontact rate 36 percent), the debates (prewave 9/20–9/29/04, postwave 10/14–10/24/04, recontact rate 41 percent), and the general election (prewave 7/15–11/1/04, postwave 11/4–12/28/04, recontact rate

43 percent). Additional details about the NAES and access to the 2000 and 2004 datasets are available in two books about the survey.[1]

MEASURING MEDIA LEANINGS

Media leanings were assessed for each media type identified by respondents. The following section reports statistics based on the 2004 RCS NAES for data collected between June 9 (the day after the final primary election) and November 1. A total of 39,338 respondents participated in the survey during this time period, though not all estimates are based on this number due to sample splits, described below.

Newspapers. Respondents were asked how many days in the past week that they read a daily newspaper. The 76 percent who stated that they had read a newspaper at least once were asked which newspaper they read most often.

These newspapers were coded into conservative and liberal categories on the basis of the newspaper's presidential endorsement, as explained in chapter 3. To determine who each newspaper endorsed, several strategies were used. Whenever possible, public information sources were consulted to determine which candidate each newspaper endorsed. This included reviewing the trade publication *Editor & Publisher,* releases over the AP Newswire, and online information about the newspapers. For the remaining newspapers, an e-mail was sent to the newspaper. E-mails were tailored by using the name of the newspaper and, when possible, the editor's name in an effort to increase response. Of the 1,076 emails sent, 537 responses were received.

These data were matched to the survey responses in the NAES. Of the 29,298 respondents who identified the newspaper they read most often, this classification strategy enabled classification of 77 percent of responses. Fifteen percent of open-ended responses were unable to be classified. This group included newspapers that could not be found and newspapers for which an endorsement could not be determined. For example, when respondents stated that they read the "Courier Post" most often in the past week, they could be referring to either the *Hannibal Courier Post,* which endorsed Bush, or the *Camden Courier Post,* which endorsed Kerry. Eight percent of respondents named newspapers that were contacted but that did not provide information about who they endorsed. Of the respondents who were able to be classified, 34 percent read a newspaper that endorsed Bush and 47 percent read a newspaper that endorsed Kerry. The remainder read newspapers that declined to endorse a candidate, read more than one paper with different editorial stances, or read a newspaper that gave two conflicting endorsements (a small minority was in the latter two categories, only 0.3 percent of the respondents). To create a measure of *reading newspapers endorsing Kerry,* respondents reading a newspaper endorsing Kerry were given a 1 and respondents reading a newspaper endorsing Bush, reading a newspaper not making an endorsement, not reading a newspaper, not able to name a newspaper that they read, or who named a newspaper that was not able to be classified were given a 0. An identical operationalization was used for *reading newspapers endorsing Bush,* with the exception that a 1 was given to respondents reading a newspaper endorsing Bush and respondents reading a newspaper endorsing Kerry were given a 0.

Radio. Forty-eight percent of respondents listened to talk radio or NPR one or more days in the past week. Respondents were asked to identify the hosts and programs to which they listened. As described in chapter 3, hosts and programs were classified as liberal or conservative on the basis of their declared leanings (e.g., Bruce Jacobs's Web site notes, "Like Rush, Bruce is grateful for the opportunity to stir things up and bring a more independent, conservative voice to Valley radio"), how they were described in the trade magazine *Talkers* (e.g., Rusty Humphries is labeled a "multi-talented conservative talker"), and the findings of prior scholarship and content analyses.[2]

Not all hosts and programs mentioned by respondents were conservative or liberal. Hosts such as David Brudnoy and Gene Burns identified as libertarian and others such as Doug Stephan and Jim Bohannon touted their moderate political positions. Several shows had multiple hosts with different political perspectives. Further, some respondents identified programs that were not political in content, such as sports talker Jim Rome and the "steward of late-night paranormal talk" George Noory.[3] All of these types of programs were coded as being neither liberal nor conservative.

Using this method, 78 percent of the radio responses were classified. The remaining responses either were unable to be located (a radio host or program that could not be found using Internet searches) or were indeterminate (such as respondents providing the frequency of the radio station without additional details, e.g., "101.1"). Based on this coding scheme, 28 percent of those listening to political talk radio listened to conservative hosts and shows and 25 percent listened to liberal hosts and shows.

As with the construction of the media consumption variables for newspaper, dichotomous variables were constructed that indicated whether or not the respondent listened to liberal-leaning radio and whether or not the respondent listened to conservative-leaning radio. Respondents listening to nonliberal, nonconservative radio programs or not listening to political talk radio were coded as 0.

Cable News. Respondents who watched cable news in the past week (66 percent) were asked to name the news network they watched most often. Thirty-four percent reported viewing Fox News most often, 45 percent CNN, and 12 percent MSNBC. As discussed in the text, CNN and MSNBC are treated as consistent exposure for liberals and Democrats and Fox News is treated as consistent exposure for conservatives and Republicans.

Political Internet. Respondents with Internet access (76 percent) who had obtained information about the campaign for president online in the past week (35 percent) were asked to identify the Web sites that they accessed. Twelve percent stated that they had accessed a candidate Web site, 60 percent a news organization Web site, and 32 percent another Web site. Responses from those identifying another Web site were coded as to whether the Web sites leaned toward conservative or liberal perspectives. A subset of responses were coded by a second coder to ensure that the classification system was reliable (*Krippendorff's* α = 0.96).[4] Of the 3,348 open-ended responses to this question, 2,714 were able to be categorized. Most respondents named nonpartisan or nonpolitical Web sites (e.g., AOL, 72 percent). Twelve percent named conservative-leaning Web sites (e.g., rushlimbaugh.com) and 14 percent named liberal-leaning Web sites (e.g., moveon.org). Again, two variables were created; one for accessing liberal-leaning Web sites and one for accessing conservative-leaning Web sites.

Indices of Media Exposure. As the media use variables formed two clusters, two indices of media exposure were created from the outlet-specific measures of partisan media use. The first index, exposure to conservative media outlets, was created by summing reading newspapers endorsing Bush, listening to conservative talk radio, watching Fox News, and accessing conservative Web sites (all survey respondents, including those who did not consume any media and thus received a 0 on this scale, M = 0.56, SD = 0.76, *range* 0 to 4). The second index, exposure to liberal media outlets, was created by summing reading newspapers endorsing Kerry, listening to liberal talk radio, watching CNN or MSNBC, and accessing liberal Web sites (M = 0.79, SD = 0.81, *range* 0 to 4). Overall, 42 percent use one or more media types categorized as conservative and 58 percent use one or more media types categorized as liberal. Just over 80 percent use at least one conservative or liberal media type. Please note that the terms "liberal media" and "conservative media" are used loosely and merely to delineate two patterns of media consumption.

MEASURING KEY POLITICAL VARIABLES

Political Knowledge. Two measures of political knowledge were used: campaign knowledge and general political knowledge. As the names imply, campaign knowledge measures contemporary knowledge about the presidential campaign, while general political knowledge aims to tap into an individual's base levels of knowledge about politics and the government in general. Using both of these constructs to evaluate the relationship between partisan selective exposure and political knowledge is important because of the questions raised about the causal direction. From a measurement perspective, general political knowledge is more likely to predict partisan selectivity because it is a more stable indicator of political aptitude. Alternatively, campaign knowledge may be more likely to be influenced by partisan selective exposure. Since these two measures are expected to differ in terms of the direction of causality with partisan selective exposure, both were tested. From a practical perspective, campaign knowledge was measured on both the pre- and postwaves of the panel surveys. General political knowledge, as a more constant indicator, was included only on the survey prewaves.

For the cross-sectional analysis, a scale of campaign knowledge was created by summing responses to nine different political knowledge questions. These items were (1) Who favors allowing workers to invest some of their Social Security contributions in the stock market—George W. Bush, John Kerry, both, or neither? (2) Who favored changing the recently passed Medicare prescription drug law to allow reimporting drugs from Canada—George W. Bush, John Kerry, both, or neither? (3) John Kerry says that he would eliminate the Bush tax cuts on those making how much money—over \$50 thousand a year, over \$100 thousand a year, over \$200 thousand a year, or over \$500 thousand a year? (4) Who was a former prosecutor—George W. Bush, John Kerry, both, or neither? (5) Who favors making the recent tax cuts permanent—George W. Bush, John Kerry, both, or neither? (6) Who favors laws making it more difficult for a woman to get an abortion—George W. Bush, John Kerry, both, or neither? (7) Which candidate favors placing limits on how much people can collect when a jury finds that a doctor has committed medical malpractice—George W. Bush, John Kerry, both, or neither? (8) Which candidate wants to make additional stem cell lines from human embryos available for federally funded research on diseases like Parkinson's—George W. Bush, John Kerry, both, or neither? (9) Which candidate favors increasing the five dollar and fifteen cent minimum wage employers must pay their workers—George W. Bush, John Kerry, both, or neither? Each of these nine items was coded as 1 if the respondent provided the correct response. A code of 0 was used when the respondent incorrectly answered the question, when the respondent did not know the answer, and when the respondent refused to answer the question. Responses were summed to create a scale (*Cronbach's* α = 0.74, M = 5.69, SD = 2.43). These items were asked of a random two-thirds of 2004 NAES respondents between October 14, 2004, and November 1, 2004. For the panel surveys, similar scales were developed.

A scale of general political knowledge was created using five items.[5] The first four items asked of survey respondents were: (1) Do you happen to know what job or political office is now held by Dick Cheney? (2) Who has the final responsibility to determine if a law is constitutional or not? Is it the president, the Congress, or the Supreme Court? (3) How much of a majority is required for the U.S. Senate and House to override a presidential veto? (4) Do you happen to know which party has the most members in the U.S. House of Representatives? Correct answers were coded as a 1 and incorrect answers (including don't know and refused) were coded as 0. The fifth measure included in the scale was the interviewer's assessment of the interviewee's knowledgeability.[6] This measure asked the interviewer to give the interviewee a grade of A through F for how knowledgeable she was during the interview. This grade was collapsed into a dichotomous measure where scores of A and B were coded as 1 and C, D, and F were coded as 0. These five measures were summed to create a measure of general political knowledge (*Cronbach's* α = 0.64, M = 3.21, SD = 1.47). The general political knowledge battery was asked of a random two-thirds of respondents and was only on the survey between July 16 and August 8; between August 20 and September 12; and between September 20 and October 24, 2004.[7]

Political Interest. Political interest was measured with the following question: "Some people seem to follow what is going on in government and public affairs most of the time, whether there is an election or not. Others are not that interested, or are interested in other things. Would you say you follow what is going on in government and public affairs most of the time, some of the time, only now and then, or hardly at all." This variable was coded such that higher values indicate higher levels of political interest (*range* = 1 to 4, M = 3.10, SD = 0.90, not included on 2004 survey 10/8–10).

Political Participation. From July 16 through September 13, 2004, participation intentions were assessed by asking participants, "How likely are you to participate in this year's presidential campaign, either by working to help one of the candidate's campaigns, by donating money to a campaign, by attending a campaign event of some kind, or by trying to convince others to vote for him as well? Would you say you are very likely to do at least one of these things (3), somewhat likely (2), or not very likely (1)?" (M = 1.89, SD = 0.88). Beginning on September 20, 2004, participation was assessed using the following items: During the presidential campaign, have you (1) talked to any people and tried to show them why they should vote for or against one of the presidential candidates; (2) gone to any political meetings, rallies, speeches, dinners, or things like that in support of a particular presidential candidate; (3) done any other work for one of the presidential candidates; (4) given money to any of the presidential candidates; (5) worn a presidential campaign button, put a campaign sticker on your car, or placed a sign in your window or in front of your house? A random one-third of respondents were asked each participation question with response options of yes, coded 1, or no, coded 0. These five items were summed to create an index whereby higher values indicate more participation (*Cronbach's* α = 0.62, M = 1.02, SD = 1.17).

Commitment to Vote for a Candidate and Time of Vote Decision. The survey questions used in creating a measure of commitment asked respondents for whom they intended to vote. Beginning on June 9, respondents were asked, "If the 2004 presidential election were being held today, would you vote for George W. Bush, the Republican; John Kerry, the Democrat; or Ralph Nader?" Beginning on July 6, 2004, a different vote intention question was added and asked of a random half of the respondents. This question read, "If the 2004 presidential election were being held today, would you vote for George W. Bush and Dick Cheney, the Republicans; John Kerry and John Edwards, the Democrats; or Ralph Nader and Peter Camejo of the Reform Party?" Beginning on July 21, 2004, the question not naming running mates was dropped in favor of the question including the names of the presidential running mates. A comparison of the response distribution of these two questions during the overlap period yielded no significant differences ($\chi^2 = 7.183$, $df = 6$, $p = 0.30$). Therefore, responses to the two versions of the vote choice question were combined for analysis.

The second set of questions used to determine respondents' commitment level asked respondents about the likelihood that they would change their mind. Respondents who answered that they intended to vote for Kerry, Bush, or Nader were asked, "Will you definitely vote for <candidate> for president, or is there a chance you could change your mind and vote for someone else?" If they indicated that there was a chance that they could change their mind, respondents were asked, "Is there a good chance you'll change your mind or would you say it's pretty unlikely?"

The final question used in creating a measure of commitment asked respondents about voting early. Beginning on September 23, respondents were asked if they had voted ("Some states allow individuals to vote before election day, that is, vote early at a polling station or by filling out an absentee ballot. How about you? Have you already voted in this year's presidential election or not?"). In total, 84 percent of respondents were unlikely to change their mind or had voted already and 16 percent believed that there was some chance that they could change their mind or did not know for whom they would vote.

Time of decision was measured by asking postelection survey respondents when they made up their mind for whom to vote: election day, the week before the election, the weekend before the election, the last week before the election, the last month before the election, earlier in the fall, during the summer, or before the summer. The variable was coded so that higher values indicate earlier decision times ($M = 6.62$, $SD = 1.79$).

Political Polarization. Political polarization was measured by computing the absolute value of the difference between thermometer ratings for each of the major party candidates. Respondents were asked, "Now for each of the following people in politics, please tell me if your opinion is favorable or unfavorable using a scale from 0 to 10. Zero means very unfavorable, and 10 means very favorable. Five means you do not feel favorable or unfavorable toward that person. Of course, you can use any number between 0 and 10." They were asked this question both for Bush ($M = 5.25$, $SD = 3.71$) and for Kerry ($M = 5.07$, $SD = 3.29$). Polarization, computed by taking the absolute value of the difference between ratings of Bush and Kerry for each respondent, had a mean of 5.56 and a standard deviation of 3.22. On average, respondents rated Bush 5 points more/less favorably than Kerry.

Most Important Problem. Survey respondents were asked in their opinion, what was the most important problem facing our country today. Though the question wording encouraged respondents to name a single issue, multiple responses were recorded. Nineteen percent of respondents named terrorism or national security as the most important problem facing the country. Twenty percent of respondents named Iraq as the most important problem facing the nation. Though there is no agreed upon way to measure issue agendas at the individual level, one method that has been used is to analyze whether or not people name a certain issue as the most important issue facing the country.[8] In this type of analysis, respondents naming Iraq as the most important issue would receive a 1 and respondents naming other issues as most important would receive a 0. More details about how the open-ended responses were coded can be found in the technical appendix for chapter 6.

Political Leanings (Political Ideology/Partisanship). There are many ways to assess political leanings. On the NAES, participants were asked to identify their political ideology (9 percent very conservative, 30 percent conservative, 39 percent moderate, 18 percent liberal, 5 percent very liberal). Partisanship was measured using three questions that asked respondents to report their partisanship, the strength of their partisanship, and whether they leaned more toward the Democratic or Republican Party. In creating a measure of partisanship, I opted to combine those identifying as weak partisans with those identifying as leaning partisans. I did this for two reasons. First, current research supports the idea that leaners are indistinguishable from those with weak party support.[9] As political scientist John Petrocik reports, "Americans who admit to feeling closer to one of the parties in the follow-up probe—the leaners—are virtually identical to those who are classified as 'weak' partisans (who are almost universally viewed as party identifiers) across a wide variety of perceptions, preferences, and behaviors."[10] Second, in terms of partisan selective exposure, leaners typically were either equally likely as weak partisans to engage in the behavior or, in some instances, more likely. This provides empirical support for treating leaners and weak partisans as identical. The resultant measure of partisanship had the following distribution: 20 percent strong Republican, 23 percent not strong/leaning Republican, 10 percent no leanings, 26 percent not strong/leaning Democrat, and 21 percent strong Democrat.

I also opted to combine the partisanship and ideology measures for three reasons. First, current scholarship documents that citizens are becoming increasingly consistent in their use of ideological and partisan labels—Democrats are liberals and Republicans are conservatives.[11] If these measurements tap into a similar underlying construct, it makes sense to combine them for analysis. Second, ideology and partisanship were significantly correlated in the datasets used. For the 2004 NAES, the correlation between the partisanship and ideology measures was 0.49 (p <0.001). Third, the empirical results for the two treated separately were remarkably similar. Presenting the results for ideology and partisanship separately would result in extensive duplication.

Measuring Control Variables

Demographics: Education (years of school completed, $M = 14.29$, $SD = 2.47$), Age ($M = 48.23$, $SD = 16.50$), Income (in thousands of dollars, $M = 64.84$, $SD = 49.96$), Gender (56 percent female), Race/ethnicity (8 percent Black/African-American, 8 percent Hispanic), Adults in home (37 percent 1 adult, 50 percent 2 adults, 14 percent 3+ adults), Phone lines (84 percent 1 line), Region (Northeast 20 percent, Midwest 25 percent, South 35 percent, West 20 percent)

Media Use (days in past week): National network news ($M = 2.57$, $SD = 2.62$), Twenty-four-hour cable news channel ($M = 3.06$, $SD = 2.84$), Local television news ($M = 3.96$, $SD = 2.77$), Read a newspaper ($M = 3.76$, $SD = 2.91$), National Public Radio (NPR, $M = 1.17$, $SD = 2.21$), Non-NPR talk radio ($M = 1.29$, $SD = 2.18$), Use Internet for information about presidential campaign ($M = 1.00$, $SD = 2.01$), Internet access (76 percent)

Media Attention (*range* = 0 to 3, higher values indicate more attention to stories about the campaign for president): National network/cable television news ($M = 1.60$, $SD = 1.09$), Local television news ($M = 1.32$, $SD = 1.07$), Newspaper coverage ($M = 1.37$, $SD = 1.12$)

Political Orientations: Political discussion in past week with friends/family (days in past week, $M = 3.22$, $SD = 2.53$), Strength of political leanings (*range* = 0 to 4, higher values indicating stronger political leanings; folded measure of ideology/partisanship, $M = 1.83$, $SD = 1.12$), Political knowledge (discussed earlier), Political interest (discussed earlier)

Political Event Exposure (included as controls only in relevant event panels): Debate exposure (*range* = 4 to 16, 4 items, *Cronbach's* α = 0.89, *M* = 10.53, *SD* = 4.37), Republican National Convention exposure (*range* = 0 to 9, 3 items, *Cronbach's* α = 0.86, *M* = 3.18, *SD* = 3.28), Democratic National Convention exposure (*range* = 0 to 9, 3 items, *Cronbach's* α = 0.85, *M* = 3.02, *SD* = 3.25)

ANALYSIS STRATEGIES

Cross-Sectional Analysis. For each variable under consideration, regression or logistic regression analyses were employed (depending on the nature of the dependent variable) to assess the relationship between partisan media use and a political variable. Interactions between ideology/partisanship and partisan media use were used to predict whether partisan selective exposure was related to each outcome variable of interest. Interactions between ideology/partisanship and the political variable of interest were used to predict whether partisans possessing certain political characteristics were more likely to use likeminded media.

The general form of the equations used was:

(1) Partisan media use = $b_0 + b_1$ (Variable of interest) + b_2 (Ideology/partisanship) + b_3 (Variable of interest * Ideology/partisanship) + b_4 (Control$_1$) + ... b_x (Control$_y$) + e

(2) Variable of interest = $b_0 + b_1$ (Partisan media use) + b_2 (Ideology/partisanship) + b_3 (Partisan media use * Ideology/partisanship) + b_4 (Control$_1$) + ... b_x (Control$_y$) + e

For each of the analyses, I evaluated the robustness of the results in numerous ways; I will describe each briefly in turn here.

1. Community Standards Robustness Check. For the cross-sectional analyses that incorporate variables associated with using Kerry-endorsing or Bush-endorsing newspapers, I evaluated whether the results would hold when taking into account voting habits within respondents' communities. I used hierarchical linear modeling where survey respondents were clustered into congressional districts and the percentage of the vote going to Bush within each congressional district was included as a control. Adding this control did not change the results in any instance.

2. Restricted Range Robustness Check. As chapter 3 shows, people tend to consume likeminded media. Thus, estimates for those who use contradictory media are based on fewer cases. Further, few respondents used four partisan media outlets. In order to ensure that these rare cases were not responsible for the results, I replicated the analysis using a different version of the liberal and conservative media use indices. Instead of an index from 0 to 4, I used an index from 0 to 2 (where all 3's and 4's are recoded to 2's). In no instance did this change the nature of the results. I also examined whether those who used more partisan media displayed stronger effects. Here, I contrasted those using two or more conservative [liberal] media types to those using no or one conservative [liberal] media types. Results were similar to the indices of media use for those using more partisan outlets.

3. Ideology and Partisanship Robustness Check. Throughout the analysis, I opted to use a combined measure of ideology and partisanship. To analyze whether the results would change if I used only one of these measures (and controlled for the other), I reran all of

the analyses using ideology and partisanship separately. In most instances, the results were unchanged. Where results were different, they tended to be in the same direction, but were somewhat weaker for ideology compared to partisanship. I also reran the analysis using dummy coding for both ideology and partisanship. Here, I entered separate variables for very conservative, conservative, liberal, and very liberal and for strong Democrats, weak Democrats, leaning Democrats, leaning Republicans, weak Republicans, and strong Republicans. I examined interactions between each set of dummy variables, controlling for the other. Looking across the analyses, the majority of relationships using the dummy variables were significant and in the expected direction. The only exception to this pattern was those identifying as weak Democrats. Although in most cases the results for weak Democrats were in the expected direction, the results were more likely to be nonsignificant than significant. Coefficients were significant and in the opposite direction from the expected relationship only rarely. It also is of note that the results were more likely to be significant and in the expected direction in the analyses including likeminded partisans and media use.

4. National Public Radio (NPR) Robustness Check. One coding decision that warrants special attention is the coding of the hosts and programs on NPR. There have been popular claims that NPR tends to be biased in the liberal direction. The limited literature on this topic does not provide a clear answer. One study found little indication of bias in *Morning Edition*'s coverage of the 2000 election.[12] A study of *All Things Considered*, however, found that the program "reported the activities of conservative presidents less favorably than it has those of liberal presidents."[13] In their study of political talk radio, Joseph Cappella, Joseph Turow, and Kathleen Hall Jamieson coded Diane Rehm of NPR as liberal and *Talk of the Nation* as moderate.[14] Given the controversy surrounding NPR, analyses were run both with and without NPR coded as a liberal outlet. In general, the results remained the same and the interpretations were unchanged.

Over-Time Analysis. To investigate the over-time analyses, panel regression analysis was used. Itzhak Yanovitzky and Joseph Cappella, for example, used a similar type of analysis in their study:

> By including a lagged measure of each respondent attitude as an explanatory variable in a regression model predicting that person's attitude in the following wave, all factors other than [political talk radio, PTR] reception that may account for change in attitudes between waves are controlled for.... Thus, to the extent that PTR reception, as an additional predictor, is shown to have an independent contribution to attitude change between two adjacent waves...PTR reception may be understood as causing attitude change.[15]

The general form of the equations used was:

(1) Partisan media use$_{time\,2}$ = b_0 + b_1 (Partisan media use$_{time\,1}$) + b_2 (Variable of interest$_{time\,1}$) + b_3 (Ideology/partisanship) + b_4 (Variable of interest$_{time\,1}$ * Ideology/partisanship) + b_5 (Control$_1$) + ...b_x (Control$_y$) + e

(2) Variable of interest$_{time\,2}$ = b_0 + b_1 (Variable of interest$_{time\,1}$) + b_2 (Partisan media use$_{time\,1}$) + b_3 (Ideology/partisanship) + b_4 (Partisan media use$_{time\,1}$ * Ideology/partisanship) + b_5 (Control$_1$) + ...b_x (Control$_y$) + e

Analysis is reported with unweighted data given debates about the use of weighted data in regression analysis.[16] All analyses were rerun using weighted data. Results for the cross-sectional analyses were identical. For the panel analyses, where the sample size was smaller, results generally remained the same. In some instances, however, weighting yielded different results. Differences sometimes yielded more support for the hypotheses and in other times, less support. As four panels were analyzed, however, the general conclusions reached throughout the book continue to hold regardless of which strategy is used. I also reran the analyses for equation (2) in both the cross-sectional and panel analyses with each media use type separately and with the two (conservative and liberal media use) together. There were no changes in the cross-sectional analysis. In the panel analysis, partisan media use variables that were significant when entered individually sometimes fell below significance when entered together. This is partially due to the correlation between liberal and conservative media use, which is strong and negative for those who use at least one liberal or conservative media type ($r = -0.61$, $p < 0.001$). The overall conclusions, however, are unchanged. In other words, in no instance does this eliminate all significant panel results such that the conclusions are no longer supported by the panel analysis.

Appendix B: Knowledge Networks Study

A nationally representative sample of subjects completed this online study between August 13 and October 15, 2008. In total, 498 respondents completed the survey. The data were gathered using the panelists from Knowledge Networks. Knowledge Networks conducts a list assisted random-digit-dial telephone survey to solicit a nationally representative panel of survey respondents. Those agreeing to participate in the panel receive reward points and Internet service in exchange for their participation in online surveys. Those respondents without Internet access are provided with Internet access so that they can complete the surveys. For the current study, the completion rate was 56 percent. Previous research has provided evidence of the representativeness of the Knowledge Networks panel.[17] The Knowledge Networks panel has been widely used in research on the media and politics.[18]

MEASUREMENT OF KEY VARIABLES

Demographics: Education (years of school completed, $M = 13.90$, $SD = 2.36$), Age ($M = 48.41$, $SD = 15.14$), Income (in thousands of dollars, $M = 64.24$, $SD = 45.70$), Gender (51 percent female), Race/ethnicity (7 percent Black/African-American, 9 percent Hispanic)

Media Use (days in past week): CNN ($M = 1.33$, $SD = 2.00$), MSNBC ($M = 0.91$, $SD = 1.72$), Fox News ($M = 1.41$, $SD = 2.22$)

Political Orientations: Strength of political leanings (*range* = 0 to 4, higher values indicating stronger political leanings; folded measure of ideology/partisanship, $M = 1.64$, $SD = 1.06$), Political knowledge (*range* = 0 to 5, $M = 3.22$, $SD = 1.57$, *Cronbach's* $\alpha = 0.71$),[19] Political interest (*range* = 1 to 4, higher values indicating more interest, $M = 2.77$, $SD = 0.82$), Partisanship (14 percent strong Republicans, 25 percent not so strong/leaning Republicans, 16 percent

Independents, 29 percent not so strong/leaning Democrats, 15 percent strong Democrats), Political ideology (6 percent very conservative, 26 percent conservative, 49 percent moderate, 15 percent liberal, 3 percent very liberal). Ideology and partisanship were combined into a single measure with higher values indicating stronger liberal Democratic leanings ($r = 0.56$, $p < 0.01$, $M = 5.89$, $SD = 1.95$).

Perceptions of Media Leanings: Respondents were asked to rate whether several news media hosts and outlets had a liberal bias, a conservative bias, or no bias: CNN (37 percent no opinion, 29 percent liberal, 27 percent no bias); MSNBC (42 percent no opinion, 27 percent liberal, 24 percent no bias); *New York Times* (43 percent no opinion, 31 percent liberal, 18 percent no bias); NPR (43 percent no opinion, 28 percent liberal, 23 percent no bias); Fox News (39 percent no opinion, 30 percent conservative, 22 percent no bias); Rush Limbaugh (30 percent no opinion, 52 percent conservative, 10 percent no bias); Bill O'Reilly (39 percent no opinion, 38 percent conservative, 17 percent no bias); *Wall Street Journal* (48 percent no opinion, 20 percent conservative, 20 percent no bias).

There were several components to this study. The first part of the study was the Google News experiment reported in chapter 3. For this study, participants were shown an image of a Google News page with either two or four different articles. Half of the articles were attributed to CNN and the other half to Fox News. This was randomly varied. The articles were about how Obama and McCain would handle domestic affairs or how the candidates would handle foreign policy. Respondents were asked to identify which one story they would most prefer to read.

The second part of the study was the clarity/bias experiment reported in chapter 4 and the agenda-setting experiment reported in chapter 6. This study evaluated whether priming people to look for bias or to look for clarity in an article influenced their perceptions of an article. An article was created by combining several articles from the mainstream news media, including articles from the *Washington Post* and Associated Press. The article was created so as to include positions on issues considered to be the strong suits of both candidates. In the 2008 election, pre-election polling broadly indicated that Obama was perceived to be more effective at handling the economy and domestic affairs, while McCain was perceived to be more effective at handling national security and foreign affairs issues. In addition, the article was created to include information about both candidates.

Subjects were randomly assigned to read one of the following two instructions, developed based on previous research that has primed subjects to approach media with different orientations.[20]

Bias Instructions: We are interested in your impressions about bias in the media. With this in mind, please read the article below. As you read, think about whether this article favors presumptive Democratic presidential nominee Barack Obama or favors presumptive Republican presidential nominee John McCain. When you finish reading, we will ask you about your thoughts on this matter.

Clarity Instructions: We are interested in your impressions of whether the average American voter is able to read and understand news coverage. With this in mind, please read the article below. As you read, think about the article's grammar, format, and structure as well as how clearly the information is presented. When you finish reading, we will ask you about your thoughts on this matter.

In addition to manipulating whether respondents were directed to look for bias or clarity, information about the candidates' issues strengths was included or excluded from the article randomly. This information is italicized in the article here.

McCain, Obama Clash on Key Issues

WASHINGTON—Sens. Barack Obama and John McCain outlined on Tuesday sharply different approaches on how to revive the economy, protect the nation's security, and direct America's foreign policy.

Speaking to a group of small-business owners in New York, McCain pushed an agenda that emphasizes reduced regulation and long-term economic growth through cuts in corporate taxes, expanded free trade agreements and cuts in government spending. McCain would also maintain tax cuts for wealthier Americans, raising the total cost of his plans to more than $300 billion a year.

In St. Louis, Obama called for expanding health insurance to all Americans, reducing income inequality and raising taxes on wealthy Americans, as part of his emphasis on providing immediate relief to hard-hit families. Obama has called for a $50 billion economic stimulus plan that would include rebate checks, aid for the unemployed, subsidies for those who cannot afford health insurance and tax cuts for middle-income Americans.

For Obama, emphasizing economic issues could be crucial to his chances. Polls show that voters favor Obama's positions over McCain's on the economy. National security and foreign policy, however, are McCain's signature issues. McCain, a former Navy pilot and Vietnam POW, may have a better chance to win if he can focus voters on these issues.

McCain has called for measures aimed at increasing pressure on Iran, including denying visas and freezing assets. McCain also has pushed for financial sanctions on the Central Bank of Iran, which he said aids in terrorism and weapons proliferation. On Iraq, McCain has adamantly opposed any kind of timetable, arguing that any troop withdrawal from Iraq should depend on the country's security and that setting a timeline would weaken the U.S. effort there.

Obama has called for open discussions with world leaders—including direct U.S.-Iran negotiations. He says that he would depart from the current policy of refusing to meet with certain nations that fail to meet preconditions. On Iraq, Obama has called for withdrawing most troops in his first two years in office. He says he would leave some troops there to defend the U.S. Embassy and to form a special strike force to carry out anti-terrorism missions, although he has not detailed how many troops those initiatives would require.

Note: Italics indicate component of the article that was randomly included or excluded.

After reading the article, subjects were asked questions about both the readability of the article and their perceptions of whether the article was biased or not. On 5-point Likert scales, respondents were asked whether they agreed or disagreed that (1) the average American voter would be able to read and understand this article and (2) this article is well written. Respondents also were asked: "Would you say that the article that you read was fairly neutral, or was it biased in favor of Barack Obama or John McCain?" on a 5-point scale: strongly biased in favor of Obama, somewhat in favor of Obama, fairly neutral, somewhat biased in favor of McCain, and strongly biased in favor of McCain.

After completing these tasks, respondents clicked to the next page of the survey and were told that the researchers were interested in obtaining additional information about the people that participated in the study. They were asked to identify the most important issue(s) facing the nation. These responses were then coded as to whether respondents mentioned (1) a domestic issue or (2) a foreign policy issue. In total, 74 percent mentioned a domestic affairs issue and 45 percent a foreign policy issue.

To examine the randomization of respondents to the following conditions: (1) bias instructions/no bias instructions, (2) candidate strengths paragraph/no candidate strengths paragraph, and (3) ideal article present in choice set/no ideal article present in choice set (see chapter 3), I tested whether the demographic, media use, and political orientation control variables previously described differed between conditions using ANOVA and chi-square analyses. In only one instance was there a significant difference ($p < 0.05$). Hispanics were less likely to have an ideal article in their choice set. Including controls for Hispanic-identifying respondents, however, did not change the results presented in chapter 3.

Appendix C: Technical Details from Chapter 3

TABLE C.I.

Logistic regression analyses predicting convention viewership with ideology/partisanship in 2008 (Figures 3.1, 3.2)

	McCain		Obama	
	B	SE	B	SE
Education	−0.01	0.04	0.02	0.04
Income	0.004**	0.002	0.002	0.002
Black	−0.42	0.35	1.20***	0.30
Hispanic	0.82+	0.44	−0.31	0.50
Female	−0.18	0.17	0.17	0.17
Age	0.03***	0.01	0.02***	0.01
Adults in home	−0.04	0.12	−0.09	0.12
Phone lines	−0.12	0.22	0.05	0.23
Region 1	−0.48+	0.26	0.13	0.24
Region 2	−0.24	0.23	0.04	0.24
Region 3	−0.05	0.22	−0.32	0.23
Campaign on television	0.21***	0.05	0.08	0.05
Campaign in newspaper	0.003	0.03	0.01	0.03
Campaign on radio	−0.003	0.03	0.04	0.03

(continued)

TABLE C.1. (Continued)

	McCain		Obama	
	B	SE	B	SE
Internet access	−0.27	0.27	−0.17	0.27
Campaign online	0.02	0.03	−0.01	0.03
Strength of IP	−0.06	0.07	−0.18**	0.07
Political discussion	0.10*	0.04	0.15***	0.04
Political knowledge	−0.05	0.08	−0.01	0.08
Follow 2008 campaign	1.18***	0.16	1.56***	0.17
Ideology/partisanship (IP)	**−0.15***	**0.04**	**0.34***	**0.04**
Constant	−6.35***	0.95	−10.57***	1.03
Nagelkerke R-square	0.32		0.44	
n	885		1,026	

2008 NAES, $^+p <$ 0.10, $^*p <$ 0.05, $^{**}p <$ 0.01, $^{***}p <$ 0.001.

TABLE C.2.

Logistic regression analyses predicting convention viewership with ideology/partisanship in 2004 (Figures 3.1, 3.2)

	Bush		Kerry	
	B	SE	B	SE
Education	0.10*	0.04	0.10*	0.04
Income	0.002	0.002	0.00	0.00
Black	−0.78$^+$	0.40	0.07	0.32
Hispanic	−0.20	0.44	−0.34	0.38
Female	0.04	0.17	0.14	0.18
Age	0.02***	0.01	0.01$^+$	0.01
Adults in home	−0.11	0.12	0.13	0.13
Phone lines	−0.04	0.21	0.33	0.22
Region 1	−0.32	0.26	−0.30	0.26
Region 2	0.07	0.24	0.00	0.24
Region 3	−0.11	0.23	−0.04	0.23
National news	0.08*	0.04	0.05	0.04
Cable news	0.08*	0.03	0.01	0.04
Local news	−0.04	0.04	−0.01	0.05
Newspaper	−0.03	0.04	−0.02	0.04
NPR	−0.03	0.04	0.04	0.04
Talk radio (non-NPR)	0.06$^+$	0.04	−0.05	0.04
Internet access	0.03	0.24	−0.02	0.25
Political Internet	0.02	0.04	0.02	0.04
National news attention	0.48***	0.10	0.61***	0.11

Local news attention	0.07	0.11	0.11	0.11
Newspaper attention	0.17	0.11	0.26*	0.11
Strength of IP	0.05	0.08	0.04	0.08
Political discussion	0.06	0.04	0.09*	0.04
Political knowledge	−0.13[+]	0.08	0.16*	0.08
Political interest	0.36**	0.13	0.24[+]	0.14
Ideology/partisanship (IP)	−0.36***	0.04	0.22***	0.04
Constant	−3.90***	0.91	−8.86***	0.95
Nagelkerke R-square	0.37		0.35	
n	1,073		1,106	

2004 NAES, [+]$p<0.10$, *$p<0.05$,**$p<0.01$, ***$p<0.001$.

TABLE C.3.

Logistic regression analyses predicting convention viewership with ideology/partisanship in 2000 (Figures 3.1, 3.2)

	Bush		Gore	
	B	SE	B	SE
Education	0.15**	0.05	−0.01	0.05
Income	0.0003	0.002	0.002	0.002
Black	0.38	0.41	0.36	0.31
Hispanic	0.58	0.42	0.29	0.40
Female	0.08	0.22	0.15	0.20
Age	0.03***	0.01	0.02*	0.01
Adults in home	0.11	0.15	−0.06	0.14
Phone lines	0.19	0.27	−0.29	0.26
Region 1	−0.26	0.34	0.06	0.31
Region 2	0.12	0.32	0.06	0.29
Region 3	0.18	0.29	−0.12	0.26
National news	0.02	0.05	0.06	0.05
Cable news	0.08*	0.04	0.004	0.04
Local news	0.001	0.06	0.04	0.05
Newspaper	−0.01	0.05	−0.01	0.05
Talk radio	0.02	0.05	0.04	0.04
Internet access	0.48	0.30	0.02	0.26
Political Internet	−0.04	0.05	0.02	0.05
National news attention	0.85***	0.15	0.75***	0.13
Local news attention	0.13	0.14	−0.04	0.13
Newspaper attention	0.07	0.13	0.05	0.12
Strength of IP	0.01	0.11	0.13	0.09

(continued)

TABLE C.3. (continued)

	Bush		Gore	
	B	SE	B	SE
Political discussion with family	0.21***	0.05	0.08	0.05
Political discussion at work	−0.03	0.06	0.12[+]	0.06
Political knowledge	−0.04	0.05	0.20***	0.05
Political interest	0.26	0.16	0.20	0.13
Ideology/partisanship (IP)	**−0.20***	**0.06**	**0.16****	**0.05**
Constant	−8.98***	1.09	−7.46***	1.02
Nagelkerke R-square	0.43		0.35	
n	849		903	

2000 NAES, [+]p<0.10, *p<0.05, **p<0.01, ***p<0.001.

TABLE C.4.

Logistic regression analyses predicting media use with ideology/partisanship (Figures 3.3, 3.5–37)

	Bush-Endorsing Newspapers		Kerry-Endorsing Newspapers		Conservative Radio		Liberal Radio	
	B	SE	B	SE	B	SE	B	SE
Education	0.01	0.01	0.04***	0.01	0.03	0.02	0.09***	0.02
Income	-0.002***	0.001	0.003***	0.0005	0.0003	0.001	0.001	0.001
Black	0.02	0.09	0.17*	0.08	-0.86***	0.17	-0.48***	0.15
Hispanic	0.20*	0.09	-0.27**	0.10	-0.43*	0.18	-0.10	0.15
Female	0.01	0.05	-0.01	0.04	-0.18*	0.07	-0.06	0.07
Age	-0.01***	0.002	0.001	0.002	0.004	0.003	-0.01**	0.003
Adults in home	0.04	0.04	0.005	0.03	0.16**	0.05	0.01	0.05
Phone lines	-0.08	0.07	0.001	0.06	-0.14	0.09	-0.01	0.10
Region 1	-0.48***	0.08	0.40***	0.07	-0.39***	0.11	0.03	0.10
Region 2	0.07	0.07	0.0002	0.06	-0.19+	0.10	-0.14	0.10
Region 3	0.01	0.06	-0.004	0.06	-0.14	0.09	-0.10	0.10
National news	-0.002	0.01	0.02-	0.01	-0.07***	0.02	0.02	0.02
Cable news	-0.01	0.01	-0.04***	0.01	0.02+	0.01	-0.05**	0.01
Local news	0.05***	0.01	0.01	0.01	0.03+	0.02	-0.03	0.02
Newspaper	0.16***	0.01	0.13***	0.01	0.03+	0.02	-0.02	0.02
NPR	-0.03*	0.01	0.02*	0.01	-0.03+	0.02	0.55***	0.01
Talk radio (non-NPR)	0.03**	0.01	0.01	0.01	0.55***	0.01	-0.25***	0.02
Internet access	0.12+	0.07	0.15*	0.06	0.34**	0.11	0.11	0.11
Political Internet	-0.01	0.01	-0.01	0.01	-0.03+	0.02	0.01	0.02

(continued)

TABLE C.4. (continued)

	Bush-Endorsing Newspapers		Kerry-Endorsing Newspapers		Conservative Radio		Liberal Radio	
	B	SE	B	SE	B	SE	B	SE
National news attention	0.03	0.03	-0.03	0.03	0.15***	0.04	-0.01	0.04
Local news attention	-0.03	0.03	-0.06*	0.03	-0.13**	0.05	-0.07	0.05
Newspaper attention	0.24***	0.03	0.37***	0.03	-0.07	0.04	0.12*	0.05
Strength of IP	0.03	0.02	0.01	0.02	0.07+	0.04	0.05	0.03
Political discussion	-0.02+	0.01	0.01	0.01	0.04*	0.02	0.01	0.02
Political knowledge	0.02	0.02	0.06**	0.02	0.24***	0.03	0.15***	0.03
Political interest	-0.03	0.03	-0.04	0.03	0.16**	0.05	0.12*	0.05
Ideology/partisanship (IP)	**-0.07***	**0.01**	**0.10***	**0.01**	**-0.39***	**0.02**	**0.20***	**0.02**
Constant	-1.90***	0.23	-3.70***	0.21	-3.52***	0.36	-5.97***	0.35
Nagelkerke R-square	0.10		0.19		0.52		0.47	
n	13,142		13,142		13,115		13,115	

	Fox News		CNN/MSNBC		Conservative Web Sites		Liberal Web Sites	
	B	SE	B	SE	B	SE	B	SE
Education	-0.05***	0.01	0.03**	0.01	0.08	0.05	0.05	0.05
Income	-0.001+	0.001	0.001**	0.0005	-0.003	0.002	-0.004*	0.002
Black	0.07	0.10	0.05	0.08	-0.74	0.73	-0.07	0.39
Hispanic	-0.29*	0.11	0.15+	0.08	-1.01	0.74	0.05	0.41
Female	0.10+	0.05	-0.05	0.04	-0.12	0.20	0.25	0.19
Age	-0.0005	0.002	-0.01***	0.002	-0.001	0.01	0.01*	0.01
Adults in home	0.10*	0.04	0.06+	0.03	0.05	0.16	-0.03	0.14
Phone lines	-0.03	0.07	0.03	0.06	0.04	0.23	-0.20	0.24

Region 1	0.04	0.08	0.03	0.07	0.03	0.31	-0.13	0.23
Region 2	0.09	0.08	0.04	0.06	0.01	0.28	-0.40	0.25
Region 3	0.21**	0.07	0.03	0.06	0.05	0.25	-0.61*	0.24
National news	-0.14***	0.01	0.07***	0.01	-0.04	0.05	-0.04	0.04
Cable news	0.30***	0.01	0.31***	0.01	-0.003	0.04	-0.04	0.04
Local news	0.01	0.01	0.01	0.01	-0.12*	0.05	-0.11*	0.05
Newspaper	0.03*	0.01	0.004	0.01	0.01	0.05	-0.11*	0.05
NPR	-0.12***	0.01	0.06***	0.01	-0.03	0.05	0.06+	0.03
Talk radio (non-NPR)	0.13***	0.01	-0.12***	0.01	0.16***	0.04	0.03	0.04
Internet access	0.12	0.07	0.18**	0.06	—a	—	—	—
Political Internet	-0.03**	0.01	-0.02+	0.01	0.35***	0.04	0.30***	0.03
National news attention	0.37***	0.03	0.22***	0.03	0.14	0.12	0.01	0.10
Local news attention	-0.02	0.03	0.06*	0.03	0.14	0.13	0.10	0.12
Newspaper attention	-0.08*	0.03	0.10***	0.03	-0.01	0.12	0.28*	0.12
Strength of IP	0.03	0.02	-0.12***	0.02	0.02	0.12	-0.17	0.12
Political discussion	0.01	0.01	-0.07***	0.01	-0.001	0.05	0.17***	0.05
Political knowledge	-0.01	0.02	-0.01	0.02	0.10	0.10	0.21*	0.10
Political interest	-0.04	0.04	-0.11***	0.03	0.06	0.18	0.08	0.17
Ideology/partisanship (IP)	**-0.34***	**0.01**	**0.27***	**0.01**	**-0.48***	**0.08**	**0.55***	**0.09**
Constant	-0.41+	0.25	-3.11***	0.20	—	0.31	—	—
Nagelkerke R-square	0.37		0.31		0.31		0.34	
n	13,154		13,154		13,143		13,143	

2004 NAES, +p<0.10, *p<0.05, **p<0.01, ***p<0.001.

a Effects not shown due to quasi-complete separation; see Paul D. Allison, *Logistic Regression Using the SAS System: Theory and Application* (Cary: SAS Institute, 1999).

The Nielsen Company Data

In the last two weeks of October 2008, 50 percent of households turned to CNN and MSNBC or to Fox News for five minutes or more during a single day, according to data gathered by The Nielsen Company. Forty-one percent watched CNN or MSNBC for five minutes or more and watched Fox News for five minutes or more. In the last two weeks of October 2004, 43 percent of households turned to CNN and MSNBC or to Fox News for five minutes or more. Forty-four percent watched CNN or MSNBC for five minutes or more and watched Fox News for five minutes or more.

When looking at those watching sixty minutes of cable news during a single day over the course of two weeks, selectivity is more prevalent. In the last two weeks of October 2008, just over 30 percent of households tuned in to CNN and MSNBC or to Fox News for sixty minutes or more. Only 18 percent watched CNN or MSNBC for sixty minutes or more and watched Fox News for sixty minutes or more. In the last two weeks of October 2004, 23 percent of households tuned in to CNN and MSNBC or to Fox News for sixty minutes or more. Twenty-two percent watched CNN or MSNBC for sixty minutes or more and watched Fox News for sixty minutes or more.

Additional Nielsen data purchased for this project are shown in Tables C5 and C6. Here, the data are based on viewing 60 or 120 minutes at any point over the course of two weeks (e.g., a viewer could watch five minutes one day, ten minutes the next, etc.).

TABLE C.5.

Cable news network viewing, household data

	% watching CNN/MSNBC for 60 min or more	% of those watching CNN/MSNBC for 60 min or more who watched Fox News for less than 15 min
April 2004	20.42%	47.31%
October 2004	20.53%	43.68%
April 2008	23.11%	52.42%
October 2008	26.79%	52.28%
	% watching Fox News for 60 min or more	% of those watching Fox News for 60 min or more who watched CNN/MSNBC for less than 15 min
April 2004	14.80%	31.20%
October 2004	15.57%	30.57%
April 2008	14.64%	30.17%
October 2008	17.64%	32.57%
	% watching CNN/MSNBC for 120 min or more	% of those watching CNN/MSNBC for 120 min or more who watched Fox News for less than 15 min
April 2004	14.72%	44.61%
October 2004	15.11%	42.29%

April 2008	17.01%	49.99%
October 2008	21.31%	50.02%
	% watching Fox News for 120 min or more	% of those watching Fox News for 120 min or more who watched CNN/MSNBC for less than 15 min
April 2004	11.33%	40.78%
October 2004	12.34%	40.30%
April 2008	11.67%	44.95%
October 2008	14.36%	45.61%

The Nielsen Company. Viewing could occur at any point during the last two weeks of the month.

TABLE C.6.

Cable news network viewing, individual data (2- to 99-year-olds)

	% watching CNN/MSNBC for 60 min or more	% of those watching CNN/MSNBC for 60 min or more who watched Fox News for less than 15 min
April 2004	10.39%	54.21%
October 2004	10.46%	50.03%
April 2008	11.73%	58.63%
October 2008	15.22%	60.14%
	% watching Fox News for 60 min or more	% of those watching Fox News for 60 min or more who watched CNN/MSNBC for less than 15 min
April 2004	8.18%	33.70%
October 2004	8.94%	33.20%
April 2008	7.93%	32.67%
October 2008	10.15%	35.73%
	% watching CNN/MSNBC for 120 min or more	% of those watching CNN/MSNBC for 120 min or more who watched Fox News for less than 15 min
April 2004	7.05%	51.35%
October 2004	7.20%	49.05%
April 2008	8.10%	56.04%
October 2008	11.25%	58.50%

(continued)

TABLE C.6. (continued)

	% watching Fox News for 120 min or more	% of those watching Fox News for 120 min or more who watched CNN/ MSNBC for less than 15 min
April 2004	5.98%	52.35%
October 2004	6.78%	50.03%
April 2008	6.22%	54.86%
October 2008	7.82%	57.18%

The Nielsen Company. Viewing could occur at any point during the last two weeks of the month.

PEW RESEARCH CENTER MEDIA CONSUMPTION SURVEY

To supplement the Internet analysis, the 2008 Biennial Media Consumption Survey, sponsored by the Pew Research Center for the People & the Press, was used to examine the relationship between ideology/partisanship and Web site selection more closely. The survey of 3,615 adults in the United States was conducted via cell and landline telephone between April 30 and June 1, 2008. Additional details about the survey methodology are available at http://people-press.org/reports/pdf/444.pdf. Note that the Pew Research Center for the People & the Press bears no responsibility for the interpretations presented or conclusions reached based on analysis of the data.

In this survey, 65 percent reported that they go online to access the Internet or to send and receive e-mail. Of those respondents, 92 percent reported going online to get news. A random half of respondents going online to get news were asked to name a few of the Web sites that they went to most often. Using an identical procedure as described in appendix A for the NAES, the open-ended responses were categorized on the basis of their political leanings (or lack thereof). Of the 973 open-ended responses, 27 percent referenced a liberal-leaning Web site and 9 percent a conservative-leaning Web site. Fifty-seven percent either had no clear partisan identity (e.g., Yahoo! News) or were unable to be classified ("local newspaper"). Six percent identified both a liberal-leaning and a conservative-leaning site. The measurement of the control variables is described below.

Demographics: Education (years of school completed, $M = 14.22$, $SD = 2.40$), Age ($M = 50.04$, $SD = 17.70$), Income (in thousands of dollars, $M = 70.59$, $SD = 54.36$), Gender (50 percent female), Race/ethnicity (10 percent Black/African-American, 6 percent Hispanic)

Media Use (range = 1 [never] to 4 [regularly]): Talk radio ($M = 2.19$, $SD = 1.14$), NPR ($M = 1.76$, $SD = 1.09$), Local news ($M = 3.22$, $SD = 1.02$), Newspaper ($M = 3.11$, $SD = 1.11$), Internet access = 65 percent, Use Internet for news (days per week, $M = 2.41$, $SD = 2.93$). Questions asking about cable news and national news viewership were asked on a survey split. A random half of respondents were asked to report their viewing habits for "the national nightly network news on CBS, ABC, or NBC." The other half were asked three separate questions about CBS, ABC, and NBC. The same was done for cable news, where one-half was asked about their viewing of "cable news networks such as CNN, MSNBC, or the Fox News cable channel" and the other half was asked about each network individually. To create a measure of cable and national news viewing for respondents asked about multiple networks individually, I took the maximum response (regularly, sometimes, hardly ever, or never) across the three questions. I then compared the two sample splits using independent sample *t*-tests. Although there were no differences between those asked about their national news viewing habits in a single question versus three questions [$M_{one\ question} = 2.63$, $SD = 1.19$; $M_{three\ questions} = 2.68$, $SD = 1.16$; $t(1,810) = 0.95$, $p = 0.34$], there was a significant difference for cable news [$M_{one\ question} = 2.93$, $SD = 1.13$; $M_{three\ questions} = 3.13$, $SD = 1.03$; $t(1,809) = 3.77$, $p < 0.001$]. To take this into account in the analysis and still control for cable news viewing, I also controlled for the sample split and for the interaction between cable news viewing and the sample split.

Political Orientations: Political knowledge (*range* = 0 to 3, $M = 1.41$, $SD = 1.11$, *Cronbach's* $\alpha = 0.64$), Enjoy keeping up with the news (*range* = 1 [not at all] to 4 [a lot], $M = 3.39$, $SD = 0.81$); Follow news about political figures and events in Washington (*range* = 1 [not at all closely] to 4 [very closely], $M = 2.84$, $SD = 0.92$), Strength of political leanings (*range* = 0 to 4, higher values indicating stronger political leanings; folded measure of ideology/partisanship, $M = 1.98$, $SD = 1.10$), Partisanship (29 percent Republicans, 8 percent leaning Republicans, 13 percent Independents, 14 percent leaning Democrats, 36 percent Democrats), Political ideology (7 percent very conservative, 34 percent conservative, 39 percent moderate, 16 percent liberal, 5 percent very liberal). As before, ideology and partisanship were combined into a single measure with higher values indicating stronger liberal Democratic leanings ($r = 0.42$, $p < 0.01$, *range* = 2 to 10, $M = 5.95$, $SD = 2.26$).

TABLE C.7

Logistic regression analyses predicting Web site use with ideology/partisanship (Figure 3.8)

	Conservative Web Sites		Liberal Web Sites	
	B	SE	B	SE
Education	−0.10	0.08	0.12*	0.05
Income	−0.001	0.003	0.001	0.002
Black	—[a]	—	0.21	0.29
Hispanic	−1.22	1.05	0.36	0.37
Female	−0.01	0.31	0.27	0.18
Age	−0.01	0.01	−0.03***	0.01
National news	−0.34*	0.14	0.09	0.09
Cable news	3.53*	1.39	−1.18+	0.64
Local news	0.13	0.16	−0.21*	0.10
Newspaper	−0.24+	0.13	−0.02	0.09
NPR	0.00	0.14	0.30***	0.08
Talk radio (non-NPR)	0.41**	0.14	−0.15+	0.08
Internet access	—	—	—	—
Political Internet	0.06	0.05	0.12***	0.03

(*continued*)

TABLE C.7 (continued)

	Conservative Web Sites		Liberal Web Sites	
	B	SE	B	SE
Sample split	3.24*	1.37	−1.12+	0.63
Cable news * Sample split	−0.90*	0.38	0.39*	0.19
News interest	0.29	0.27	0.19	0.15
Political news interest	0.07	0.22	−0.02	0.12
Strength of IP	0.02	0.15	0.03	0.08
Political knowledge	0.25	0.17	0.25**	0.10
Ideology/partisanship (IP)	**−0.21****	**0.08**	**0.19****	**0.04**
Constant	—	—	—	—
Nagelkerke R-square	0.33		0.39	
n	1,302		1,302	

2008 Pew Research Center, $^{+}$p <0.10, *p <0.05, **p <0.01, ***p <0.001.
[a]Effects not shown due to quasi-complete separation, Allison, *Logistic Regression Using the SAS System.*

NATIONAL ANNENBERG ELECTION SURVEY PANELS

As there were four different panels conducted as part of the 2004 NAES and several analyses per political variable per panel, the number of results is too unwieldy to present in full form. Instead, I first present an example of the panel analyses conducted using data from the general election panel (Table C.8). I then summarize the results for the remainder of the analyses by displaying the coefficients for ideology/partisanship (Table C.9).

TABLE C.8

Partisan selective exposure panel regression analyses, General election panel

	Media use (postwave)			
Dependent Variable	Conservative Media		Liberal Media	
	B	SE	B	SE
Education	−0.002	0.005	0.02***	0.01
Income	0.0002	0.0002	0.0005+	0.0003
Black	−0.005	0.04	−0.02	0.05
Hispanic	−0.002**	0.04	−0.05	0.05
Female	−0.03	0.02	−0.04+	0.02
Age	0.002	0.001	0.0001	0.001
Adults in home	0.02	0.01	0.004	0.02
Phone lines	−0.02	0.03	0.06+	0.03
Region 1	−0.05+	0.03	0.03	0.03
Region 2	0.01	0.03	−0.03	0.03

Region 3	−0.003	0.03	−0.02	0.03
National news	−0.01**	0.005	0.01+	0.01
Cable news	0.01*	0.004	0.01**	0.005
Local news	0.01	0.01	−0.003	0.01
Newspaper	−0.004	0.005	0.01*	0.01
NPR	−0.01**	0.004	0.02***	0.01
Talk radio (non-NPR)	0.03***	0.005	−0.02***	0.01
Internet access	−0.02	0.03	−0.01	0.03
Political Internet	0.002	0.005	0.01	0.01
National news attention	−0.002	0.01	−0.01	0.01
Local news attention	0.003	0.01	−0.01	0.01
Newspaper attention	0.01	0.01	0.01	0.01
Strength of IP	0.03***	0.01	−0.01	0.01
Political discussion	0.01+	0.005	0.01	0.01
Political knowledge	0.01	0.01	0.02	0.01
Political interest	0.02	0.01	−0.002	0.02
Media use (prewave)	0.62***	0.01	0.48***	0.02
Ideology/partisanship (IP)	**−0.05***	**0.005**	**0.06***	**0.01**
Constant	0.25*	0.10	−0.48***	0.11
R-square	0.57		0.45	
n	3,340		3,340	

2004 General Election Panel NAES, +p<0.10, *p<0.05, **p<0.01, ***p<0.001.

TABLE C.9

Summary of panel analyses predicting media use with ideology/partisanship

	Panel Surveys			
	DNC	RNC	Debate	General Election
Outlet-by-outlet				
Bush-endorsing newspaper	0.05	−0.04	−0.04	−0.03
Kerry-endorsing newspaper	0.17*	0.06	0.08	0.05*
Conservative radio	−0.38***	−0.20*	−0.45***	−0.35***
Liberal radio	0.09	0.04	0.34**	0.25***
Fox News	−0.23*	−0.08	−0.26***	−0.34***
CNN/MSNBC	0.05	0.17**	0.25***	0.21***
Conservative Web sites	—	—[a]	−1.25	−0.23*
Liberal Web sites	—	—	0.17	0.72**

(continued)

TABLE C.9 (continued)

	Panel Surveys			
	DNC	RNC	Debate	General Election
Indices				
Conservative media use	−0.03**	−0.02	−0.05***	−0.05***
Liberal media use	0.03*	0.04**	0.06***	0.06***
n	550	585	680	3,340

2004 NAES, +p <0.10, *p <0.05, **p <0.01, ***p <0.001. Table shows unstandardized coefficients for ideology/partisanship in predicting use of each media type across four different panels. Negative values indicate that conservative Republicans are more likely to use the media type; positive values indicate that liberal Democrats are more likely to use the media type. Analysis controls for demographics, political orientations, media use, event exposure, and the prewave use of each media type. Controls not shown. Logistic regression analyses used for the individual media types, regression analyses used for the indices of media use.
[a]Effects not shown due to quasi-complete separation, Allison, *Logistic Regression Using the SAS System*.

MAGAZINE EXPERIMENT

An experiment was designed to evaluate whether partisan selective exposure would change when people were faced with more political media options from which to choose and more diverse political content across the options. This study used political magazines in order to vary the number of options and the diversity of political content. Each subject was given a certain combination of magazines (a choice set) from which to choose. The number of magazines in a subject's choice set and the diversity of political viewpoints expressed within the choice set were manipulated based on a 2 (number of choices) by 2 (diversity) design. Further, subjects were able to make magazine selections in two contexts: browsing magazines in a waiting room and choosing a magazine subscription.

Choice was manipulated by including either three or five magazines in the respondent's choice set. Diversity was manipulated by including more ideologically extreme magazine options in a high-diversity condition in comparison to a low-diversity condition. Participants were randomly assigned to one of the four conditions and were unobtrusively observed in the waiting room.

After their subscription selection, subjects completed a questionnaire asking them to give their perceptions of the partisan and ideological leanings of each magazine in their choice set. Subjects were informed that their magazine selections had been recorded with the intent of analyzing whether people's political beliefs were related to their magazine selection. Once informed of the study purpose, subjects were asked to provide their consent for the data to be used. All subjects provided consent. Subjects were paid in exchange for their time and were given their magazine subscription.

Materials. Prior to the experiment, a pretest was conducted to select magazines for this study. Sixteen magazines were pretested to evaluate people's perceptions about the political leanings of the magazines. Based on the pretest, magazines were arranged into conditions such that each condition included an equal number of conservatively rated magazines and liberally rated magazines. In each condition, a magazine that people did not consistently perceive to have clear political leanings was included in the choice set, the *Economist*. Low-diversity conditions included magazines that respondents to the pretest did not find to be as ideologically extreme as those magazines included in the high-diversity conditions.

Based on the pretest, magazines were arranged into the following conditions:

Low Choice, Low Diversity: *American Spectator, Economist, Atlantic*

Low Choice, High Diversity: *National Review, Economist, Nation*

High Choice, Low Diversity: *American Spectator, Weekly Standard, Economist, Atlantic, Harper's*

High Choice, High Diversity: *National Review, American Spectator, Economist, Atlantic, Nation*

The selected magazines provided subjects with several cues that allowed them to infer the partisan leanings of the content. First, the covers contained cues about the magazine's political leanings. For example, while *The Nation* headline chided, "In your face: Bush's war on the press," the *National Review* cover headline boasted, "We're winning: How the U.S. learned the art of counterinsurgency in Iraq." Second, articles and commentaries also provided clues about the magazine's political leanings.

Measures: Independent Variables. Participants were asked to indicate their ideological leanings on a 7-point scale from (1) extremely conservative to (7) extremely liberal. Eight percent identified as extremely liberal, 18 percent liberal, 7 percent slightly liberal, 35 percent moderate, 10 percent slightly conservative, 14 percent conservative, and 5 percent extremely conservative. Participants also were asked about their partisan leanings: 27 percent of participants identified as strong Democrats, 21 percent not strong Democrats, 24 percent leaning Democrats, 3 percent independents, 8 percent leaning Republicans, 5 percent not strong Republicans, and 12 percent strong Republicans. The partisanship and ideology measures were combined to create a measure of ideology/partisanship ($r = 0.51, p < 0.001, range = 2$ to $14, M = 9.05, SD = 3.19$). Higher values indicate more liberal Democratic leanings.

Measures: Covariates. General political knowledge was measured by asking respondents a series of ten questions such as those on the NAES survey (*Cronbach's α = 0.81, M = 6.36, SD = 2.88*). An ANOVA revealed that there were some differences in political knowledge across conditions. In particular, those in high-choice conditions were more knowledgeable than those in low-choice conditions [$F(1, 103) = 4.02, p < 0.05$]. For this reason, general political knowledge was included as a covariate throughout the analysis. Political interest was measured using identical wording to the NAES; response options included most of the time (36 percent), some of the time (33 percent), only now and then (23 percent), and hardly at all (7 percent). Interest did not differ across conditions.

Participants. One hundred and five community members in the Philadelphia area participated in the study in the summer of 2005. Sixty-three percent of subjects were female, 31 percent identified as white or Caucasian, and 64 percent identified as Black or African-American. Chi-square tests of gender and race by condition revealed no significant differences between the experimental conditions. The average age of the participants was 32 ($SD = 12, range = 18$ to 74) and the average number of years of education was 14 ($SD = 2, range = 7$ to 18). ANOVAs demonstrated that neither age nor education differed across the experimental conditions. Since there were no differences across conditions for these demographic measures, they were not included as covariates in the analysis.

Manipulation and Stimulus Check. A manipulation check was conducted to confirm that respondents perceived the magazines to have the same political leanings as found in the pretest. Participants rated each magazine in their choice set on three scales: whether the magazine seemed to be liberal/conservative, whether the magazine seemed to be Democrat/Republican, and whether they thought the magazine favored Bush/Kerry in the 2004 presidential election. An average of these measures was calculated to create a scale of magazine leanings for each magazine (average magazine *Cronbach's* α = 0.75). This measure ranged from 1 (very conservative/Republican/supportive of Bush) to 5 (very liberal/Democrat/supportive of Kerry), with 3 indicating that on average, the magazine was perceived as having no clear political leanings. One-tailed *t*-tests were used to evaluate whether perceptions of each magazine differed from 3, as anticipated in the experimental design. All of the magazines classified as liberal based on the pretest were evaluated by the experimental subjects as liberal and all of the magazines classified as conservative based on the pretest were evaluated by the experimental subjects as conservative. In addition, the mean ideological rating for the *Economist*, the magazine selected as the neutral magazine, was not significantly different from 3 $[t(80) = 1.00, p > 0.10]$.

According to the hostile media phenomenon, perceptions of the media vary such that people perceive "neutral" media to be biased against their own viewpoint. Perceptions of the *Economist*, the neutral magazine in the present study, follow this very pattern. In a regression analysis predicting ratings of the *Economist* (controlling for general political knowledge and the experimental manipulations), ideology/partisanship was related to ratings ($B = -0.05, SE = 0.03, p < 0.10$) such that conservative Republicans rated the *Economist* as more liberal leaning than did others, and liberal Democrats rated the *Economist* as more conservative leaning than did others.

Not only was it necessary to document that the magazines were perceived to lean in the same direction as the pretest, but it was also necessary to evaluate whether the high-diversity condition was perceived to consist of more politically diverse options in comparison to the low-diversity condition. To evaluate the perceived diversity of the options, the variance of the perceived political leanings of the magazines evaluated by each respondent was computed. The average variance of political leanings in the high-diversity condition was compared to the average variance of political leanings in the low-diversity condition using a *t*-test. Though the difference between the conditions was in the correct direction (*Low-diversity average variance* = 0.80, *SE* = 0.15; *High-diversity average variance* = 1.09, *SE* = 0.18), it was not significant $[t(81) = 1.23, p > 0.10]$. Unfortunately, there was little indication that the diversity manipulation was successful. For this reason, I do not discuss this manipulation further, although I do control for it in the analyses.

In the present study, 32 percent of participants did not view a magazine in the waiting room. Analysis confirmed that not viewing a magazine did not differ by condition. Further, though subjects were permitted to browse as many magazines as they wanted, looking at more than one magazine in the waiting room was relatively rare. Of the subjects who opted to view a magazine in the waiting room, 72 percent looked at only one. Analysis revealed that reading more than one magazine was unrelated to condition, however.

TABLE C.10

Regression analyses of percentage of time spent with magazines (Figure 3.9)

	Conservative Magazines		Liberal Magazines	
	B	SE	B	SE
General political knowledge	−0.03	0.02	0.03	0.02
Ideology/partisanship	−0.04*	0.02	0.02	0.02
Choice[i]	−0.25+	0.15	0.35*	0.14
Diversity	−0.10	0.15	0.10	0.14
Choice * diversity	−0.16	0.23	−0.13	0.23
Constant	0.88***	0.17	−0.04	0.16
R-square	0.18		0.15	
N	66		66	

Magazine experiment, +p<0.10, *p<0.05, **p<0.01, ***p<0.001.
[i]The main effect of choice is intriguing. A *t*-test revealed that in the high choice condition, participants spent more time with liberal magazines (*High choice % of time with liberal magazines M*=0.50, *SE*=0.08; *Low choice M*=0.21, *SE*=0.07; *t*(67)=−2.81, *p*<0.01) and less time with conservative magazines (*High choice % of time with conservative magazines M*=0.31, *SE*=0.08; *Low choice M*=0.62, *SE*=0.07; *t*(67)=2.78, *p*<0.01) compared to the low choice condition. The data at hand don't allow for a definitive conclusion about hwy this occurred, but it is controlled throughout the analyses.

TABLE C.11

Discrete choice analyses of browsing a magazine in the waiting room[a]

	Conservative Magazine Leaning		Liberal Magazine Leaning	
	B	SE	B	SE
Magazine leaning (ML)	1.55**	0.53	−1.10+	0.60
ML * # of options in choice set	−1.28+	0.68	1.49*	0.74
ML * Diversity of options	−0.32	0.72	0.40	0.81
ML * # of options * Diversity	−0.60	1.09	−0.52	1.10
ML * Political knowledge	−0.03	0.09	0.02	0.09
ML * Ideology/partisanship	−0.15+	0.08	0.10	0.08
Likelihood ratio χ^2	15.24*		7.40	
Wald χ^2	13.37*		6.66	
n	66		66	

Magazine experiment, +p <0.10, *p <0.05, **p <0.01, ***p <0.001.
[a] Note that for discrete choice models, variables with fixed values across all of a person's choices (e.g., the number of choices available, ideology/partisanship, and whether the ideal article was present in the choice set) can be included in the model only using interaction terms. Allison, *Logistic Regression Using the SAS System*.

TABLE C.12

Discrete choice analyses of magazine subscription decisions

	Conservative Magazine Leaning		Liberal Magazine Leaning	
	B	SE	B	SE
Magazine leaning (ML)	1.50*	0.69	0.05	0.70
ML * # of options in choice set	−1.12	0.83	−0.68	0.93
ML * Diversity of options	−0.16	0.82	0.01	0.80
ML * # of options * Diversity	−0.95	1.18	−0.03	1.18
ML * Political knowledge	−0.37*	0.11	0.24*	0.12
ML * Ideology/partisanship (IP)	**−0.17+**	**0.09**	**0.15**	**0.15**
ML * IP * # of options	**n.s.**		**0.36+**	**0.22**
Likelihood Ratio χ^2	25.65***		22.81**	
Wald χ^2	19.14**		14.67*	
n	85		85	

Magazine experiment, n.s. $p>0.10$, $^+p<0.10$, $^*p<0.05$, $^{**}p<0.01$, $^{***}p<0.001$.

Results for Tables C.11 and C.12 persist if liberal and conservative magazine choices are included in the same model. Results for Table C.11 also replicate if instead of modeling all choices in the waiting room, I look only at the last magazine chosen by the respondent.

GOOGLE NEWS EXPERIMENT

This experiment was conducted as part of the Knowledge Networks study detailed in appendix B. To begin the analysis, I coded whether an "ideal article" was in the choice set for each individual. An ideal article was operationalized as follows:

1. The presence of a CNN article about domestic issues for liberals or Democrats naming only domestic issues as most important
2. The presence of a CNN article about foreign policy for liberals or Democrats naming only foreign policy as most important
3. The presence of a Fox News article about domestic issues for conservatives or Republicans naming only domestic issues as most important
4. The presence of a Fox News article about foreign policy for conservatives or Republicans naming only foreign policy as most important

TABLE C.13

Discrete choice analyses of selecting Google article

	All Respondents		Those with a *Different* Opinion of CNN and Fox News	
Article labeled CNN	−0.24	(0.16)	−0.17	(0.21)
Article labeled CNN * Number of choices	0.51*	(0.22)	0.22	(0.30)
Article labeled CNN * Ideal article in choice set	−0.14	(0.24)	n.s.	
Article labeled CNN * Ideology/partisanship (IP)	0.02	(0.06)	0.15*	(0.07)
Article labeled CNN * Ideal article in choice set * IP	0.22+	(0.13)	n.s.	
Economy article	0.04	(0.38)	0.08	(0.51)
Economy article * Number of choices	0.95***	(0.27)	0.63+	(0.36)
Economy article * Domestic affairs most important	0.99**	(0.34)	0.97*	(0.44)
Economy article * Foreign policy most important	−0.14	(0.24)	−0.15	(0.37)
Likelihood ratio χ^2	138.87***		59.93***	
Wald χ^2	100.60***		46.60***	
n	421		212	

2008 Knowledge Networks Study, n.s. $p > 0.10$, $^+p < 0.10$, $^*p < 0.05$, $^{**}p < 0.01$, $^{***}p < 0.001$. Note that the interaction between Economic article * Domestic problem most important * Ideal article in choice set was not significant and is not displayed. Interactions with the number of choices were not significant.

Appendix D: Technical Details from Chapter 4

NATIONAL ANNENBERG ELECTION SURVEY

TABLE D.I

Logistic regression analysis predicting knowledge of newspaper endorsement (Figure 4.1)

	B	SE
Education	0.03	0.03
Income	0.003*	0.001
Black	−0.53*	0.26
Hispanic	0.08	0.32
Female	0.27*	0.11
Age	0.03***	0.004
Adults in home	0.01	0.09
Phone lines	−0.20	0.15
Region 1	0.02	0.17
Region 2	0.13	0.16
Region 3	−0.07	0.15
National news	−0.05*	0.03
Cable news	−0.01	0.02
Local news	−0.01	0.03
Newspaper	0.12***	0.03
NPR	−0.003	0.02
Talk radio (non-NPR)	0.04$^+$	0.02
Internet access	0.07	0.17

Political Internet	0.03	0.03
National news attention	−0.01	0.07
Local news attention	−0.12	0.08
Newspaper attention	0.17*	0.08
Strength of IP	0.05	0.05
Political discussion	0.06*	0.03
Political knowledge	**0.29***	0.06
Political interest	**0.14**	0.09
Ideology/partisanship (IP)	0.06*	0.03
Read Kerry-endorsing newspaper	0.24*	0.11
Constant	−5.15***	0.62
Nagelkerke R-square	0.24	
n	1,680	

2004 NAES postwave general election panel, $^+p < 0.10$, $^*p < 0.05$, $^{**}p < 0.01$, $^{***}p < 0.001$. This analysis is among the half of respondents who read a newspaper at least once in the past week and who read a newspaper endorsing Bush or Kerry. Here, the independent variables are measured in the prewave and the dependent variable is measured in the postwave. Results are similar if postwave values of the independent variables are used, although the coefficient for political interest drops to near zero.

KNOWLEDGE NETWORKS STUDY

TABLE D.2A

Logistic regression analyses predicting believing source is *liberally* biased (Figure 4.2)

	CNN Liberal Bias		MSNBC Liberal Bias		New York Times Liberal Bias		NPR Liberal Bias	
	B	SE	B	SE	B	SE	B	SE
Education	0.16*	0.07	−0.004	0.07	0.12	0.07	0.07	0.07
Income	0.001	0.003	0.002	0.003	−0.003	0.003	0.002	0.003
Black	1.22*	0.58	−0.24	0.62	0.55	0.67	−0.34	0.76
Hispanic	−1.25*	0.60	−0.49	0.49	−0.56	0.51	0.41	0.48
Female	−0.26	0.30	0.40	0.30	−0.20	0.31	−0.19	0.28
Age	0.01	0.01	−0.02	0.01	0.01	0.01	−0.01	0.01
CNN	−0.14	0.09	−0.24*	0.10	−0.01	0.10	0.11	0.10
MSNBC	−0.02	0.09	0.003	0.10	−0.09	0.10	−0.21*	0.10
Fox News	0.28***	0.08	0.41***	0.09	0.28**	0.10	0.08	0.08
Strength of IP	0.27+	0.16	0.28+	0.14	0.16	0.16	0.07	0.14
Political interest	−0.27	0.23	0.28	0.23	0.17	0.24	−0.19	0.22
Political knowledge (PK)	**0.47*****	**0.13**	**0.37****	**0.12**	**0.65*****	**0.14**	**0.61*****	**0.13**
Ideology/ partisanship (IP)	**−0.37*****	**0.09**	**−0.16***	**0.08**	**−0.30*****	**0.09**	**−0.23****	**0.08**
PK * IP	**−0.13***	**0.06**	n.s.		n.s.		n.s.	

Constant	-4.00**	1.24	-0.55	1.13	-2.22$^+$	1.22	-0.97	1.15
Nagelkerke R-square	0.47		0.37		0.43		0.30	
n	305		281		274		276	

2008 Knowledge Networks Study, n.s. $p > 0.10$, $^+p < 0.10$, $^*p < 0.05$, $^{**}p < 0.01$, $^{***}p < 0.001$. Note that these analyses are only for those respondents who had an opinion about the political leanings of these outlets. If I rerun the analysis including those who did not have an opinion as *not* perceiving a liberal bias, the results are generally the same. Only two effects change and narrowly miss significance: PK * IP in predicting CNN liberal bias and IP in predicting NPR liberal bias. Although the interactions between general political knowledge and ideology/partisanship are not always significant, it is of note that in all equations in this table, the interactions are negative, consistent with the hypothesis. A combined measure of perceiving that CNN, MSNBC, *New York Times*, and NPR are liberally biased is significantly predicted by the interaction between general political knowledge and ideology/partisanship such that politically knowledgeable conservative Republicans perceive more bias compared to other respondents.

TABLE D.2B

Logistic regression analyses predicting believing source is *conservatively* biased (Figure 4.2)

	Fox News Conservative Bias		O'Reilly Conservative Bias		Limbaugh Conservative Bias		Wall Street Journal Conservative Bias	
	B	SE	B	SE	B	SE	B	SE
Education	0.14*	0.07	0.22**	0.08	0.28***	0.08	0.20**	0.07
Income	0.004	0.003	−0.004	0.003	−0.002	0.004	0.001	0.003
Black	0.17	0.69	0.19	0.83	0.49	0.70	0.07	0.67
Hispanic	0.51	0.47	0.28	0.52	−0.29	0.53	−0.16	0.52
Female	−0.18	0.28	−0.05	0.31	−0.27	0.33	−0.30	0.31
Age	−0.005	0.01	0.01	0.01	−0.01	0.01	−0.004	0.01
CNN	0.01	0.08	−0.07	0.08	0.04	0.10	−0.07	0.10
MSNBC	0.05	0.10	0.14	0.11	−0.18	0.12	−0.09	0.11
Fox News	0.11+	0.07	−0.07	0.07	0.20+	0.10	−0.02	0.08
Strength of IP	0.58***	0.15	0.31+	0.17	0.45*	0.18	0.28+	0.17
Political interest	−0.10	0.22	0.29	0.23	0.70**	0.25	0.13	0.24
Political knowledge (PK)	**0.39***	**0.12**	**0.81***	**0.14**	**0.75***	**0.14**	**0.20**	**0.14**
Ideology/partisanship (IP)	**0.20***	**0.08**	**0.05**	**0.10**	**−0.13**	**0.10**	**0.31***	**0.10**
PK * IP	**0.14***	**0.05**	**0.21***	**0.07**	**n.s.**		**0.14***	**0.07**

	Constant							
Constant	−3.37**	1.13	−3.27**	1.24	−2.69*	1.29	−3.28**	1.23
Nagelkerke R-square	0.31		0.43		0.49		0.31	
n	296		295		340		249	

2008 Knowledge Networks Study, n.s. $p > 0.10$, $+p < 0.10$, $*p < 0.05$, $**p < 0.01$, $***p < 0.001$. Note that these analyses are only for those respondents who had an opinion about the political leanings of these outlets. If I rerun the analysis including those who did not have an opinion as *not* perceiving a conservative bias, the results are generally the same. Only one effect changes: PK * IP narrowly misses significance in predicting *Wall Street Journal* conservative bias. Although the interactions between general political knowledge and ideology/partisanship are not always significant, it is of note that in all equations in the table, the interactions are positive, consistent with the hypothesis. A combined measure of perceiving that Fox News, O'Reilly, Limbaugh, and *Wall Street Journal* are conservatively biased is significantly predicted by the interaction between general political knowledge and ideology/partisanship such that politically knowledgeable liberal Democrats perceive more bias compared to other respondents.

TABLE D.3

Regression analysis predicting the perception of bias in a news article (Figure 4.3)

	B	SE
Ideology/partisanship	0.09***	0.02
Bias instructions	−0.16*	0.08
Constant	2.80***	0.06
R-square	0.07	
n	363	

2008 Knowledge Networks Study, ⁺p<0.10, *p<0.05, **p<0.01, ***p<0.001.

2009 STUDENT SAMPLE STUDY

A sample of students from southwestern universities participated in a second study to replicate the results from the Knowledge Networks study reported previously. In total, 426 students participated between March and April of 2009. On average, participants were 20.36 years old ($SD = 2.67$) and 68 percent were women. Ideology/partisanship was computed in the same way as the NAES ($r = 0.60, p <0.01, M = 6.00, SD = 2.12$). As described in the text, the article and prompts used for this study differed from the Knowledge Networks study. The article used in this study is included here.

WASHINGTON—President Barack Obama savored his first major victory in Congress with the newly passed $787 billion economic stimulus package aimed at combating the worst economic crisis since the Great Depression of the 1930s.

The bill passed Friday with lawmakers largely voting along party lines, allowing Democratic leaders to deliver on their promise of clearing the legislation by mid-February.

The Senate approved the measure 60–38 with three Republican moderates providing crucial support. Hours earlier, the House vote was 246–183, with all Republicans opposed to the package of tax cuts and federal spending that Obama has made the centerpiece of his plan for economic recovery.

Obama "now has a bill to sign that will create millions of good-paying jobs and help families and businesses stay afloat financially," said Sen. Max Baucus, a Democrat who was a leading architect of the measure.

"It will shore up our schools and roads and bridges, and infuse cash into new sectors like green energy and technology that will sustain our economy for the long term," he added in a statement.

Despite Obama's early bipartisan goals, Republican opposition was nearly unanimous to the $787 billion package. Conservatives in both houses have been relentless critics, arguing the plan is filled with wasteful spending and that greater tax cuts would be more effective in creating jobs.

"A stimulus bill that was supposed to be timely, targeted and temporary is none of the above," Senate Republican Leader Mitch McConnell said in remarks Friday on the Senate floor. "And this means Congress is about to approve a stimulus that's unlikely to have much stimulative effect."

Sen. Lisa Murkowski, in the Republicans' radio address Saturday, contended Democrats settled "on a random dollar amount in the neighborhood of $1 trillion and then set out to fill the bucket."

The legislation, among the costliest ever considered in Congress, provides billions of dollars to victims of the recession through expanded unemployment benefits, food stamps, medical care, job retraining and more. Tens of billions are ticketed for financially strapped states to offset cuts they might otherwise have to make in aid to schools and local governments, and there is more than $48 billion for transportation projects such as road and bridge construction, mass transit and high-speed rail.

Republicans pointed out a bevy of questionable spending items that made the final cut in House-Senate negotiations, including money to replace computers at federal agencies, inspect canals, and issue coupons for convertor boxes to help people watch TV when the changeover to digital signals occurs this summer.

"This measure is not bipartisan. It contains much that is not stimulative," said Sen. John McCain, R-Ariz., Obama's rival for the White House. "And is nothing short—nothing short—of generational theft" since it burdens future generations with so much debt, he added.

TABLE D.4

Regression analysis predicting the perception of bias in a news article (Figure 4.4)

	B	SE
Ideology/partisanship	0.09***	0.02
Bias instructions	−0.35**	0.11
Clarity instructions	−0.005	0.11
Constant	3.02***	0.08
R-square	0.07	
n	399	

2009 Student Sample Study, ⁺$p<0.10$, *$p<0.05$, **$p<0.01$, ***$p<0.001$.

KNOWLEDGE NETWORKS STUDY

Based on the analysis from Table D.2, two scales were created: perceptions of conservative bias by summing those perceiving a conservative bias in Fox News, Bill O'Reilly, Rush Limbaugh, and the *Wall Street Journal* (*Cronbach's* α = 0.76, *range* = 0 to 4, M = 1.40, SD = 1.41), and perceptions of liberal bias by summing those perceiving a liberal bias in CNN, MSNBC, the *New York Times,* and National Public Radio (*Cronbach's* α = 0.77, *range* = 0 to 4, M = 1.14, SD = 1.39). Analysis confirmed that these were better treated as two factors (perceptions of liberal bias and perceptions of conservative bias) than as a single factor solution (perceptions of partisan bias).

TABLE D.5

Regression analyses predicting use of cable news networks (Figure 4.5)

	MSNBC		CNN		Fox News	
	B	SE	B	SE	B	SE
Education	−0.04	0.04	−0.02	0.04	−0.09*	0.04
Income	−0.0004	0.002	0.001	0.002	−0.002	0.002
Black	0.09	0.32	0.56	0.37	−0.35	0.38
Hispanic	0.10	0.27	0.34	0.32	0.38	0.32
Female	0.04	0.15	0.01	0.18	0.42*	0.18
Age	0.0001	0.01	0.01*	0.01	0.02***	0.01
Strength of IP	−0.15*	0.08	−0.17+	0.09	0.01	0.09
Political knowledge	−0.03	0.06	−0.02	0.08	−0.21**	0.08
Political interest	0.63**	0.11	0.57**	0.13	0.75**	0.13
Ideology/partisanship (IP)	0.13**	0.04	0.10*	0.05	−0.19***	0.05
Perceive conservative bias	0.18*	0.07	0.19*	0.08	0.20*	0.08
Perceive liberal bias	0.02	0.07	−0.002	0.08	0.42***	0.08
Constant	−0.24	0.57	−0.69	0.68	−0.53	0.69
R-square	0.15		0.12		0.29	
n	480		481		478	

2008 Knowledge Networks Study, $^+p<0.10$, $^*p<0.05$, $^{**}p<0.01$, $^{***}p<0.001$.

NATIONAL ANNENBERG ELECTION SURVEY

TABLE D.6

Regression analyses predicting partisan media use with political knowledge and ideology/partisanship (Figures 4.6, 4.7)

	Conservative Media Use		Liberal Media Use	
	B	SE	B	SE
Education	−0.004	0.003	0.02***	0.003
Income	−0.0004**	0.0001	0.001***	0.0001
Black	−0.07**	0.02	0.01	0.02
Hispanic	−0.03	0.02	−0.01	0.02
Female	0.01	0.01	−0.02	0.01
Age	0.0002	0.0004	−0.002***	0.0005
Adults in home	0.02**	0.01	0.01	0.01
Phone lines	−0.03*	0.02	−0.001	0.02
Region 1	−0.08***	0.02	0.09***	0.02
Region 2	−0.002	0.02	−0.01	0.02
Region 3	0.01	0.02	−0.01	0.02
National news	−0.03***	0.003	0.01***	0.003
Cable news	0.04***	0.002	0.05***	0.003
Local news	0.01**	0.003	−0.002	0.003
Newspaper	0.03***	0.003	0.02***	0.003
NPR	−0.02***	0.003	0.09***	0.003
Talk radio (non-NPR)	0.10***	0.003	−0.04***	0.003
Internet access	0.04**	0.02	0.05**	0.02
Political Internet	0.003	0.003	0.01*	0.003
National news attention	0.07***	0.01	0.03***	0.01
Local news attention	−0.02**	0.01	−0.01	0.01
Newspaper attention	0.01	0.01	0.09***	0.01
Strength of IP	0.05***	0.01	0.002	0.01
Political discussion	0.01**	0.003	−0.01*	0.003
Political interest	0.01	0.01	−0.01	0.01
Political knowledge (PK)	0.02***	0.005	0.02**	0.01
Ideology/partisanship (IP)	−0.08***	0.003	0.08***	0.003
IP * PK	−0.03***	0.002	0.03***	0.002
Constant	0.08	0.05	0.10	0.06
R-square	0.34		0.32	
n	13,090		13,090	

2004 NAES, $^+p<0.10$, $^*p<0.05$, $^{**}p<0.01$, $^{***}p<0.001$.

TABLE D.7

Regression analyses predicting partisan media use with political interest and ideology/partisanship

	Conservative Media Use		Liberal Media Use	
	B	SE	B	SE
Education	−0.002	0.003	0.02***	0.003
Income	−0.0004**	0.0001	0.001***	0.0001
Black	−0.05*	0.02	−0.001	0.02
Hispanic	−0.02	0.02	−0.01	0.02
Female	0.003	0.01	−0.01	0.01
Age	0.0002	0.0004	−0.002***	0.0005
Adults in home	0.03**	0.01	0.01	0.01
Phone lines	−0.03+	0.02	−0.003	0.02
Region 1	−0.08***	0.02	0.09***	0.02
Region 2	0.002	0.02	−0.01	0.02
Region 3	0.02	0.02	−0.01	0.02
National news	−0.03***	0.003	0.01***	0.003
Cable news	0.04***	0.002	0.05***	0.003
Local news	0.01**	0.003	−0.003	0.003
Newspaper	0.03***	0.003	0.02***	0.003
NPR	−0.02***	0.003	0.09***	0.003
Talk radio (non-NPR)	0.10***	0.003	−0.04***	0.003
Internet access	0.04*	0.02	0.06***	0.02
Political Internet	0.004	0.003	0.01*	0.003
National news attention	0.07***	0.01	0.03***	0.01
Local news attention	−0.02**	0.01	−0.01	0.01
Newspaper attention	0.01	0.01	0.09***	0.01
Strength of IP	0.05***	0.01	0.003	0.01
Political discussion	0.01*	0.003	−0.01+	0.003
Political knowledge	0.02***	0.005	0.02***	0.01
Political interest (PI)	0.01	0.01	−0.01	0.01
Ideology/partisanship (IP)	−0.09***	0.003	0.09***	0.003
IP * PI	−0.05***	0.003	0.04***	0.003
Constant	0.03	0.05	0.01	0.06
R-square	0.34		0.31	
n	13,090		13,090	

2004 NAES, $+p<0.10$, $*p<0.05$, $**p<0.01$, $***p<0.001$.

For the panel analysis in Table D.8, the general form of the equation used for analysis was:

$$\text{Partisan media use}_{time2} = b_0 + b_1 (\text{Partisan media use}_{time1}) + b_2 (\text{Ideology/partisanship}) + b_3$$
$$(\text{General political knowledge}) + b_4 (\text{Ideology/partisanship} * \text{General political knowledge})$$
$$+ b_5 (\text{Control}_1) + \ldots b_x (\text{Control}_y) + e$$

Note that all the same controls from the cross-sectional analysis were incorporated into the panel analysis, as were controls for viewing the RNC, DNC, and debates for each of these panels. As there were four different panels conducted as part of the 2004 NAES and several analyses per political variable per panel, the number of results is too unwieldy to present in full form. Instead, I summarize the results in the Table D.8, where b_2, b_3, and b_4 correspond with the previously listed equation.

TABLE D.8

Summary of panel regression analyses predicting liberal and conservative media use with general political knowledge and ideology/partisanship

	Conservative Media Use	Liberal Media Use
DNC Panel		
b_2	−0.03*	0.02
b_3	0.02	0.04
b_4	−0.01	0.03**
RNC Panel		
b_2	−0.01	0.03*
b_3	0.02	0.01
b_4	−0.01	0.02+
Debate Panel		
b_2	−0.04***	0.05***
b_3	0.01	0.05*
b_4	−0.01	0.02+
General Election Panel		
b_2	−0.05***	0.05***
b_3	0.01	0.02+
b_4	−0.01**	0.02***

2004 NAES, +$p<0.10$, *$p<0.05$, **$p<0.01$, ***$p<0.001$.

For the panel analysis in Table D.9, the general form of the equations used for analysis was:

Equation 1:   Political interest$_{time2}$ = b_0 + b_1 (Political interest$_{time1}$) + b_2 (Ideology/partisanship$_{time1}$) + b_3 (Partisan media use$_{time1}$) + b_4 (Ideology/partisanship$_{time1}$ * Partisan media use$_{time1}$) + b_5 (Control$_1$) +.... b_x (Control$_y$) + e

Equation 2:   Partisan media use$_{time2}$ = b_0 + b_1 (Partisan media use$_{time1}$) + b_2 (Ideology/partisanship$_{time1}$) + b_3 (Political interest$_{time1}$) + b_4 (Ideology/partisanship$_{time1}$ * Political interest$_{time1}$) + b_5 (Control$_1$) +.... b_x (Control$_y$) + e

TABLE D.9

Summary of panel regression analyses for media use, political interest, and ideology/partisanship

	Equation 1		Equation 2	
	DV: Political Interest b_3: Conservative Media Use	DV: Political Interest b_3: Liberal Media Use	DV: Conservative Media Use b_3: Political Interest	DV: Liberal Media Use b_3: Political Interest
DNC panel				
b_2	−0.01	−0.004	−0.03*	0.02+
b_3	−0.001	−0.02	0.04	−0.03
b_4	0.01	−0.01	−0.01	0.02
RNC panel				
b_2	0.001	−0.002	−0.01	0.04**
b_3	0.05	−0.02	0.01	−0.01
b_4	0.002	0.01	−0.02	0.01
Debate panel				
b_2	−0.004	−0.0003	−0.05***	0.06***
b_3	−0.03	0.005	0.05	0.01
b_4	0.004	0.005	−0.01	0.02
General election panel				
b_2	−0.001	−0.002	−0.05***	0.05***
b_3	0.02	0.005	0.02	−0.001
b_4	−0.005	−0.01	−0.01*	0.02***

2004 NAES, +p <0.10, *p <0.05, **p <0.01, ***p <0.001.

For the panel analysis in Table D.10, the general form of the equations used for analysis was:

Equation 1:   Campaign knowledge$_{time2}$ = b_0 + b_1 (Campaign knowledge$_{time1}$) + b_2 (Ideology/partisanship$_{time1}$) + b_3 (Partisan media use$_{time1}$) + b_4 (Ideology/partisanship$_{time1}$ * Partisan media use $_{time1}$) + b_5 (Control$_1$) +.... b_x (Control$_y$) + e

Equation 2:   Partisan media use$_{time2}$ = b_0 + b_1 (Partisan media use$_{time1}$) + b_2 (Ideology/partisanship$_{time1}$) + b_3 (Campaign knowledge$_{time1}$) + b_4 (Ideology/partisanship$_{time1}$ * Campaign knowledge$_{time1}$) + b_5 (Control$_1$) +.... b_x (Control$_y$) + e

TABLE D.10

Summary of panel regression analyses for media use, campaign knowledge, and ideology/partisanship (Figure 4.8)

	Equation 1		Equation 2	
	DV: Campaign Knowledge b_3: Conservative Media Use	DV: Campaign Knowledge b_3: Liberal Media Use	DV: Conservative Media Use b_3: Campaign Knowledge	DV: Liberal Media Use b_3: Campaign Knowledge
DNC panel				
b_2	−0.03	−0.04	−0.03**	0.03+
b_3	−0.15[1]	0.08	−0.01	−0.003
b_4	−0.05	0.08*	0.00004	0.01
RNC panel				
b_2	0.06*	0.04	−0.01	0.04**
b_3	0.10	0.05	0.002	−0.02
b_4	−0.01	0.04	−0.01	0.01
Debate panel				
b_2	−0.03	−0.04	−0.05***	0.05***
b_3	−0.08	0.08	0.03*	0.01
b_4	−0.05	0.04	−0.01	0.01+
General election panel				
b_2	0.09**	0.07*	−0.03**	0.03***
b_3	0.15	0.02	0.01	0.01
b_4	−0.03	0.02	−0.01*	0.01**

2004 NAES, +p <0.10, *p <0.05, **p <0.01, ***p <0.001.

Appendix E: Technical Details from Chapter 5

The general form for the cross-sectional analysis was:

$$\text{Political variable} = b_0 + b_1 \text{ (Ideology/partisanship)} + b_2 \text{ (Partisan media use)} + b_3 \text{ (Ideology/partisanship * Partisan media use)} + b_4 \text{ (Control}_1) + \dots b_x \text{ (Control}_y) + e$$

TABLE E.1

Regression analysis predicting participation with media use and ideology/partisanship (Figure 5.1)

	B	SE
Education	0.01	0.01
Income	0.0003	0.0004
Black	0.12[+]	0.07
Hispanic	0.10	0.08
Female	0.05	0.04
Age	0.001	0.001
Adults in home	−0.07*	0.03
Phone lines	0.11*	0.05
Region 1	−0.06	0.06
Region 2	0.06	0.05
Region 3	0.002	0.05

National news	0.01	0.01
Cable news	0.01	0.01
Local news	−0.02*	0.01
Newspaper	0.01	0.01
NPR	0.02	0.01
Talk radio (non-NPR)	0.03**	0.01
Internet access	0.01	0.05
Political Internet	0.05***	0.01
National news attention	−0.01	0.02
Local news attention	0.09***	0.02
Newspaper attention	0.07**	0.02
Strength of IP	0.20***	0.02
Political discussion	0.11***	0.01
Political knowledge	0.02	0.02
Political interest	0.06*	0.03
Ideology/partisanship (IP)	0.03**	0.01
Conservative media use (CMU)	−0.02	0.03
IP * CMU	−0.04**	0.01
Liberal media use (LMU)	0.05+	0.03
IP * LMU	0.06***	0.01
Constant	−0.60***	0.18
R-square	0.32	
n	2,892	

2004 NAES, +$p<0.10$, *$p<0.05$, **$p<0.01$, ***$p<0.001$.

The general form for the panel analyses in E.2 through E.4, E.6, E.7, and E.9 was:

Equation 1: Political variable$_{time2}$ = b_0 + b_1 (Political variable$_{time1}$) + b_2 (Ideology/partisanship$_{time1}$) + b_3 (Partisan media use$_{time1}$) + b_4 (Ideology/partisanship$_{time1}$ * Partisan media use$_{time1}$) + b_5 (Control$_1$) +....b_x (Control$_y$) + e

Equation 2: Partisan media use$_{time2}$ = b_0 + b_1 (Partisan media use$_{time1}$) + b_2 (Ideology/partisanship$_{time1}$) + b_3 (Political variable$_{time1}$) + b_4 (Ideology/partisanship$_{time1}$ * Political variable$_{time1}$) + b_5 (Control$_1$) +....b_x (Control$_y$) + e

Note that all the same controls from the cross-sectional analysis were incorporated into the panel analysis, in addition to controls for watching events when the panel spans an event (RNC, DNC, and debates). As before, the number of results is too unwieldy to present in full form. Instead, I summarize the results in the Table E.2, where b_2, b_3, and b_4 correspond with the previously listed equations.

Given the limited evidence, I evaluated the relationship between participation (from the post-wave) and partisan selective exposure controlling for intentions to participate (from the prewave). Note, therefore, that Table E.5 does not exactly follow equations 1 and 2 listed previously because the control variable is not the prewave value of the dependent variable.

TABLE E.2

Summary of panel regression analyses of intentions to participate, media use, and ideology/partisanship

	Equation 1		Equation 2	
	DV: Intentions to Participate b_3: Conservative Media Use	DV: Intentions to Participate b_3: Liberal Media Use	DV: Conservative Media Use b_3: Intentions to Participate	DV: Liberal Media Use b_3: Intentions to Participate
DNC panel				
b_2	0.04*	0.03*	−0.03*	0.03+
b_3	0.05	0.01	−0.07*	0.06+
b_4	0.02	0.005	−0.003	0.01
RNC panel				
b_2	0.03+	0.02	−0.01	0.02+
b_3	0.03	−0.003	0.04	0.05
b_4	−0.02	0.02	−0.02	0.03*

2004 NAES, +p <0.10, *p <0.05, **p <0.01, ***p <0.001.

TABLE E.3

Summary of panel regression analyses of participation, media use, and ideology/partisanship

	Equation 1		Equation 2	
	DV: Participation b_3: Conservative Media Use	DV: Participation b_3: Liberal Media Use	DV: Conservative Media Use b_3: Participation	DV: Liberal Media Use b_3: Participation
Debate panel				
b_2	0.03	0.03	−0.06**	0.06**
b_3	0.04	−0.05	−0.004	0.06+
b_4	0.002	0.02	−0.01	0.01
General election panel				
b_2	0.03+	0.03+	−0.04***	0.03**
b_3	−0.08+	0.03	−0.004	−0.02
b_4	−0.03+	0.02	−0.01	−0.003

2004 NAES, +p <0.10, *p <0.05, **p <0.01, ***p <0.001.

TABLE E.4

Summary of panel regression analyses of participation, media use, and ideology/partisanship (controlling for intentions to participate measured in the prewave)

	Equation 1		Equation 2	
	DV: Participation b_3: Conservative Media Use	DV: Participation b_3: Liberal Media Use	DV: Conservative Media Use b_3: Intentions to Participate	DV: Liberal Media Use b_3: Intentions to Participate
General election panel				
b_2	0.03	0.02	−0.05***	0.07***
b_3	−0.02	0.03	0.02	0.02
b_4	−0.08**	0.04*	−0.01	0.02*

2004 NAES, +p <0.10, *p <0.05, **p <0.01, ***p <0.001.

TABLE E.5

Logistic regression analysis predicting commitment with media use and ideology/partisanship (Figure 5.2)

	B	SE
Education	−0.06***	0.01
Income	0.0005	0.001
Black	0.30**	0.10
Hispanic	0.04	0.10
Female	−0.02	0.06
Age	0.005*	0.002
Adults in home	0.02	0.04
Phone lines	0.05	0.08
Region 1	−0.14	0.09
Region 2	−0.26**	0.08
Region 3	−0.15*	0.08
National news	−0.01	0.01
Cable news	0.002	0.01
Local news	0.001	0.01
Newspaper	0.02	0.01
NPR	0.002	0.01
Talk radio (non-NPR)	0.004	0.01
Internet access	−0.09	0.07
Political Internet	0.02	0.02
National news attention	0.11**	0.04
Local news attention	0.004	0.04
Newspaper attention	−0.03	0.04
Strength of IP	0.57***	0.03
Political discussion	0.08***	0.01
Political knowledge	0.09***	0.02
Political interest	0.14***	0.04
Ideology/partisanship (IP)	−0.02	0.02
Conservative media use (CMU)	0.03	0.05
IP * CMU	−0.09***	0.02
Liberal media use (LMU)	−0.04	0.04
IP * LMU	0.10***	0.02
Constant	0.34	0.25
Nagelkerke R-square	0.15	
n	12,708	

2004 NAES, +p<0.10, *p<0.05, **p<0.01, ***p<0.001.

TABLE E.6

Summary of panel regression analyses of commitment to vote for a candidate, media use, and ideology/partisanship

	Equation 1		Equation 2	
	DV: Commitment b_3: Conservative Media Use	DV: Commitment b_3: Liberal Media Use	DV: Conservative Media Use b_3: Commitment	DV: Liberal Media Use b_3: Commitment
DNC panel				
b_2	0.20[+]	0.21[*]	−0.03	0.01
b_3	−0.21	0.14	−0.05	−0.06
b_4	−0.09	0.27[*]	0.001	0.02
RNC panel				
b_2	−0.04	−0.07	0.03	−0.03
b_3	0.24	0.12	0.07	−0.10
b_4	−0.08	0.05	−0.05	0.08[+]
Debate panel				
b_2	0.10	0.05	−0.02	0.05
b_3	0.31	0.02	−0.002	−0.001
b_4	−0.10	0.11	−0.03	0.01

2004 NAES, [+]$p <0.10$, [*]$p <0.05$, [**]$p <0.01$, [***]$p <0.001$.

TABLE E.7

Summary of panel regression analyses of time of decision, media use, and ideology/partisanship (controlling for commitment measured in prewave)

	Equation 1		Equation 2	
	DV: Time of Decision b_3: Conservative Media Use	DV: Time of Decision b_3: Liberal Media Use	DV: Conservative Media Use b_3: Commitment	DV: Liberal Media Use b_3: Commitment
General election panel				
b_2	0.03[*]	0.03[*]	0.01	0.02
b_3	0.02	−0.09[*]	0.05[+]	0.01
b_4	−0.02	0.05[**]	−0.07[***]	0.04[*]

2004 NAES, [+]$p <0.10$, [*]$p <0.05$, [**]$p <0.01$, [***]$p <0.001$.

TABLE E.8

Regression analysis predicting polarization with media use and ideology/partisanship (Figure 5.3)

	B	SE
Education	−0.11***	0.01
Income	0.0001	0.001
Black	0.16	0.10
Hispanic	−0.15	0.10
Female	0.40***	0.05
Age	0.02***	0.002
Adults in home	−0.05	0.04
Phone lines	0.07	0.07
Region 1	−0.04	0.08
Region 2	−0.10	0.08
Region 3	0.09	0.07
National news	−0.02	0.01
Cable news	0.02	0.01
Local news	−0.02+	0.01
Newspaper	−0.02	0.01
NPR	−0.01	0.01
Talk radio (non-NPR)	0.04**	0.01
Internet access	−0.19**	0.07
Political Internet	0.05***	0.01
National news attention	0.13***	0.03
Local news attention	0.02	0.03
Newspaper attention	0.04	0.03
Strength of IP	0.78***	0.02
Political discussion	0.19***	0.01
Political knowledge	0.01	0.02
Political interest	0.26***	0.04
Ideology/partisanship (IP)	−0.03*	0.01
Conservative media use (CMU)	−0.06	0.05
IP * CMU	−0.08***	0.02
Liberal media use (LMU)	−0.13**	0.04
IP * LMU	0.13***	0.02
Constant	3.08***	0.24
R-square	0.21	
n	12,841	

2004 NAES, +$p<0.10$, *$p<0.05$, **$p<0.01$, ***$p<0.001$.

TABLE E.9

Summary of panel regression analyses for partisan media use, polarization, and ideology/partisanship

	Equation 1		Equation 2	
	DV: Polarization b_3: Conservative Media Use	DV: Polarization b_3: Liberal Media Use	DV: Conservative Media Use b_3: Polarization	DV: Liberal Media Use b_3: Polarization
DNC panel				
b_2	0.10*	0.08+	−0.03*	0.03+
b_3	0.02	−0.10	0.002	0.01
b_4	−0.10+	0.09+	−0.001	0.004
RNC panel				
b_2	−0.04	−0.04	−0.01	0.03*
b_3	0.08	−0.19	0.001	−0.001
b_4	−0.06	0.10*	−0.005	0.01+
Debate panel				
b_2	0.09*	0.08*	−0.04***	0.06***
b_3	0.15	−0.03	−0.002	0.002
b_4	0.0003	0.004	−0.01	0.004
General election panel				
b_2	−0.05**	−0.05*	−0.05***	0.06***
b_3	−0.03	−0.12*	0.01	−0.002
b_4	−0.06*	0.04¹	−0.005**	0.004*

2004 NAES, +p <0.10, *p <0.05, **p <0.01, ***p <0.001.

Appendix F: Technical Details from Chapter 6

Content Analysis of Bush and Kerry Campaign Rhetoric

Party platforms, convention speeches, and candidate speeches were coded sentence by sentence for the presence of mentions of Iraq and terrorism. Intercoder reliability was assessed by having two separate coders assess sentences from two speeches (one Bush, one Kerry). Krippendorff's *alpha* was computed with the sentence as the unit of analysis.[21] The average Krippendorff's *alpha* across issues and coders was 0.78. Advertisements were coded as to whether Iraq or terrorism was mentioned. Intercoder reliability was assessed by having an additional coder evaluate fifteen Kerry advertisements and fifteen Bush advertisements. The average Krippendorff's *alpha* across issues was 0.90. Weighting each advertisement by the number of times it was shown yields a similar pattern to the one shown in Table 6.1. For Bush, 7 percent name Iraq and 37 percent terrorism. For Kerry, 15 percent name Iraq and 23 percent terrorism.

All Bush speeches were available online. Some Kerry speeches, however, could not be located. For all locations where Kerry made an appearance and the transcript was not available from his staff, coverage of the event in local newspapers was reviewed. This was done by using Lexis Nexis and searching for articles in the state of the speech on the day of his stop and the day following his stop. Each article was required to contain Kerry's name and any variant of the following terms: visit, stop, or speech. All articles discussing Kerry's speech using this method were evaluated (*n* = 44). Each sentence paraphrasing Kerry's speech or directly quoting Kerry was included in the analysis. Of all sentences, a total of fifty mentioned terrorism and sixty-six mentioned Iraq.

Most Important Problems

Respondents were asked to name the most important problem facing the country. SRBI, the firm managing the NAES data collection, had trained coders review the open-ended responses and code them into categories. The percentages based on this scheme are displayed in Table F.1. As a check on the validity of the employed coding scheme, 100 survey responses were randomly selected from the survey. The responses were recoded using the SRBI coding criteria. A comparison of the sample recoding and the coding done by SRBI yielded a Krippendorff's *alpha* of 0.86.

Though SRBI created a scheme of issue codes based on the survey responses, there is no inherent reason to maintain the same coding scheme for my purposes.

TABLE F.I

Most frequently mentioned important problems facing the nation

Issue	% of Respondents
Iraq War/Iraq Situation	19%
Economy	16%
Terrorism/War on Terrorism	14%
Other	10%
Unemployment/Job Security/Layoffs	8%
National Security/Homeland Security	5%
Lack of Moral Values/Family Values	5%

2004 NAES.

To create a measure of naming terrorism as the most important problem facing the nation, responses of terrorism/war on terrorism and national/homeland security were combined. These items were combined for two reasons. First, they were often discussed in combination during the campaign. For example, one frequent line in Bush's campaign speeches was, "We will fight the terrorists overseas so we do not have to face them here at home." Kerry also frequently equated terrorism and homeland security; in one speech, he noted, "Border inspectors tell us they lack the basic training and ready access to information they need to keep terrorists out." Second, the results of three logistic regression analyses with the following dependent variables were compared: (1) naming terrorism as the most important problem, (2) naming national security as the most important problem, and (3) naming either of these issues as the most important problem. If combining were appropriate, one would anticipate that the Nagelkerke R-square value from the combined terrorism/national security measure would be higher than the Nagelkerke R-square value associated with either the terrorism or national security measure. To do this, a battery of demographic, political orientation, and media use variables were included as independent variables in a logistic regression analysis predicting the most important problem named by the respondent. Combining these two issues resulted in an increase in the Nagelkerke R-square value. Predicting naming terrorism as the most important problem facing the country yielded a Nagelkerke R-square value of 0.14 and predicting naming national security yielded a Nagelkerke R-square value of 0.08. Predicting naming terrorism *or* national security yielded a Nagelkerke R-square value of 0.17, an improvement over either measure by itself. Nineteen percent of respondents named terrorism or national security as the most important problem facing the country. Twenty percent of respondents named Iraq as the most important problem facing the nation.

TABLE F.2

Logistic regression analysis predicting naming Iraq the most important problem with media use and ideology/partisanship (Figure 6.1)

	B	SE
Education	−0.02*	0.01
Income	−0.0001	0.001
Black	0.09	0.08
Hispanic	0.27**	0.09
Female	0.29***	0.05
Age	0.01***	0.002
Adults in home	−0.04	0.04
Phone lines	0.12+	0.07
Region 1	−0.01	0.07
Region 2	−0.11	0.07
Region 3	−0.03	0.07
National news	0.01	0.01
Cable news	−0.001	0.01
Local news	−0.01	0.01
Newspaper	0.01	0.01
NPR	0.04***	0.01
Talk radio (non-NPR)	−0.03*	0.01
Internet access	−0.05	0.06
Political Internet	−0.01	0.01
National news attention	0.03	0.03
Local news attention	0.001	0.03
Newspaper attention	0.08**	0.03
Strength of IP	−0.07**	0.02
Political discussion	−0.01	0.01
Political knowledge	−0.13***	0.02
Political interest	−0.02	0.03
Ideology/partisanship (IP)	0.13***	0.01
Conservative media use (CMU)	−0.09*	0.04
IP * CMU	n.s.	
Liberal media use (LMU)	0.01	0.04
IP * LMU	n.s.	
Constant	−1.27***	0.22
Nagelkerke R-square	0.06	
n	12,823	

2004 NAES, n.s. p>0.10, +p <0.10, *p <0.05, **p <0.01, ***p <0.001.

TABLE F.3

Logistic regression analysis predicting naming terrorism the most important problem with media use and ideology/partisanship (Figure 6.2)

	B	SE
Education	0.03*	0.01
Income	0.003***	0.001
Black	−0.33**	0.11
Hispanic	0.15	0.10
Female	−0.03	0.05
Age	−0.002	0.002
Adults in home	−0.02	0.04
Phone lines	−0.11	0.07
Region 1	0.22**	0.08
Region 2	0.05	0.07
Region 3	0.002	0.07
National news	−0.02	0.01
Cable news	0.04***	0.01
Local news	−0.002	0.01
Newspaper	−0.02	0.01
NPR	−0.05***	0.01
Talk radio (non-NPR)	0.04***	0.01
Internet access	0.03	0.07
Political Internet	−0.02	0.01
National news attention	0.15***	0.03
Local news attention	−0.07*	0.03
Newspaper attention	−0.04	0.03
Strength of IP	−0.07**	0.03
Political discussion	0.02+	0.01
Political knowledge	0.02	0.02
Political interest	0.08*	0.04
Ideology/partisanship (IP)	−0.26***	0.01
Conservative media use (CMU)	0.25***	0.05
IP * CMU	−0.05**	0.02
Liberal media use (LMU)	−0.12**	0.04
IP * LMU	−0.03+	0.02
Constant	−2.40***	0.23
Nagelkerke R-square	0.19	
n	12,823	

2004 NAES, +p<0.10, *p<0.05, **p<0.01, ***p<0.001.

The general form for the panel analysis was:

$$\text{Most Important Problem}_{\text{time2}} = b_0 + b_1 (\text{Most Important Problem}_{\text{time1}}) + b_2 (\text{Ideology/partisanship}) + b_3 (\text{Partisan media use}_{\text{time1}}) + b_4 (\text{Ideology/partisanship * Partisan media use}_{\text{time1}}) + b_5 (\text{Control}_1) + \ldots b_x (\text{Control}_y) + e$$

TABLE F.4

Summary of panel logistic regression analyses predicting naming Iraq or terrorism the most important problem, with media use and ideology/partisanship

	Iraq		Terrorism	
	b_3: Conservative media use	b_3: Liberal media use	b_3: Conservative media use	b_3: Liberal media use
DNC Panel				
b_2	0.25***	0.27***	−0.18*	−0.19*
b_3	−0.23	−0.04	−0.07	−0.02
b_4	n.s.	n.s.	−0.27*	n.s.
RNC Panel				
b_2	0.13	0.17*	−0.32***	−0.30***
b_3	−0.96**	0.26	0.34	−0.45*
b_4	n.s.	n.s.	n.s.	n.s.
Debate Panel				
b_2	0.10	0.09	−0.29***	−0.32***
b_3	−0.003	0.05	0.16	0.08
b_4	n.s.	n.s.	n.s.	n.s.
General Panel				
b_2	0.11***	0.11***	−0.20***	−0.20***
b_3	−0.10	0.03	0.22**	−0.26***
b_4	n.s.	n.s.	n.s.	n.s.

2004 NAES, +p<0.10, *p<0.05, **p<0.01, ***p<0.001.

Content Analysis of Iraq, Terrorism Media Coverage in 2004

Articles from four newspapers that endorsed Kerry in 2004 (the *New York Times, Washington Post, San Francisco Chronicle*, and *Boston Globe*) and four newspapers that endorsed Bush in 2004 (*Chicago Tribune, New York Daily News, New York Post*, and *Houston Chronicle*) were analyzed. Efforts were made to balance the reach of the newspapers included in this analysis; summing the circulations for each of these newspapers, the circulation figure for those newspapers endorsing Kerry was 2,859,560 and the circulation figure for those newspapers endorsing Bush was 2,608,258. Broadcast transcripts for Fox News and CNN also were coded.[22] All available content between October 26 and November 1, 2004 (the week before the general election) was gathered using the online database Lexis Nexis. To isolate only the relevant media content, I developed a search string that would limit the analysis to only those articles that were primarily about either Iraq or terrorism.[23]

A codebook was created that included popular claims made during this time period. Although it was not possible to evaluate all the claims made, it was possible to evaluate the *same* claims across media outlets. Therefore, I am able to compare the percentage of times a claim was made across outlets. Reliability analysis was conducted on a subset of 50 articles. Reliabilities for the items ranged from 0.71 to 1.00 (*mean Krippendorff's* α = 0.82). All transcripts and newspaper articles were blinded so that there were no distinguishing features that would allow coders to make assumptions about the content of the article on the basis of the source. For newspaper articles, this involved removing the byline, newspaper name, and any contact or location information. For broadcast transcripts, this involved removing all mentions of anchors, hosts, reporters, station identification, references to well-known segments, and locations. The content analysis was conducted in two parts. One part examined articles and transcripts that discussed Iraq (CNN = 54, Fox News = 22, Kerry-endorsing newspapers = 266, Bush-endorsing newspapers = 135) and another part examined articles and transcripts that discussed terrorism (CNN = 24, Fox News = 15, Kerry-endorsing newspapers = 116, Bush-endorsing newspapers = 84). Note that transcripts from the same show that were separated in Lexis Nexis were combined for this analysis. The percentages in Table 6.2 correspond to the Iraq analysis with the exception of the following four claims: "Iraq diverted from the war on terror," "Iraq increased the threat of terrorism," "Iraq success helps in the war on terror," and "Iraq linked to war on terror."

KNOWLEDGE NETWORKS STUDY OF AGENDA SETTING AND ISSUE OWNERSHIP

TABLE F.5

Logistic regression analyses predicting naming domestic or foreign issues as most important based on issue ownership details included in the article and ideology/partisanship (Figure 6.3)

	Domestic[i]		Foreign	
	B	SE	B	SE
Paragraph of candidate strengths (CS)	0.09	0.29	0.02	0.19
Ideology/partisanship (IP)	0.31**	0.10	0.09	0.07
CS * IP	−0.14	0.14	−0.18[+]	0.10
Constant	1.73***	0.21	−0.07	0.14
Nagelkerke R-square	0.05		0.01	
n	431		431	

2008 Knowledge Networks Study, $^+p<0.10$, $^*p<0.05$, $^{**}p<0.01$, $^{***}p<0.001$. Note that ideology/partisanship remains significant in predicting naming domestic issues if the non-significant interaction is removed.

[i] Note that the results are the same if I analyze only mentions of the economy, not any domestic affairs issue.

Based on the results from chapter 4, I again used the variable for "perceive liberal bias."

TABLE F.6

Logistic regression analysis predicting naming foreign issues as most important based on issue ownership details included in the article, the ability to detect liberal cues, and ideology/partisanship (Figure 6.4)

	Foreign	
	B	SE
Paragraph of candidate strengths (CS)	0.05	0.20
Ideology/partisanship (IP)	0.15[+]	0.08
CS * IP	−0.20*	0.10
Perceive liberal bias (PLB)	−0.01	0.08
PLB * IP	−0.10*	0.04
Constant	−0.04	0.15
Nagelkerke R-square	0.03	
n	431	

2008 Knowledge Networks Study, $^+p<0.10$, $^*p<0.05$, $^{**}p<0.01$, $^{***}p<0.001$. The same does not occur for perceiving conservative biases. Interactions with PCB and CS were not significant.

NOTES

1. Daniel Romer, Kate Kenski, Kenneth Winneg, Christopher Adasiewicz, and Kathleen Hall Jamieson, *Capturing Campaign Dynamics 2000 & 2004: The National Annenberg Election Survey* (Philadelphia: University of Pennsylvania Press, 2006); Daniel Romer, Kate Kenski, Paul Waldman, Christopher Adasiewicz, and Kathleen Hall Jamieson, *Capturing Campaign Dynamics: The National Annenberg Election Survey: Design, Method, and Data* (New York: Oxford University Press, 2004).

2. C. Richard Hofstetter, David Barker, James T. Smith, Gina M. Zari, and Thomas A. Ingrassia, "Information, Misinformation, and Political Talk Radio," *Political Research Quarterly* 52, 2 (1999): 353–69; Joseph N. Cappella, Joseph Turow, and Kathleen Hall Jamieson, *Call-In Political Talk Radio: Background, Content, Audiences, Portrayal in Mainstream Media* (Philadelphia: Annenberg Public Policy Center, 1996); William G. Mayer, "Why Talk Radio is Conservative," *Public Interest* 156 (2004): 86–103; Michael Harrison, "New Format for Heavy Hundred: The 100 Most Important Hosts Now Ranked Leading Elite Group of 250," *Talkers Magazine* 165 (2006); Kathleen Hall Jamieson and Joseph N. Cappella, *Echo Chamber: Rush Limbaugh and the Conservative Media Establishment* (New York: Oxford University Press, 2008). Using these criteria, statements that the hosts or programs were liberal, progressive, Democratic, anti-Bush, pro-Kerry, or supportive of issue positions known to be related to the Democratic Party were coded as liberal. Statements that hosts or programs were conservative, Republican, pro-Bush, anti-Kerry, or supportive of issue positions known to be related to the Republican Party were coded as conservative.

3. Harrison, "New Format for Heavy Hundred."

4. Klaus Krippendorff, *Content Analysis: An Introduction to its Methodology* (Thousand Oaks, CA: Sage, 2004), 2.

5. Michael X. Delli Carpini and Scott Keeter, *What Americans Know about Politics and Why It Matters* (New Haven, CT: Yale University Press, 1996).

6. John Zaller, *Analysis of Information Items in the 1985 NES Pilot Study* (National Election Studies, 1986).

7. These two measures of political knowledge are correlated ($r - 0.58, p < 0.001$) though they are not identical, as the results document.

8. Many previous analyses of agenda setting have relied on aggregate-level data and have compared the issue agenda for a sample of a population to the issue agenda of a media outlet; as McCombs noted, a great deal of agenda-setting evidence comes from studies conducted at the aggregate level. See Maxwell McCombs, *Setting the Agenda: The Mass Media and Public Opinion* (Cambridge: Polity Press, 2004); Yariv Tsfati, "Does Audience Skepticism of the Media Matter in Agenda Setting?" *Journal of Broadcasting & Electronic Media* 47, 2 (2003): 157–76.

9. John Richard Petrocik, "Measuring Party Support: Leaners Are Not Independents," *Electoral Studies* 28 (2009): 562–72.

10. Ibid., 563.

11. Matthew Levendusky, *The Partisan Sort: How Liberals Become Democrats and Conservatives Become Republicans* (Chicago: The University of Chicago Press, 2009).

12. Timothy Boudreau, "Down to the Wire: NPR's 'Morning Edition' Coverage of the 2000 Presidential Election Campaign," Paper presented at the Association for Education in Journalism and Mass Communication, Toronto, Canada (2004).

13. Mary. S. Larson, "Presidential News Coverage and 'All Things Considered': National Public Radio and News Bias," *Presidential Studies Quarterly* 19, 2 (1989): 347–54.

14. Cappella, Turow, and Jamieson, *Call-In Political Talk Radio*.

15. Itzhak Yanovitzky and Joseph N. Cappella, "Effect of Call-In Political Talk Radio Shows on Their Audiences: Evidence from a Multi-wave Panel Analysis," *International Journal of Public Opinion Research* 13, 4 (2001): 385–6.

16. See, for example, Andrew Gelman, "Struggles with Survey Weighting and Regression Modeling," *Statistical Science* 22, 2 (2007): 153–64.

17. See Linchiat Chang and Jon A. Krosnick, "National Surveys via RDD Telephone Interviewing versus the Internet: Comparing Sample Representativeness and Response Quality," *Public Opinion Quarterly* 73, 4 (2009): 641–78.

18. See, for example, D. Sunshine Hillygus and Todd G. Shields, *The Persuadable Voter: Wedge Issues in Presidential Campaigns* (Princeton: Princeton University Press, 2008); Vincent Price, Lilach Nir, and Joseph N. Cappella, "Framing Public Discussion of Gay Civil Unions," *Public Opinion Quarterly* 69, 2 (2005): 179–212; Markus Prior, *Post-Broadcast Democracy: How Media Choice Increases Inequality in Political Involvement and Polarizes Elections* (New York: Cambridge University Press, 2007).

19. Using the Internet to assess political knowledge can be problematic because respondents may use the Internet to look up answers to unknown questions. In an attempt to remedy this issue, respondents were given only one minute to answer each knowledge question and they were reminded not to consult other sources.

20. Linda M. Isbell and Robert S. Wyer Jr., "Correcting for Mood-Induced Bias in the Evaluation of Political Candidates: The Roles of Intrinsic and Extrinsic Motivation," *Personality and Social Psychology Bulletin* 25, 2 (1999): 237–49; Milton Lodge, Kathleen M. McGraw, and Patrick Stroh, "An Impression-Driven Model of Candidate Evaluation," *American Political Science Review* 83, 2 (1989): 399–419.

21. Krippendorff, *Content Analysis*.

22. The content analysis includes CNN and Fox News coverage as these networks are the most popular twenty-four-hour cable news networks.

23. I used Lexis Nexis Smart Indexing to isolate those articles that had a 90 percent or higher rating in one or more topically related areas. To focus the search on those articles that were about Iraq, articles were required to be about Iraq or Hussein. To focus the search on articles about terrorism, articles were required to be about counterterrorism, September 11 attacks, terrorism, terrorist organizations, or Osama bin Laden.

Index

Accidental selective exposure. *See* incidental
   selective exposure
Accuracy goals. *See* motivated reasoning
Agenda setting, 12, 143–58, 164–5, 172, 177–8
Al Qaeda, 4, 106, 148
Allen, Mike, 47
The American Voter, 27
AOL News, 73
Associated Press, 73
Austin American Statesman, 46–7, 169

Baum, Matthew, 102–3
BBC (British Broadcasting Corporation), 72
Beck, Glenn, 53
Berelson, Bernard, 28, 64, 172
Bias. *See also* hostile media phenomenon
   elite accusations of, 4–7, 87–9, 111, 161, 182
   in information seeking, 15, 18–9, 74, 77, 127–8
   perceptions of, 74, 89–103, 142, 146, 179–82
Biased assimilation, 21
Bill of Rights, 175
Bishop, Bill, 28–9
Blitzer, Wolf, 5–7, 9
Boomerang effects, 131–2
Boston Globe, 154–9
Brown, Aaron, 52

Bush, George H. W., 3, 88, 153–4
Bush, George W.
   attitudes toward, 132–3
   convention speeches, 43–4
   Fahrenheit 9/11 and, 45, 132
   issue coverage in newspapers endorsing, 154–8
   issue emphasis, 148–50, 159
   knowledge about, 109
   news media coverage of, 4, 29, 52–3, 103
   political discussion with those favoring, 28
   Press Secretary Tony Snow, 7
   use of newspapers endorsing, 47–50, 61, 66,
      90–1, 122
Business Week, 52

Cable news. *See also* CNN, Fox News, and MSNBC
   bundling versus á la carte, 69
   issue coverage on, 147, 156–8
   number of choices on, 29, 66
   online, 73
   partisan leanings of, 89
   perceptions of, 101–2, 170
   selective exposure and, 30–1, 52–8, 61–3,
      77–8, 87
   selective exposure and political
      polarization, 132